Deb Bickford

THE FIRST-YEAR EXPERIENCE
MONOGRAPH SERIES No. 13

Designing Successful Transitions:
A Guide for Orienting Students to College

Jeanine A. Ward-Roof and Cathie Hatch, Editors   2nd Edition

N⊕DA

National Orientation Directors Association

NATIONAL RESOURCE CENTER FOR THE FIRST-YEAR EXPERIENCE® & STUDENTS IN TRANSITION
UNIVERSITY OF SOUTH CAROLINA, 2003

Cite as:

Ward-Roof, J. A., & Hatch, C. (Eds). (2003). *Designing successful transitions: A guide for orienting students to college* (Monograph No. 13, 2nd ed.). Columbia, SC: University of South Carolina, National Resource Center for The First-Year Experience and Students in Transition.

Sample Chapter Citation:

Austin, D. (2003). The role of family influence on student success. In J. A. Ward-Roof & C. Hatch (Eds)., *Designing successful transitions: A guide for orienting students to college* (Monograph No. 13, 2nd ed.) (pp. 137-163). Columbia, SC: University of South Carolina. National Resource Center for The First-Year Experience and Students in Transition.

Additional copies of this monograph may be obtained from the National Resource Center for The First-Year Experience and Students in Transition, University of South Carolina, 1629 Pendleton Street, Columbia, SC 29208. Telephone (803) 777-6029. Telefax (803) 777-4699.

Special gratitude is expressed to Amy Murray, Editorial Assistant, for copy editing; to Holli Armstrong, Editorial Assistant, for design and layout; to Jimmie Gahagan, Graduate Assistant, and Scott Slawinski, free-lance editor, for proofing; to Barbara Tobolowsky, Associate Director, for copy editing; and to Tracy Skipper, Editorial Projects Coordinator, for project management and copy editing.

Designing successful transitions : orienting students to college / Jeanine Ward-Roof and Cathie Hatch, editors.-- 2nd ed.
    p. cm. -- (The first-year experience monograph series ; no. 13)
Includes bibliographical references.
 ISBN 1-889271-41-1
 1. College student orientation--United States. 2. College freshmen--United States. I. Ward-Roof, Jeanine. II. Hatch, Cathie. III. National Orientation Directors Association. IV. National Resource Center for the First-Year Experience & Students in Transition (University of South Carolina) V. Series.

 LB2343.32.D47 2003
 378.1'98--dc21

                                      2003008698

Contents

Chapter Nine

Chapter Ten

Chapter Eleven

Chapter Twelve

Chapter Thirteen

Chapter Fourteen

Chapter Fifteen

Appendix

About the Contributors

Foreword

In 1993, the National Orientation Directors Association, in partnership with the National Resource Center for The Freshman Year Experience, published *Designing Successful Transitions: A Guide for Orienting Students to College*. Nine years and two print runs later, we are pleased to introduce the second edition of this monograph.

In this nine-year period the National Resource Center for The Freshman Year Experience has become the National Resource Center for The First-Year Experience and Students in Transition, reflecting a significant semantic and philosophical change and growth in scope and mission. Rather than looking at only the first year of college, the Center now focuses on all significant transitions for college students in its publications, research, and conference series. The National Orientation Directors Association has also expanded its mission from a focus on orientation programming to its current role as a leader in the field of college student orientation, transition programs, and retention. This growth is reflected in a new addition to this monograph: a chapter addressing the growing numbers of nontraditional learners on college and university campuses. Other chapters have been revised and expanded to reflect the changes in higher education in general and orientation in particular.

Designing Successful Transitions is written for all practitioners who are interested in the social and academic success of new college and university students. In the increasingly competitive higher education arena, educators search for the "magic formula" that will successfully connect students to the institution and increase their persistence throughout the first year and on to graduation. Suggestions for creating and maintaining successful transitions for an increasingly diverse student body are found throughout the pages of this monograph. As professional practitioners and faculty, the chapter authors provide examples of best practices, creative strategies, and innovative solutions for developing exemplary programs and partnerships in a changing higher education landscape.

The National Orientation Directors Association and the National Resource Center for The First-Year Experience and Students in Transition are proud of our ongoing partnership and the collaborations that have resulted in valuable resources for those who devote themselves to the orientation, transition, and retention of college and university students. We will continue to work together to expand the number and types of publications available for professionals working in these areas.

We express our appreciation to Jeanine Ward-Roof and Cathie Hatch for serving as editors, to Tracy Skipper for her management of the project, and to each author who dedicated time, energy, and passion to the success of this publication. We know that you will enjoy and benefit from this valuable resource, the second edition of *Designing Successful Transitions: A Guide for Orienting Students to College*.

Mary Stuart Hunter, Director
National Resource Center for The First-Year Experience and Students in Transition

Cindy Payne, Immediate Past President
National Orientation Directors Association

Reflections on the Future of Orientation

M. Lee Upcraft

What is the future of orientation? Perhaps I should follow the advice of Yogi Berra, who supposedly said, "I never predict nothing, especially the future!" But as my career as a student affairs professional winds down, the offer to speculate on the future of orientation was one I just couldn't refuse. So here are my thoughts on what orientation might look like in the years ahead as we continue the noble task of helping new students make a successful transition to college.

First, new students of the future will continue to be more diverse by age, race, ethnicity, geography, sexual orientation, ability, and other characteristics. They will be more likely to commute, study part-time, transfer to other institutions, stop out, and study from a distance. The number of first-generation students will continue to increase, and more students will come from single-parent or blended families. Because college costs increase faster than rates of inflation, college may become less affordable for more students. Alcohol and other drug abuse, which are facts of life for more students prior to their enrollment, will continue to plague them during their college years. And as these differences become the reality of student life, relationships among students based on these differences must be addressed.

Second, orientation will rely even more heavily on technology to acquaint entering students with what they need to know before and during their first year of college. Prior to college, they will know more about the campus through virtual tours, student services web sites, interactive question and answer sites, chat rooms with faculty and staff, as well as returning and entering students, and even opportunities to take college courses online. Once on campus, students will continue the transition to college by taking a mixture of virtual and traditional classes, including first-year seminars; communicating electronically with faculty; researching, submitting, and receiving feedback on homework assignments; and engaging in other activities not yet imaginable. Because of the increased availability of online courses and degrees, students may even enroll at more than one institution at the same time, which means that they may be participating in several orientations at the same time.

Third, orientation will continue to become more academically focused, with more faculty involvement and more emphasis on programs that help entering students successfully attain their educational goals. Of course, programs designed to help students make a successful interpersonal transition to college will still be important, but, to use Tinto's (1993) terms, there must be a better balance between social and academic integration. Orientation will become better integrated with academically focused efforts such as first-year seminars, learning communities, service-learning, developmental education, academic advising, and Supplemental Instruction.

Fourth, demonstrating the effectiveness of orientation through systematic assessment studies will become even more important in the future. Institutions must know who their entering students are—their needs, their satisfaction with orientation programs and services, the campus climate with which they interact—and most important, must assess the relationship between what's done in orientation and desirable outcomes such as student learning, grades, and persistence to graduation. Orientation programs will also be "benchmarked" against similar programs at comparable institutions.

All of these trends will have enormous implications for orientation practitioners. We will become managers of the orientation process rather than program planners and deliverers. We will become more knowledgeable and skillful in the academic transition of entering students, which means becoming as familiar with learning theorists such as Jean Piaget, Howard Gardner, and David Kolb as we are with developmental theorists such as Arthur Chickering, Carol Gilligan, William Perry, and Laurence Kohlberg. When possible, we will teach or team-teach academic courses, particularly first-year seminars, and this means, among other things, knowing more about classroom instruction and earning relevant advanced degrees. We will have to stay current with technological advances and integrate technology into orientation program delivery systems, and we will have to assess orientation programs to determine how effective they are and how they might be improved.

Of course, all these predictions are very speculative. Some will come to pass, while others will not. But of one thing I am sure: Working with entering students will continue to be for you, as it has been for me, one of the most exciting, challenging, and rewarding ways of earning a living that anyone could ask for. Enjoy!

References

Tinto, V. (1993). Leaving college: Rethinking the causes and cures of student attrition (2nd ed.). Chicago: University of Chicago Press.

Notes on the Second Edition

Jeanine A. Ward-Roof and Cathie Hatch

The second edition of *Designing Successful Transitions: A Guide for Orienting Students to College* represents the continued collaboration between the National Orientation Directors Association and the National Resource Center for The First-Year Experience and Students in Transition. The successful collaborative effort, on the part of these two entities, has once again created a valuable resource for orientation, transition, and retention professionals.

The vision for and completion of the first comprehensive edition of *Designing Successful Transitions* filled a major gap in the literature of higher education, particularly in the area of orientation. We would be remiss if we did not acknowledge the authors, editors, and staff of the National Resource Center who worked on the first edition. Without their vision and persistence with the project, this second edition would not exist. Specifically, we need to thank Dick Mullendore and the NODA Board of Directors for the original vision for this monograph and John Gardner and the staff of the National Resource Center for believing in and supporting this vision. Additionally, we need to recognize M. Lee Upcraft's (1984) landmark publication, *Orienting Students to College*, and its influence on the first edition as well as Lee's efforts as the editor-in-chief of the first edition. When the first edition was released, these were some of the only comprehensive publications focusing on orientation.

The second edition continues to close the gap in the literature and to offer orientation, transition, and retention professionals validation and support for their work. The monograph addresses many types of student and family orientation programs from the perspective of current practitioners and faculty, creating a valuable resource for educators within a variety of institutional settings. The second edition of *Designing Transitions* updates and expands the insights into student populations, university and college environments, and expectations for the orientation process provided by the publications mentioned above. New and seasoned professionals alike will find this monograph a comprehensive resource for orientation program development on university and college campuses.

As shown in the first edition, many trends shape how we offer programs and services to our students. For example, decreasing levels of financial and human resources, increasing levels of consumerism, higher expectations for accountability, increasing demands for the use and availability of technology, and increasing diversity among students all influence how we interact with new students. This monograph defines, describes, and outlines current and future issues for orientation professionals and offers suggestions for how to deal with these issues. Many of the authors are current practitioners facing the same challenges as the readers of this monograph; thus, we believe their insights are especially relevant. In addition, many of the authors are active members of the National Orientation Directors Association, an organization whose mission includes supporting those involved in orientation, transition, and retention activities. Thus, they have an awareness of current practice and the wide range of resources available to support work in these areas.

Editors' Notes

The chapters in the monograph are evenly balanced between a focus on the populations served by orientation and a focus on how best to design and administer orientation programs. Throughout the monograph, the concept of orientation and specific recommendations for implementation are supported by student development theory, research on college students and transition issues, and national standards for practice. The practitioner will also find helpful examples of orientation and transition services from a wide range of institutional types.

The monograph opens by laying the philosophical and theoretical groundwork for orientation and transition services. In Chapter 1, Tony Cawthon and Michael Miller describe today's students and provide a foundation for understanding the population served. The second chapter, by Michael Dannells and Maureen Wilson, includes an overview of student development theory and provides a model for applying theory to program design. This chapter proves to be a good review for those who studied student development theories or a good introduction for those who did not. Chapter 3, by Gerry Strumpf, Greg Sharer, and Matthew Wawrzynski, moves away from the theoretical basis of orientation to provide a glimpse of the current state of affairs in orientation. The authors offer the reader a glimpse into the trends of orientation programming drawn from their analysis of the most recent *NODA Data Banks*.

Once this groundwork has been laid, the monograph takes up issues related to the design of orientation programs. In Chapter 4, Becky Smith and Dick Brackin outline the major components of orientation programs with supporting research from various higher education entities. The next chapter, updated by Jim Zakely, builds on Smith and Brackin's discussion and highlights how the design of orientation programs impact academic and social integration and ultimately retention. In Chapter 6, Jimmy Abraham, Bryan Nesbit, and Jeanine Ward-Roof continue the focus on the administration of orientation, taking up issues related to placement of orientation within the institutional hierarchy, staffing, and funding.

The next five chapters look more closely at the populations served by orientation. In Chapter 7, Bonita Jacobs and Brian Bowen discuss the needs of a number of special student populations and offer suggestions for their meaningful inclusion in the orientation process. Because of their increasing presence on our campuses, the needs of two student populations are taken up in chapter-length discussions—those of transfer students and adult learners. In Chapter 8, Jeanine Ward-Roof, Patricia Kashner, and Valerie Hodge describe the transfer population and highlight programs designed to help ease the transition to a new educational environment. In a new chapter for this edition, Cathie Hatch provides an analysis of nontraditional learners, their unique needs, and their learning preferences. She also offers suggestions for creating an effective and appropriate orientation process for a nontraditional population. Chapter 10, by Les Cook, Betty Cully, and Deneece Huftalin, looks not only at a large population within American higher education but also considers a unique institutional setting—those students enrolling at two-year institutions. In addition to discussing issues related to orientation in this setting, the authors highlight best practices in orientation and transition services in two-year colleges. Parents and families of new students are another significant population served by orientation. In Chapter 11, Diane Austin discusses family influence on student success and outlines the process for developing a family orientation program.

The majority of topics presented in the monograph focus on what might be seen as traditional or highly focused orientation programs, but Chapter 12 explores extending the benefits of orientation throughout the first semester. Mary Stuart Hunter, Tracy Skipper, and Carrie Linder discuss the origins and structure of first-year seminars in American higher education and highlight the benefits to student development, academic success, and retention. In a similar vein, Gary Kramer explores technology and its potential for enhancing the benefits associated with orientation, retention, and transition programs.

In Chapter 14, by Dick Mullendore, Gary Biller, and Ralph Busby, we return to a discussion of the administration of orientation programs. Here, the authors outline the importance of evaluation and assessment in developing and maintaining an orientation program, and they offer a process for completing such activities. In the final chapter, John Gardner and Dave Hansen reflect on the value of orientation and offer observations for how it might, and perhaps should, change in the coming years. Throughout, their discussion underscores the issues raised by other authors in this volume.

In conclusion, we are grateful for the efforts of the authors, editors, reviewers, NODA Board members, and National Resource Center staff who agreed to collaborate on this very important project. Thank you to each of you for the time and energy you committed to this project.

We hope that orientation, retention, and transition professionals (among others) find support for the incredible work accomplished each day in the field of higher education in *Designing Successful Transitions: A Guide for Orienting Students to College*.

Today's Students and Their Impact on Orientation and First-Year Programs

Tony W. Cawthon and Michael Miller

The purpose of this chapter is to create a snapshot of today's college student—the student at the beginning of the 21st century. Attempting to create a single snapshot is problematic, because the American college student population of 2003 is no longer the ethnically, socially, and culturally homogenous group it was during the mid-20th century. Increasingly, the student population on American college campuses shows a widening diversity in terms of gender, age, social class, and ethnicity. So, rather than a clear image, our snapshot features something more closely resembling a double exposure.

By and large, traditional orientation programs are still designed and delivered with a single audience in mind—the student between the ages of 18 and 24. As the chapters on nontraditional learners, transfer students, and diverse student populations attest, orientation professionals are also designing more specialized programs in recognition of these student populations. This chapter will focus on traditional-aged students who, while no longer the defining population on America's campuses, are still the primary customers for orientation programs. Because this chapter presents an incomplete picture of today's college student, readers are encouraged to explore the chapters on adult learners and diverse student populations to understand how their needs may differ from the students described here.

Student Demographic Characteristics

Since World War I, society has chosen labels to describe generations of young people. These terms, including the Lost Generation, the Depression Generation, the Silent Generation, Baby Boomers, the Me Generation, Generation X, 13th Generation, Baby Busters, the Repair Generation, and Generation Y, often have produced confusion and conflicting views of our students. The most recent generational label, the Millennial, is attached to those students born in or after 1982 (Howe & Strauss, 2000). The Millennials are large in number, team-oriented, ethnically diverse, and upbeat. Additionally, Howe and Strauss (2000) describe them as idealistic, sheltered, committed to changing the world, and valuing relationships. College juniors in the year 2002 are on the leading edge of this generation. They, along with their younger peers, will impact our campuses in the coming years, and like previous generations, this generation is unique and distinct from its predecessors.

The Millenials are also culturally different from preceding generations of college students. Each year the staff at Beloit College assembles data on cultural reference points designed to increase faculty knowledge of the entering class. For example, students in the Class of 2005 have always had answering machines, never experienced a television with only 13 black and white channels, and have always had a VCR. They have no memories of the Cold War, are too young to recall the explosion of the Space Shuttle Challenger, and attach little, if any, meaning to Tianamen Square (Nief, n.d).

In 1991, Strauss and Howe made several predictions about this generation, most of which appear to be true. They predicted that future Millennials would score higher on aptitude tests due to increased home and school emphasis on math and science and that they would receive better childcare. Also, they predicted that Millennials would not understand the behavior of Baby Boomers (their parents and other adults) whom these students perceive as ill-behaved and sexually promiscuous. Strauss and Howe also expected that this generation of college students would experience a decline in substance abuse, crime, suicide, teenage pregnancies, and truancy. In fact, the largest abusers of drugs in 2002 are those Americans aged 35 to 48 (the end of the Baby Boomer generation), and alcohol use is declining among children and young teens (Gerardy, 2002). While campus behavior may not reflect this trend, the percentage of abstainers and very light drinkers appears to be increasing (Gerardy). More important, our knowledge of generation theory provides additional insights into the potential impact of Millennials on higher education, even though society and campuses may not see that impact immediately. Social and media attention on the Millenials is considerable, but generation theory suggests that full media attention to a generation usually takes place when its oldest members are approximately 25 to 30 years of age. Thus, we may not understand the complete impact of Millennials on our campuses until the years 2007 to 2012 (Gerardy).

Understanding both the empirical research and the somewhat whimsical anecdotal evidence of student characteristics gives professionals insights into generational differences. These differences are reflected in an increasing demographic diversity and in changing student attitudes and values. Ultimately, campus staff and faculty must be prepared to embrace these differences if they are to help students make smooth transitions to higher education and help them succeed academically. For example, Howe and Strauss (2000) note the increasing ethnic diversity of the college-age population; 35% of Millennials are non-white or Latino, compared to 14% of the GI generation (World War II generation). These changing demographics and student characteristics have a tremendous impact on campus environments and how we deliver campus services.

> *"The Millennials are large in number, team-oriented, ethnically diverse, and upbeat. Additionally, Howe and Strauss (2000) describe them as idealistic, sheltered, committed to changing the world, and valuing relationships."*

Moreover, the college population is expected to increase significantly in future years. With the start of the 2000 school year, the National Center for Education Statistics (2001) reported a record attendance of 53 million students in elementary and secondary schools. Record attendance levels are projected to continue until 2008, and by 2010, college populations will increase by 19%. This increase will have a significant impact on academic and student life on campuses, class size and course offerings, the delivery of orientation, and the development of campus and residence hall community.

Racial/Ethnic Diversity

Since the 1960s, higher education has been increasingly accessible to groups historically denied access (Upcraft, 1993). For example, by 1999, minority student enrollment had increased to 28.1% of total enrollment on college and university campuses (*The Chronicle of Higher Education*, 2001), up from 22.2% in 1990 and 18.7% in 1980 (Upcraft, 1993).[1]

An examination of the overall college enrollment by race and ethnicity between 1980 and 1999 reflects a 22.4% increase in minority participation compared with a 4.4% increase among white students during the same period. In particular, minority participation during the 1980s and 1990s reflects an increase of 48.2% for Blacks, a 21.8% increase for Asian Americans, a

17.9% increase for Hispanics, a 73% increase for American Indians, and a 69.3% increase for international students (*The Chronicle of Higher Education*, 2001).

A closer examination of the 1999 data reveals uneven enrollment patterns by type of institution. For all student groups, 37.8% attend two-year institutions and 62.2% attend four-year institutions. While 35.8% of White students attend two-year institutions, this percentage is higher for other racial/ethnic groups: American Indians (49.6%), Asians (39.1%), Blacks (41.1%), and Hispanics (55.8%) (*The Chronicle of Higher Education*, 2001).

The story is different when examining racial and ethnic enrollment at public versus private institutions. For all students enrolled, 76.5% attend public institutions and 23.5% attend private institutions. The enrollment of White students (76% public, 24% private), Black students (76.4% public, 23.6% private), and Asian students (78.5% public, 21.5% private) mirrors these overall percentages. Attendance for American Indians and Hispanics, however, is higher at public institutions, 85.4% and 83.4% respectively (*The Chronicle of Higher Education*, 2001).

As expected, these increases have impacted our campuses. Orientation and other student affairs professionals are expected to be knowledgeable about different ethnic/racial groups, their history, and their needs. The prudent professional understands that while student populations have similarities and differences *across* groups, that significant diversity also exists *within* groups. For this reason, terms such as Asians, American Indians, and Hispanics should be applied with discretion. The term Asian American, for example, applies to some 43 different cultural groups (28 Asian and 15 Pacific Islands) (Baruch & Manning, 1999)—all with unique cultural characteristics. Likewise, the term American Indian encompasses more than 505 federally and 365 state-recognized tribes, while the term Hispanic represents a variety of Spanish-speaking cultures. Hispanics are the fastest growing student population on our campuses, and the term incorporates Mexican Americans, Spanish Americans, Puerto Ricans, Chicanos, Salvadorians, Guatemalans, and Latin Americans (Baruch & Manning, 1999).

The racial and ethnic background of students enrolled in colleges and universities also varies greatly by geographic region. The areas where the enrollment of racial and ethnic minority groups is 34% or greater include Hawaii, California, New Mexico, District of Columbia, Texas, Mississippi, Florida, Maryland, and Louisiana (*The Chronicle of Higher Education*, 2001). The greater minority enrollment in these areas reflects the increased presence of minority groups in the general population for these regions.

Millennials respond to this increasing ethnic and racial diversity in interesting ways. They are less likely to identify themselves as White or Black and are less prejudiced about race. For Millennials diversity does not mean Black/White; rather, it represents individuals of varying skin colors from numerous countries (Howe & Strauss, 2000).

Gender

Early in U.S. history, enrollments in institutions of higher education were confined to White, upper-class males; women, Blacks, American Indians, and others were denied access to higher education (Brazzell, 1996). In 1836, almost 200 years after the founding of Harvard, the first institutions of higher education for women were established. Examples of these early institutions developed for women's education were Wesleyan College in Macon, Georgia (1836), Mount Holyoke (1837), Rockford College (1849), and Vassar College (1865), and by 1870, approximately 11,000 women were enrolled in some type of higher education (Horowitz, 1984).

In the 1980s, significant increases in enrollment occurred, with women's enrollment surpassing that of men's on college and university campuses (El-Khawas, 1996). In examining enrollment data for the last 20 years, this pattern is evident. In 1976, 53% of students enrolled were male and 47% were female, but by 1980 a shift had occurred; 48.5% of college students were male and 51.5% were female. By 1990 the percentages were 45.5% male and 54.5% female (Upcraft, 1993). This gap had widened even more by 1999 when females rose to 56.1% and males had decreased to 43.9% (*The Chronicle of Higher Education*, 2001). The gender gap on college campuses is expected to continue to widen. *The Chronicle of Higher Education's* Almanac Issue 2001-02 (2001) projects that women will comprise 58% of total enrollment by 2010.

Enrollment Status

Unlike the clear shift of increasing numbers of women in higher education, the data reflecting enrollment status is not as straightforward. Since World War II, the number of part-time students has continually increased (El-Khawas, 1996). In 1976, 39% of students were enrolled part time, and in 1990, this percentage had risen to 43.3%; however, by 1999, the number of part-time students enrolled was only 40.6%. Based on projections for 2000-2011, this percentage is expected to remain approximately 40% (*The Chronicle of Higher Education*, 2001).

Because more students are likely to attend part time or temporarily stop out to pursue other opportunities, the time necessary to complete an undergraduate degree is increasing. The financial implications of this trend are of concern to students and their families and to the general public and government officials. Astin, Tsui, & Avalos (1996) report that only two in five students complete their bachelors' degree in four years. While research suggests that taking longer than four years to complete the degree is commonplace, most students believe they will finish their undergraduate degrees in four years of continuous enrollment at a single institution. According to the fall 2000 Cooperative Institutional Research Program (CIRP) survey of entering full-time first-year students, only 6.7% believed they would need extra time to complete their degree requirements, only 1% believed they would drop out temporarily, only 6.6% believed they would transfer, and less than 1% believed they would drop out permanently (*The Chronicle of Higher Education*, 2001). Thus, there is a marked contrast between the reality and perception of length and method of obtaining a college degree.

Age

Another significant change for higher education is the age diversity of students attending colleges and universities. The passage of the GI Bill, the growth of women in the workplace, and the changing nature of educational needs/skills in the workplace have led to increased numbers of older students enrolling in higher education.

TIAA-CREF (1998) reports that in recent years the number of traditional-aged college students has decreased and the number of nontraditional students (those students 25 years and older) has increased. Due to a shift in recent demographics, TIAA-CREF reports that by 2010, more than 11% of all Americans between 25 and 64 years of age will be enrolled in some type of higher education institution. If so, the percentages of adults aged 25 years and older will increase from the current enrollment of 37.3% in fall 2000 to 50% of those students enrolled in higher education by 2010 (TIAA-CREF, 1998). Nontraditional students tend to be commuters, have families of their own, and are more likely to attend part time (Beneshoff & Bundy, 2000). Chapter 9 provides a more detailed discussion of the characteristics of nontraditional students. At the same time that enrollment of nontraditional students is increasing, the National Center for Education Statistics (2001) predicts an increase of enrollment from traditional-aged students based on record attendance in elementary and secondary schools. The convergence of these two trends suggest that orientation professionals must be knowledgeable about the needs of both groups and should anticipate designing programs that will address the concerns of students spanning a wide age spectrum.

Students With Disabilities

Section 504 of the 1973 Rehabilitation Act has provided unprecedented access for individuals with disabilities to attend higher education institutions. The act has also brought greater diversity to campuses and provided guidance on how educational institutions should serve students with disabilities. Additionally, the Americans With Disabilities Act of 1990 has further broadened educational environments for individuals with disabilities. As Henderson (1995) notes, "the percentage of freshmen who report having a disability has tripled" (p. iii) since the 1970s and passage of section 504.

The Heath Resource Center of the American Council on Education (Henderson, 2001) provides the most comprehensive overview of students with disabilities. According to the 1998 Heath report, 9% of all students enrolled in higher education reported having a disability. CIRP data suggest that the number of full-time, first-year college students reporting disabilities remained fairly stable during the 1990s, increasing from 6% in 1988 to 8% in 2000. Of those reporting disabilities in 2000, 54% attended public institutions, 42% independent colleges and universities, and 4% historically black colleges and universities (Henderson, 2001).

While the number of students reporting disabilities increased only slightly, the types of disabilities reported changed dramatically. In 1988, the predominant disability reported by first-year students was a visual impairment; however, in 2000, the number one disability was a learning disability. The percentage of first-year students reporting a learning disability increased from 16% in 1988 to 40% in 2000 (Henderson, 2001).

The significant increase of students reporting a learning disability has a tremendous impact on both academic and student affairs administrators. Academic procedures must be developed to allow these students maximum academic performance. Developing these procedures underscores the need for collaboration between the academic community and student affairs professionals as campuses provide testing centers, tutoring, and other resources for students with learning disabilities.

Sexual Orientation

Lesbian, gay, bisexual, and transgender (LGBT) students have been referred to as the invisible population on our college campuses (Sanlo, 1998). As such, determining their campus numbers is difficult. The literature on sexual orientation suggests that 10% of the American population is homosexual, but no definite consensus exists on the number of LGBT college students. Sherrill and Hardesty (1994) cite studies estimating that one in six college students are LGBT, and Howe and Strauss (2000) cite various polls indicating that between 3% and 10% of teenagers either identify themselves as gay, lesbian, or bisexual or are questioning their sexual identity. While the number of LGBT college students is not definitive, studies have shown

> "*Campuses must create environments and communities that allow for students' exploration of their multiple identities as part of their college experience.*"

that LGBT college students have increasing influence on campuses (D'Augelli, 1994; Rhoads, 1994; Rhoads, 1997). The amount of influence should not be overestimated. While LGBT may be more successful in having their voices heard, many students continue to report that campus environments are not supportive or accepting (Liddell & Douvanis, 1994).

To work effectively with the LGBT students on our campuses, individuals must be knowledgeable about the coming out process, the numerous homosexual identity development models, and the issue of multiple identities arising from the intersections of sexual identity with race/ethnicity, cultural background, religion, or gender. Creating a unified identity from these multiple identities may be an extremely challenging and lonely experience for some students. For example, LGBT students of color may experience abundant support for exploring their racial and ethnic identities but very little support for exploring their homosexual identity (Icard, 1986). Campuses must create environments and communities that allow for students' exploration of their multiple identities as part of their college experience.

International Students

Participation of international students in higher education institutions has risen steadily since the 1980s. In 1980, 2.5% of students who enrolled on American college campuses were international students; by 1990, this percentage had increased to 3.5%. While the actual percentage enrolled may not appear significant because total student enrollment has also risen, this actually reflects a 70% increase in the number of international students enrolled (*The Chronicle of Higher Education*, 2001). According to the Institute for International Education (2001), 547,867 international students were enrolled in U.S. colleges and universities. This number represents a 6.4% increase over the previous year and is the highest increase since 1980. Growth of international students on U.S. campuses has risen significantly since 1997, after years of minimal growth.

Countries with the highest participation of students include China, India, Japan, Korea, Taiwan, Canada, Indonesia, Thailand, Turkey, and Mexico. In 2001, India surpassed Japan in the number of students enrolling in American higher education. Overall, growth from Asian countries has decreased due to the troubled economic situation in the Far East (Institute for International Education, 2001).

Despite the fact that international students constitute only 3% of total enrollment, the impact of these students is great. According to the Institute for International Education (2001), more than 146 institutions had international enrollments of 1,000 or more, and at the 25 campuses with the largest international enrollments, this enrollment exceeded 3,000 students. For the 2000-01 year, the institutions reporting the highest international enrollments included New York University, the University of Southern California, Columbia University, Purdue University (Main Campus), Boston University, and the University of Texas at Austin. Also, the top programs of study for the 2000-01 year include business and management, engineering, and mathematics and computer science. Participation in mathematics and computer science actually increased 18.4% from the previous year (Institute for International Education, 2001).

Of particular note regarding the increase of international students is that since 1993, the total number of international students at all types of institutions has risen 15%. This growth is particularly evident in the community college system where the increase since 1993 has been 50%.

Campuses must be sensitive to the needs of these students. Language barriers, differing cultural expectations and norms, communication styles, and attitudes regarding gender roles may make this transition more difficult for international and American students both socially and academically. Developing social and academic support services for international students provides an excellent opportunity for collaboration between student affairs and academic affairs professionals. Such services become even more critical in the post-September 11, 2001 environment so that international students feel welcomed and safe on American campuses.

> *"According to the Institute for International Education (2001), more than 146 institutions had international enrollments of 1,000 or more, and at the 25 campuses with the largest international enrollments, this enrollment exceeded 3,000 students."*

Changing Student Characteristics

Attitudes and Values

The early emphasis on group activities for students in the Millennial generation may be one reason why they have been identified as very social (Cuneo & Krol, 1998; Rosenthal, 1998). They are also less ethnocentric than previous generations, more open to cultural differences, and more willing to interact with those different from themselves. They are more tolerant of both ambiguity and process than their predecessors in Generation X, but they are also more results-oriented than Generation X, demonstrated in their focus on career and success (Murray, 1997).

The educational aspirations of students has increased. In 2000, only 12% of entering first-year students planned to earn only a bachelor's degree compared to 28% in 1991. Nearly 47% planned to earn a master's degree, as compared to 35% a decade earlier, and 27% planned to earn some form of doctoral degree, as compared to 19% in 1991. While these students are more likely to be involved in community service activities, they are also much less likely to participate in student elections, and are much more likely to participate in some form of organized student demonstration (*The Chronicle of Higher Education*, 1992; 2001).

The impact of the events of September 11, 2001 are also beginning to be felt, as students report paying greater attention to the emotional and personal aspects of their lives. While the long-term effects on entering classes has not been studied, September 11 may have a triggering effect on student desires to stay focused and not 'lose time,' or conversely, to enjoy institutional surroundings and friends more and place a greater value on the present (Brownstein & Hoover, 2001).

Family Influence

Students entering college during the next decade will continue to come from a variety of family structures. Many of these students have been part of families that have experienced divorce and parental remarriage. The impact of the blended family on social and emotional development has not been fully explored, and many children find the socialization with new brothers and sisters who accompany parental remarriage difficult. Parental involvement in their children's activities has changed. Rather than merely completing registration forms and arranging transportation, parents now are active supporters and spectators (Murray, 1997). Children's activities now play a central, rather than peripheral, role in family life. This early involvement can have any number of effects on a student's or parent's relationship to the college and to each other. For example, it may lead to increased attention to academic successes and the expectation of greater institutional responsiveness to student and parent needs. Additionally, students may be more reliant on their parents to intervene on their behalf in various collegiate settings (e.g., resources, bursar's payments, housing), forcing the institution to respond in ways different from previous decades (Jacobs & With, 2002).

Another substantial change resulting from this involvement in planned activities is the focus on group learning, activity, and teamwork (Omelia, 1998). Students in this new generation of college students have been socialized to participate in groups, and it is therefore easier and more natural for them to solve problems, learn, and work in groups rather than individually (Wellner, 1999; Cuneo & Krol, 1998).

Academic Preparation

Entering college students are better prepared academically than they were a decade ago, as evidenced in the rise in ACT and SAT scores. ACT scores rose modestly from an average of 20 to 21, but SAT scores rose more dramatically from 422 on the verbal section and 474 on the mathematics section, both in 1991, to 505 and 514, respectively, in 2001 (*The Chronicle of Higher Education*, 1992; 2001). The academic performance of students continues to increase, as evidenced by overall grade distributions. Rojstaczer (1999), however, suggests that claims of increased student performance are exaggerated and largely due to faculty's inflating grades to attract larger enrollments.

Mental and Physical Health

Historically, campuses have relied on various sources to identify college students' mental and physical health problems. These sources, all designed to provide insights into the psychological problems faced by college students, include using diagnostic systems (Callis, 1965; Heppner, Kivlighan, Good, Roehlke, Hills, & Ashby, 1994), clients self-reported problems via checklist (Anton & Reed, 1991), and data collected via large data banks such as the College and University Counseling Center Data Bank (Magoon, 1998) and the national survey of Counseling Center Directors (Gallager, Gill, & Goldstrohm. 1998). Examining these different sources provides campus officials with a good picture of the mental and physical health of college students.

In the 1998 National Survey of Counseling Center Directors, 75% of institutions surveyed reported an increase in the number of students with learning disabilities and psychological problems, a 48% increase in sexual abuse, and a 45% increase in alcohol use and abuse (Gallagher et al., 1998). Additionally, of these counseling center directors surveyed, 86% identified the necessity of hospitalizing students with psychological concerns and 27% reported at least one student suicide during the previous year. This data appears to support the findings of Levine and Cureton (1998), whose survey of chief student affairs officers (CSAO) indicated that a majority of CSAOs believed students currently entering college were coming to campus with more psychological damage than previous students.

In looking at health behavior and health risk, several studies examining alcohol use and sexual activity are helpful. The Harvard School of Public Health (Wechsler & Wuethrich, 2002) found that 44% of students at the 120 four-year institutions included in the study reported engaging in behavior classified as binge drinking. Ullman, Karabatsos, and Koss (1999) connected the use of alcohol to additional campus problems such as unsafe sexual practices, sexual assaults, and increased occurrence of sexually transmitted diseases.

According to Simon (1993), students report using contraceptives and limiting the number sexual contacts; however, students continue to engage in unsafe sexual practices (Pendergast, 1994). Rennison's (1999) data show that forced sexual assault continues to be a problem among college students.

Four studies illustrate the state of mental health among students. Sax, Astin, Korn, and Mahoney (1998) indicated that students are reporting record levels of stress and increased substance use and abuse, eating disorders, and sexually transmitted diseases. A later study by Sax, Lindholm, Astin, Korn, and Mahoney (2001) reported that first-year students who rated their physical and mental health as above average reached record lows, and the percentage of college students anticipating a need for personal counseling reached a 28-year high at 6.6%, compared to 3.5 % in 1989. Bishop, Bauer, and Becker (1998) confirm the results of earlier studies reflecting that more than one third of students surveyed reported negative issues related to personal relationships, anxiety, depression, self-esteem, weight, and the fear of failure. Additionally, the Higher Education Research Institute, examining the impact of depression and use of antidepressants among first-year college students, reported that 9.3% of these students experienced depression during the previous year, and 65.9% of those experiencing depression reported taking prescribed antidepressants (Sax, Astin, et al., 1998).

Financing Education

Students continue to be concerned about how they will finance their college education, although for the entering class in 2001, 87% felt confident that they would have enough funds to pay for college. One fifth of entering college students chose their college based on affordability, and 42% of the entering class planned to get a part-time job to help pay for tuition. This trend reflects a change from the 1991 cohort where nearly one quarter planned to hold a part-time job and 5% planned to hold a full-time job while attending college (*The Chronicle of Higher Education*, 1992; 2001). In other words, college students worry somewhat about how they will pay for college and are willing to get a job and work part-time to pay for college.

Additionally, in terms of financial aid, fewer students are getting support from all funding sources. Federal aid to all entering students dropped from 42% to 39%, state aid dropped from 21% to 16%, and institutional aid to new stu-

> *"One fifth of entering college students chose their college based on affordability, and 42% of the entering class planned to get a part-time job to help pay for tuition."*

dents dropped the most, from 24% to 15% (National Center for Public Policy and Higher Education, 2002). Other trends noted by the National Center for Public Policy and Higher Education suggest that (a) tuition increases have made college less affordable to most American families; (b) state and federal aid has not kept pace with these tuition increases; (c) more students and their families are borrowing record levels of money to pay for college; and (d) despite increased state support for higher education, tuition increases have outpaced appropriations. The Center's major conclusion is that the college experience is becoming increasingly less affordable.

Technology Exposure

Students enter campus with greater technological savvy than many of the faculty possess. Personal computer use has grown from 37% for the 1991 entering class to nearly 80% for the entering 2001 class (*The Chronicle of Higher Education*, 1992; 2001). These students do far more than use personal computers for homework. Rakoff (2001) notes that 75% of those age 18 to 29 and 45% of all children have access to or use the Internet. Additionally, 64% of middle-income and 28% of low-income families use computers and access the Internet. These figures represent a cultural mindset change from even a decade ago (Tapscott, 1998). This cultural mindset permeates all that new college students do and expect from campus services; college students now increasingly expect a high degree of technological sophistication from the colleges they choose. Technology and technological reliance also represent a need to consider a more flexible approach toward time and space availability; office hours and resources need not be bound by traditional work schedules. Instead, resources, personnel, and advising can be provided on demand.

Access to technology is far from universal, especially for those from rural communities with poor technological infrastructures. The digital divide has the potential to affect at-risk students or students from rural communities negatively (Katsinas & Moeck, 2002). With such strong national trends to integrate sophisticated technological applications in both the business and academic aspects of attending college, students without a firm grounding in technology, including at the very least basic computing skills, will be placed at a distinct disadvantage. Students will be less capable of thriving on campus and less prepared to succeed academically and perhaps socially.

What This Means for Orientation

> *"Given the more social nature of new students arriving on campus, loosely structured social events may be more appropriate than highly structured ice breaker activities."*

New student and transfer orientation programs are designed with a wide range of goals and from a wide array of perspectives. This chapter has attempted to highlight the ways in which students arriving on campuses today are more diverse than they have been in previous decades. And because they are different, orientation professionals need to think about how and why orientation and transition programs can and should be different. The overarching concerns continue to be deciding what orientation is intended to accomplish and outlining goals with professional and student staff. All too often orientation does not have a lasting impact because incoming students have changed to the extent that once stellar activities no longer accomplish needed or desired objectives.

One of the major areas of change for orientation programs is the socialization function in transitioning new students to campus (Hadlock, 2000). This socialization is one of the historical pillars of orientation programming, and orientation typically is designed around the idea that a social support network of peer students needs to be constructed for students to succeed. As an increasingly diverse, more social group of students arrive on campus, orientation professionals need to think strategically about what types of socialization development activities are included in precious orientation programming time. Given the more social nature of new students arriving on campus, loosely structured social events may be more appropriate than highly structured ice breaker activities.

Similarly, new students are team focused, and orientation programs that rely on traditional information-sharing lectures or large-group activities may be ineffective. Instead, team-based approaches to personal discovery can maximize transitional learning opportunities. While individualized attention is expected, resources also need to be in place for new students to access meaningful and well-structured information anytime, anywhere. These students expect a high level of customer service in the technical areas of campus life, orientation, and admissions, and universities must be ready to meet these expectations (Boening & Anderson, 2000).

Students' attitudes toward achievement will also need to be considered when developing orientation activities. These students may be impressed with large-scale activities that sell the institution, but the bottom-line is increasingly important, and students want to know what it takes to succeed (Jones, 2002). This does not mean simply getting a faculty volunteer to discuss 'tips from the prof,' but it does mean that speakers are involved, are polished, and have a high degree of "fit" between their content and the objectives of orientation.

Lastly, these students want to find purpose in their time investment in orientation. Activities need to fit into an overarching orientation philosophy and theme, and although these programs take on a wide variety of objectives, a unifying purpose to the activities selected should be apparent. There needs to be a reason for participation in orientation, and that reason needs to be conveyed to new students (Nadler & Miller, 1999). Orientation professionals, therefore, need to be aware of how students can benefit from orientation programs and the college's intended orientation outcomes. The match of student benefits and orientation outcomes must be strongly articulated, and the orientation professional should understand how the results of powerful transition experiences translate into increased academic achievement and retention rates (Gardner & Hansen, 1993).

Changes in college populations have been more gradual at times than they have been over the last few decades. The failure to pay attention to student profiles can be costly to the institution and the student. Efforts by associations such as the National Orientation Directors to identify student characteristics and offer reports of best-practices and benchmarks are especially helpful as institutions struggle to define both their own student's characteristics and their purposes for offering and implementing orientation, retention, and transition programs. Ultimately, though, it is the responsibility of orientation professionals to understand who their students are and to assess what needs to be accomplished, working with those student characteristics and goals to build programs that truly make a difference.

Notes

[1] The most recent statistics on college populations can be found in the annual *Chronicle of Higher Education Almanac Issue*; this annual issue of *The Chronicle of Higher Education* provides readers with an overview of facts about higher education in the United States. Data on students, faculty and staff, and resources are included.

References

Anton, W. D., & Reed, J. R. (1991). *College adjustment scales professional manual.* Odessa, FL: Psychological Assessment Resources.

Astin, A. W., Tsui, L., & Avalos, J. (1996). *Degree attainment rates at American colleges and universities: Effects of race, gender, and institutional type.* Los Angeles: University of California, Higher Education Research Institute.

Baruch, L., & Manning, M. (1999). *Multicultural counseling and psychotherapy: A lifespan perspective* (2nd ed.). Upper Saddle River, NJ: Merrill.

Beneshoff, J. M., & Bundy, A. P. (2000). Nontraditional students. In D. C. Davis & K. M. Humphrey (Eds.), *College counseling: Issues and strategies for a new millennium* (pp. 133-151). Alexandria, VA: American Counseling Association.

Bishop, J. B., Bauer, K. W., & Becker, E. T. (1998). A survey of counseling needs of male and female students. *Journal of College Student Development, 39,* 205-210.

Boening, C. H., & Anderson, M. L. (2000). Writing apprehension and academic achievement among undergraduate honors students. *Journal of College Orientation and Transition, 8*(1), 7-12.

Brazzell, J. C. (1996). Diversification of postsecondary institutions. In S. R. Komives, D. B. Woodley, Jr., & Associates (Eds.), *Student services: A handbook for the profession* (3rd ed., pp. 43-63). San Francisco: Jossey-Bass.

Brownstein, A., & Hoover, E. (December 14, 2001). Destination unknown, for many students September 11 changed everything. *Chronicle of Higher Education*, p. A 35.

Callis, R. (1965). Diagnostic classification as a research tool. *Journal of Counseling Psychology, 12*, 238-247.

The Chronicle of Higher Education. (1992). *Almanac, 1992-1993.* Washington, DC: Author.

The Chronicle of Higher Education. (2001). *Almanac, 2001-2002.* Washington, DC: Author.

Cuneo, A., & Krol, C. (1998). Marketing finding Gen Y a profitable playground. *Advertising Age, 69*(1), 57.

D'Augelli, A. R. (1994). Identity development and sexual orientation: Toward a model of lesbian, gay, and bisexual development. In E. J. Trickett, R. J. Watts, & D. Birman (Eds.), *Human diversity: Perspectives on people in context* (pp. 312-333). San Francisco: Jossey-Bass.

El-Khawas, E. (1996). Student diversity of today's campuses. In S. R. Komives, D. B. Woodley, Jr., & Associates (Eds.), *Student services: A handbook for the profession* (3rd ed., pp. 64-80). San Francisco: Jossey-Bass.

Gallagher, R. P., Gill, A. M., & Goldstrohm, S. L. (1998). *National survey of counseling center directors.* Alexandria, VA: International Association of Counseling Services.

Gardner, J. N., & Hansen, D. A. (1993). Perspectives on the future of orientation. In M. L. Upcraft, R. L. Mullendore, B. O. Barefoot, & D. S. Fidler (Eds.), *Designing successful transitions: A guide for orienting students to college* (Monograph No. 13) (pp. 183-194). Columbia, SC: University of South Carolina, National Resource Center for The Freshman Year Experience.

Gerardy, M. (2002, June). Generational theory. Paper presented at the meeting of the Mid-Managers Institute, Williamsburg, VA.

Hadlock, H. L. (2000). Orientation programs: A synopsis of their significance. *Journal of College Orientation and Transition, 7*(2), 27-32.

Henderson, C. (1995). *College freshmen with disabilities.* Washington, DC: American Council on Education.

Henderson, C. (2001). *2001 College freshmen with disabilities: A biennial statistical profile.* Washington, DC: American Council on Education.

Heppner, P. P., Kivlighan, D. M., Good, G. E., Roehlke, H. J., Hills, H. I., & Ashby, J. S. (1994). Presenting problems of university counseling center clients: A snapshot and multivariate classification scheme. *Journal of Counseling Psychology, 41,* 315-324.

Horowitz, H. L. (1984). *Alma mater: Design and experience in the women's colleges from their nineteen-century beginnings to the 1930s.* New York: Knopf.

Howe, N., & Strauss, W. (2000). *Millennials rising: The next great generation.* New York: Vintage Books.

Icard, I. (1986). Black gay men and conflicting social identities: Sexual orientation versus racial identity. *Journal of Social Work and Human Sexuality, 4,* 83.

Institute for International Education. (2001). *Open doors, 1992-93: Report on international education exchange.* New York: Author.

Jacobs, B., & With, E. (2002). Orientation's role in addressing the developmental stages of parents. *Journal of College Orientation and Transition, 9*(2), 37-43.

Jones, P. F. (2002). The value of the liberal arts and what it means for orientation professionals. *Journal of College Orientation and Transition, 9*(2), 13-18.

Katsinas, S. G., & Moeck, P. (2002). The digital divide and rural community colleges: Problems and prospects. *Community College Journal of Research and Practice, 26*(3), 207-224.

Levine, A., & Cureton, J. (1998). *When hope and fear collide.* San Francisco: Jossey-Bass.

Liddell, D. L., & Douvanis, C. J. (1994). The social and legal status of gay and lesbian students: An update for colleges and universities. *NASPA Journal, 31,* 121-129.

Magoon, T. M. (1998). *College and university counseling centers data bank.* College Park: University of Maryland Counseling Center.

Murray, N. (1997). Welcome to the future: The millennial generation. *Journal of Career Planning and Employment, 57*(3), 36-40, 42.

Nadler, D. P., & Miller, M. T. (1999). Designing transitional programs to meet the needs of multi-ethnic first-year students. *Journal of College Orientation and Transition, 6*(2), 20-27.

National Center for Educational Statistics. (2001). Welcome to the National Center for Education Statistics. Retrieved June 2, 2002 from http: //nces.ed.gov/

National Center for Public Policy and Higher Education (2002). *Losing ground: A national status report on the affordability of American higher education.* San Jose, CA: Author.

Nief, R. (n.d). Beloit College releases annual mindset list for entering class of 2005. Retrieved April 14, 2002 from http://www.beloit.edu/~pubaff/releases/mindset-2005.htm.

Pendergast, M. L. (1994). Substance use and abuse among college students: A review of recent literature. *Journal of American College Health, 43,* 99-112.

Omelia, J. (1998). Understanding Generation Y: A look at the next wave of consumers. *Drug and Cosmetic Industry, 163*(6), 90.

Rakoff, J. S. (2001). E-boredom? *University Business, 4*(3), 16.

Rennison, C. M. (1999). *National crime victim survey 1998: Changes 1997-1998 with trends 1993-1998* (NCG Publication No. 176353). Washington, DC: U.S. Department of Justice.

Rhoads, R. A. (1994). *Coming out in college: The struggle for a queer identity.* Westport, CT: Bergin & Garvey.

Rhoads, R. A. (1997). Implications from the coming out experiences of college males. *The Journal of College Student Development, 36,* 67-74.

Rojstaczer, S. (1999). *Gone for good: Tales of university life after the golden age.* New York: Oxford University.

Rosenthal, N. (1998). The boom tube. *MediaWeek, 8*(2), 44.

Sanlo, R. L. (1998). Working with lesbian, gay, bisexual, and transgender college students: A handbook for faculty and administrators. Westport, CT: Greenwood Press.

Sax, L. J., Astin, A. W., Korn, W. S., & Mahoney, K. M. (1998). *The American freshman: National norms for Fall 1998.* Los Angeles: University of California, Higher Education Research Institute.

Sax, L. J., Lindholm, J. A., Astin, A. W., Korn, W. S., & Mahoney, K. M. (2001). *The American freshman: National norms for Fall 2001.* Los Angeles: University of California, Higher Education Research Institute.

Sherrill, J. M., & Hardesty, C. A. (1994). *The gay, lesbian, and bisexual students' guide to colleges, universities, and graduate schools.* New York: New York University Press.

Simon, T. (1993). Sexuality on campus '90s style. *Change, 25*(5), 50-56.

Strauss, W., & Howe, N. (1991) *Generations: The history of America's future, 1584-2069.* New York: Morrow.

Tapscott, D. (1998). *Growing up digital.* New York: McGraw-Hill.

TIAA-CREF. (1998, March). Higher education: Enrollment trends and staffing needs. *Research dialogues, 55.* Retrieved on September 10, 1999 from http://www.tiaa-cref.org/rds/rd55/rd55htm.

Ullman, S. E., Karabatsos, G., & Koss, M. P. (1999). Alcohol and sexual assault in a national sample of college women. *Journal of Interpersonal Violence, 14,* 603-605.

Upcraft, M. L. (1993). Orienting today's students. In M. L. Upcraft, R. H. Mullendore, B. Barefoot, & D. Fidler (Eds.), *Designing successful transitions: A guide for orienting students to college* (pp. 1-8). Columbia, SC: University of South Carolina, The National Resource Center for The Freshmen Year Experience.

Wechsler, H., Wueth, H., & Wuethrich, B. (2002). *Dying to drink on college campuses.* Emmaus, PA: Rodale Press.

Wellner, A. (1999). Get ready for generation next. *Training, 36*(2), 42-44, 46, 48.

Theoretical Perspectives on Orientation

Michael Dannells and Maureen E. Wilson*

Chapter Two

This chapter addresses a range of student development theories and campus environment models, the need for them, their evolution, their basic elements, and their uses in orientation practice. The primary focus is on some of the most widely used theories in student affairs, with a greater emphasis on those most relevant to orientation professionals. The chapter makes the case for using theory in practice and describes various theories and models that may be of use to the orientation practitioner. Lastly, the theory-to-practice gap is considered, and a process for using theory in practice is outlined.

Theory Justification

Strange (1994) contends "that what distinguishes professionals at work is their ability to bring reasoned explanations, grounded in evidence, to the phenomena about which they claim expertise" (p. 584). Hence, theory is one of the tools that can inform professional practice, and practitioners use informal theories daily. For instance, they have "theories" about orientation programs—what works and what does not, what is appropriate content, how to sequence programs effectively, and how various students will respond to different aspects of orientation. These informal theories (or explanations and predictions) are based on practical experience, implicit assumptions, presumptions, and biases that subtly influence decisions and generally guide practice. They are informal in that they are not operationally defined, explicitly stated, or systematically tested.

Formal theory provides a framework through which to construct interpretations and understanding. It makes "the many complex facets of experience manageable, understandable, meaningful, and consistent rather than random" (McEwen, 1996, p. 148). A theory's explicitness enables us to test our work against it, measure our outcomes, and craft the kinds of quality programs that characterize professionalism in our work. Ultimately, theories make the difference between practice and informed practice.

The Evolution of Student Development Theory

The practice of the earliest student affairs professionals was guided by the philosophy of *in loco parentis*. That is, the college acted "in the place of the parent," especially in disciplinary situations. Colleges in the colonial and early federal periods had as their primary purpose students' moral and religious development. Students were generally younger than they are today and were sent to college with the expectation that they would learn the classical disciplines as well as self-discipline as it was defined by their churches, families, and society. College officers, like parents, were presumed to know best what their young charges needed.

---

* Maureen Wilson joins Michael Dannels in revising and updating his contribution from the first edition.

As colleges in general grew more secular, their campuses larger, and their students older, *in loco parentis* became less and less defensible as a way of relating to students. The seeds of a more scientific and professional approach to working with college students are found in *The Student Personnel Point of View* (American Council on Education, 1937, 1949). Although the 1937 and 1949 documents clearly focus on service delivery, they are nonetheless developmental in their approach as they are grounded in principles from individual, humanistic, and holistic psychology and philosophy (Creamer, 1990). By the mid-20th century, what vestiges of *in loco parentis* remained were further diminished by increasing student activism, court decisions about disciplinary processes (Dannells, 1997), and the growing body of psychological and sociological theories on human development (Upcraft, 1989). These developmental theories burgeoned and became more focused on college students in the 1960s and 1970s.

Building on the work of Erikson (1950, 1968) and Sanford (1962, 1967), social scientists of that time sought answers to such questions as, How do college students grow and change? What most influences those processes? How do college environments affect students and their development? We still seek answers to those fundamental questions, with growing recognition and appreciation of the complexity of human nature and the variability of the increasingly diverse populations now represented in college. (For a more complete treatment of the evolving nature of student development theory, see Creamer & Associates, 1990; Evans, Forney, & Guido-DiBrito, 1998; Moore, 1990.)

The Categories of Theories

There are several taxonomies or classification systems of theories about college student development and about the interaction of students and their environments. For the purpose of providing structure for most of the remainder of this chapter, we will use the taxonomy of Knefelkamp, Widick, and Parker (1978), as modified by Rodgers (1989a) and adapted by Pascarella and Terenzini (1991), and discuss major student development theories, campus environment and interactionist models, and impact models.

The Major Student Development Theories

The psychosocial cluster. Psychosocial theories address the personal and interpersonal aspects of development. Psychosocial development concerns the issues, tasks, and events of the lifespan and a person's resolution of and adaptation to them (Rodgers, 1989a). Two basic principles of human development proposed by Sanford, one of the earliest social scientists to study college students and their environment, undergird the theories in this grouping. First, he postulated that development is expressed in increasing differentiation—that is, increasing specialization of the parts of the personality and in greater integration and a higher level of communication and organization between those parts (Sanford, 1962). Second, Sanford (1966, 1967) argued that students develop optimally when they are presented with the right balance of challenge and support in the college environment.

Following the work of Erikson and Sanford, Chickering's (1969) and Chickering and Reisser's (1993) theory of identity development is perhaps the most influential of all psychosocial theories in its focus on traditional-aged college students and its prescriptive value in student affairs programming (Pascarella & Terenzini, 1991). Growing out of Erikson's model of human development, Chickering (1969) postulated seven vectors of development in his landmark book, *Education and Identity*. Chickering and Reisser (1993) revisited and refined his theory. The seven vectors of identity development include

1. Developing competence (intellectual, physical/manual, and interpersonal)
2. Managing emotions (awareness, acknowledgment, and control)
3. Moving through autonomy toward interdependence (functioning with relative self-sufficiency, responsibility for self-chosen goals, less bound by opinions of others)
4. Developing mature interpersonal relationships (tolerance and appreciation of differences, capacity for intimacy)
5. Establishing identity (emergence of solid sense of self)
6. Developing purpose (being intentional, assessing interests and options, clarifying goals, making plans, persisting in the face of obstacles)
7. Developing integrity (humanizing and personalizing values, developing congruence between values and behaviors). (pp. 45-51)

Chickering and Reisser also identified seven key influences on student development: (a) clarity and consistency of institutional objectives, (b) institutional size, (c) student-faculty relationships, (d) curriculum, (e) teaching, (f) friendships and student communities, and (g) student development programs and services.

Marcia's work (as cited in Evans et al., 1998), like Chickering's, builds on Erikson's concept of identity. She proposes that, in addition to experiencing a conscious "crisis" when choosing between competing but meaningful alternatives, the individual must make a commitment or an investment in each of four values areas: occupational, religious, political, and sexual. Marcia's work served as a foundation for Josselson's (1987, 1996) significant research on the identity formation of women from their first year of college to age 43.

Early theories focused on late adolescence, but the development of older or nontraditional college students has seen increasing attention. For example, Schlossberg (1984; Schlossberg, Lynch, & Chickering, 1989) studied adults in transition. In this context, "transition" is defined as "any event, or non-event, that results in changed relationships, routines, assumptions, and roles" (Schlossberg, Waters, & Goodman, 1995, p. 27). Given that entering college is a time of significant transition for students, Schlossberg's work may be particularly applicable to the work of orientation professionals. She discussed three steps in mastering change resulting from transitions. First, approaching change involves examining life changes and their extent. Second, taking stock of one's resources for coping with change is important. Individual strengths and weaknesses, external supports, and strategies for coping are some common resources for managing change. The type of transition being experienced may determine the effectiveness of individual resources. Third, taking charge requires maximizing one's resources to master change. Hence, orientation professionals can help students assess the extent of life changes in their transition to college and marshall the resources necessary to master the changes. Furthermore, all students, but perhaps more important, underrepresented students of all kinds, have a need to feel they matter, that someone in the college setting cares about them. If they do not have this sense of mattering, they tend to feel marginalized and are less likely to succeed in college. The transition to college—where students must take on new roles, master new competencies, and build new social networks—may intensify feelings of marginality.

Many student development theories grew out of research on White adolescent males. Researchers have challenged some of these theories for failing to describe the development of women or members of racial and ethnic groups adequately. A small but growing subset of the research on human development addresses particular ethnic and racial groups. For example, Helm's (1990) theory of racial identity formation delineates three parts of racial identity: (a) a personal identity, (b) a reference group orientation, and (c) an ascribed identity — "the individual's deliberate affiliation or commitment to a particular racial group" (p. 5). Racial identity is "resolved" as the individual assigns relative weights to each of these three components. Because space limitations do not permit a balanced review of models of development from the perspective of particular ethnic groups, the reader is referred to Trickett, Watts, and Birman (1994) for an introduction to this important body of literature.

A variety of factors and characteristics, including sexual orientation, will affect the development of college students along psychosocial dimensions. On campuses and in society, gay, lesbian, bisexual, and transgender (GLBT) students often feel marginalized. The increasing number of GLBT student services offices (Sanlo, 2000) and a growing body of research (e.g., see Evans & Levine, 1990) highlight particular concerns of these students. Cass's (1979, 1984) model of homosexual identity formation delineates six stages: identity confusion, comparison, tolerance, pride, and synthesis. In contrast to stage models such as Cass's, D'Augelli (1994) presents an identity development model that acknowledges the influence of cultural and sociopolitical contexts. His model is less linear than Cass's and describes six concerns: (a) exiting heterosexual identity, (b) developing a personal lesbian-gay-bisexual (LGB) identity status, (c) developing an LGB social identity, (d) becoming an LGB offspring, (e) developing an LGB intimacy status, and (f) entering an LGB community. Recent scholarship (e.g., Wall & Evans, 2000), addresses many issues in promoting safe and welcoming campus environments that will promote the development of gay, lesbian, bisexual, and transgender students. As many students come out in college (Evans & Broido, 1999), they may expect more programs and services from campuses to aid in that process. This heightens the need for orientation staff to be explicit in highlighting available resources and sending early messages to *all* students that they are valuable members of the campus community.

While some theories focus on particular subpopulations, others (e.g., Jones, 1997; Jones & McEwen, 2000) consider multiple dimensions of identity. For example, how do class, culture, gender, race, religion, and sexual orientation interact to shape identity? Factors within a campus environment can influence the development of identity as well.

The cognitive-structural cluster. These theories address how people think, reason, and make meaning of their experiences (Evans et al., 1998). Building on Piaget's research, Perry's (1970) model, or "scheme," of intellectual and ethical development describes nine positions of a continuum along which students move from a simplistic view of the world to a more relativistic perspective in which they may make commitments. The nine stages are best summarized by four general clusters (King, 1978):

1. Dualism (positions 1-2). Students see the world in dualistic, discrete, categorical absolutes; whatever is deemed to be "right" is determined by established authority and is unquestioned.
2. Multiplicity (positions 3-4). Students acknowledge multiple perspectives, but uncertainty is temporary and different beliefs are held as simply wrong or not subject to evaluation.
3. Relativism (positions 5-6). Students view knowledge as contextual and relative; multiple perspectives are subject to objective, comparative evaluation, and multiple "truths" may be appreciated, often resulting in indecision.
4. Commitment in relativism (positions 7-9). Students make "an active affirmation of themselves and their responsibilities in a pluralistic world, establishing their identities in the process." (p. 39)

These commitments, in such areas as marriage, career, and religion, are modifiable and are consistent with the individual's self-identity and personalized view of the world.

Influenced by the work of Perry, Dewey, and others, King and Kitchener (1994) studied intellectual development, resulting in the Reflective Judgment Model. Reflective judgments "involve integrating and evaluating data, relating those data to theory and well-formed opinions, and ultimately creating a solution to [vexing problems] that can be defended as reasonable or plausible" (p. xvi). The model presents a developmental progression in reasoning and concepts of justification. King and Kitchener describe seven distinct sets of assumptions (stages) about knowledge and how it is acquired. For a comparison of Perry's scheme with King and Kitchener's model, see Rodgers (1989a). Marcia Baxter Magolda (1992, 2001) has also built on the work of other cognitive-structural theorists to describe gender-related patterns in the intellectual development of college students and young adults.

Closely related to theories of intellectual development is Kohlberg's (1971) attempt to define the cognitive stages of moral development, with each stage seen as a mode or structure of thought. Rather than focusing on the content of moral decisions, which may be socially or culturally influenced, Kohlberg focused on the universal cognitive processes—the how and why—of decision making about moral problems. He identified six stages, which may be summarized by three levels:

1. Preconventional, in which right is defined as following the rules and avoiding punishment (Stage 1) or what is fair or mutually agreeable (Stage 2)
2. Conventional, in which right is being a "good person" and conforming to expectations (Stage 3) or being loyal to and maintaining the social order and obligations (Stage 4)
3. Postconventional, autonomous, or principled, in which right promotes fundamental human rights and values (Stage 5) or universal, generalizable principles (Stage 6) (Evans et al., 1998, pp. 174-175)

In her book, *In a Different Voice*, Gilligan (1982) addresses what she perceives as a misrepresentation of women's moral development in Kohlberg and others. Gilligan argues that Kohlberg mistakenly labels women deficient in moral development because his theory stresses concepts of separation, autonomy, and justice without recognizing connectedness, responsibility to others, and care—what she calls the feminine "care voice." Much like Kohlberg, she views development as occurring through stages of decreasing egocentricity and increasing other-centeredness, moving to a universal perspective. Although the "justice voice" may predominate among men and the "care voice" among women, Gilligan proposes that both voices are inherent in the life cycle. Her focus on women's development has been extended into the realm of cognitive development through a critique and refinement of Perry's scheme by Belenky, Clinchy, Goldberger, and Tarule (1986).

Arguably at the interface of the psychosocial and cognitive development clusters, Fowler's (1981) theory of growth in faith provides an age-stage model of thinking about spiritual development, a dimension of human development largely ignored in the secular body of student development literature (Upcraft & Moore, 1990a, 1990b). Parks built on Fowler's theory and "emphasized the interrelatedness of cognitive development; affective states; and interpersonal, social, and cultural influences" (as cited in Love, 2002, p. 359). Both cognitive development and spiritual development theories focus on "the ways in which people make meaning of the world they live in and the experiences they have" (Love, 2002, p. 372). Whether or not a student practices a religion or participates in other spiritual activities, this process of meaning making is an essential component of the college experience.

The typological cluster. Typology theories do not explain the nature or process of development but represent stylistic differences in approaches to the world (Evans et al., 1998) or "relatively stable differences among individuals" (Pascarella & Terenzini, 1991, p. 36). These persistent individual differences may be found in such diverse, and often global, dimensions as cognitive style (Witkin, 1962, 1976), learning style (Kolb, 1976, 1984), level of maturity (Heath, 1964), personality (Myers, 1980; Myers & McCaulley, 1985), character and temperament (Kiersey & Bates, 1978), and sociodemographic characteristics (Cross, 1971, 1981). Certainly the most popular and the one with most obvious application to orientation programs is the Myers-Briggs Type Indicator (MBTI) (Myers, 1980; Myers & McCaulley, 1985). Based on the writings of Carl Jung, the MBTI types individuals according to preferences, or habitual patterns of thinking, along four dimensions (Rodgers, 1989a):

1. Orientation to the world—extraversion (E) and introversion (I)
2. Ways of perceiving—sensing (S) and intuition (N)
3. Ways of judging—thinking (T) and feeling (F)
4. Relating to the external environment—judging (J) and perceiving (P)

Using the MBTI to arrive at a score and assigning a letter of the preferred mode in each dimension, an individual's personality might be classified into one of 16 types: INFP, for example. MBTI types have been used as a basis for roommate assignments, and the MBTI is used often in training paraprofessional staff (among other groups). A thorough understanding of type and an appreciation of the strengths of various types can be very useful in orientation programs. For instance, while more extraverted personalities might be obvious candidates for student orientation leader positions, introverts should not be overlooked as they can bring special talents to the job.

Campus Environment and Interactionist Models

In contrast to the foregoing student development theories, which tend to focus on intra-individual development, campus environment and interactionist models attend more to the environmental origins of or influences on student behavior. In terms of Lewin's (1936) classic formula of human behavior, B = f(P X E), or behavior is a function of the interaction of person and environment, the models in this grouping give relatively more attention to the X (interaction) and to the E (environment). One substantial subset of this grouping, the so-called college "impact models" (Pascarella & Terenzini, 1991), merits separate attention.

Impact models. According to Pascarella and Terenzini (1991), college impact models have several features in common. First, they tend to be primarily sociological, giving greater credence to the context within which the individual functions. Second, they view the individual as an active participant whose behavior and development is influenced by the nature and intensity of environmental stimuli, including institutional size, type, policies, programs (both academic and non-academic), procedures, services, attitudes, values, and behaviors of others. Third, they concentrate on the origins and processes of student change, but with less specific explication of the particular changes undergone.

Astin's theory of student involvement (Astin, 1984, 1985, 1996) is unquestionably the best known of the impact models. Simply stated, his research has shown that "[s]tudents learn by becoming involved" (Astin, 1985, p. 133). He measures involvement by the amount and quality of psychological and physical energy a student devotes to an activity. The amount of learning, or development, is directly related to the quantity and quality of the student's involvement, and the educational quality of any policy or program is related to its capacity to induce student involvement. Astin saw students as active players in this equation, occupying a central role in determining the nature and extent of their growth by the choices they make and the energy they invest in the opportunities and resources they find in college.

Tinto's (1993) theory of student departure, a longitudinal model of institutional impact, attempts to explain the college student attrition process. He argues that student retention (or attrition) is a function of the degree of fit or integration between the characteristics and skills the student brings to college and the corresponding elements in the college environment. Student attributes and institutional variables interact in both academic and social systems, leading to some degree of academic and social integration, which is defined as the extent to which the individual shares the attitudes and values of peers and faculty and conforms to the expectations of the community. Negative experiences reduce integration and lead to distancing from the college's academic and social communities, increasing marginality, and perhaps culminating in withdrawal. Tinto's idea of integration has been compared to Astin's "involvement" and Pace's "quality of effort" (Pascarella & Terenzini, 1991). Tinto (1993) also suggests that this process of integration occurs in three stages: (a) separation, in which first-year students disassociate from memberships in former communities; (b) transition, which bridges the old and the new; and (c) incorporation, which is characterized by full membership in the new social and academic communities of college.

> *"Astin saw students as active players in this equation, occupying a central role in determining the nature and extent of their growth by the choices they make and the energy they invest in the opportunities and resources they find in college."*

Both Pascarella (1985) and Pascarella and Terenzini (1991) propose a general causal model for assessing change that, unlike Tinto's, gives explicit consideration to the institution's organizational and structural characteristics and to the quality of student effort. Pascarella's model accounts for the influence on student development of five sets of variables: (a) students' background and precollege characteristics, (b) features of the institution (e.g., size, selectivity), (c) the college environment, (d) students' interaction with socializing agents on the campus (peers, faculty), and (e) quality of student effort. In this model, an institution's structural and organizational characteristics (e.g., size or student-to-faculty ratio) indirectly influence students through their effect on the general college environment and on students' interactions with peers and faculty within that environment.

Unlike Pascarella and Terenzini, Weidman (1989) looks outside the institution to external social structures. His model of undergraduate socialization incorporates both psychological and social influences on students, giving particular attention to how the process of socialization in college affects students' career choices, lifestyle preferences, aspirations, and values. He explicitly considers the continuing influence of parents and other non-college socializing forces and how those forces interact with the socialization process in college.

Braxton (2000) builds on Tinto's work on student departure by examining it through the lens of organizational behavior. He reminds us that organizational models and behaviors of institutional leaders may influence students' social and academic integration, which may, in turn, impact students' departure or retention decisions. In his formulation, student departure presents an ill-structured problem that warrants the use of multiple theoretical perspectives.

Person-environment interaction theories. Huebner (1989) offers "several overarching theoretical propositions" (p. 180) that may be said to define the person-environment interaction theories as a group. The first and most basic is the focus on the "interactional-transactional relationship between persons and the environment" (p. 180). The interactionist paradigm holds that the person and the environment are involved in a process of continuous, mutual feedback. The second proposition is that the individual is an active and intentional participant in this process. Third, in their attempts to cope with environments that may be incompatible with their unique characteristics, individuals "may react negatively or fail to develop desirable qualities" (p. 181). Fourth, optimal person-environment fit "is not absolute, perfect, or similar for all individuals . . . [and] . . . some amount of incongruence (such as challenge) amidst a generally congruent situation (such as support) will stimulate development" (p. 182). Last, citing Blocker (1977, 1978), Huebner identified seven essential "ingredients for growth" in learning environments: involvement, challenge, support, structure, feedback, application, and integration.

Barker's (1968) theory of behavior settings focuses on the external, physical environment of individuals and how it influences behavior. He suggests that "behavior settings"—"standing patterns of behavior . . . that persist when the participants change" (p. 18)—select and shape the actions of different people in similar ways. Campus-related examples of behavior settings might include a sporting event, a class meeting, or a student senate meeting. Such settings are complex milieus of people, places, and things that exert powerful influence over individuals, and an understanding of them can be useful in predicting behavior.

Holland's (1966, 1985) work on vocational choice is an example of a human aggregate model, which describes the environment and its influence on people by the characteristics of the people in that environment. His theory is based on four assumptions:

1. People can be categorized into one of six basic personality types (realistic, investigative, artistic, social, enterprising, conventional) that correspond to vocational choices.
2. There are six "model environments" that correspond to those personality types.
3. People seek out environments that are congruent for them, their skills, attitudes, and values.
4. Person-environment congruence, or lack thereof, influences and can be used to predict behavior in the areas of personal development, stability, creativity, vocational choice, and achievement.

Moos (1976) conceptualized the environment in terms of the "social climate" of those who are in it. He identified three broad categories of the dimensions of social climates: (a) the relationship dimensions, which involve how people interact in the environment; (b) the personal development dimensions, which are the opportunities for personal growth and for task performance; and (c) the system maintenance and change dimensions, which describe the behavioral expectations and the ways the system maintains control and responds to change.

Stern (1970), working from the theories of Lewin (1936) and Murray (1938), developed a "need-press" model, which holds that the person and the environment must be studied on equal terms, giving equal weight to each in the analysis of any situation. Personal "needs" are "organizational tendencies which appear to give unity and direction to a person's behavior" (Stern, 1970, p. 6). These needs are inferred from the preferences students report when asked about various activities. Environmental "presses" are situational pressures to act in certain ways. They are inferred from the aggregated self-reports of the perceptions of those in the situation. In Stern's model, behavior is studied in terms of congruence or dissonance between needs and presses.

In his transactional theory, Pervin (1968) argues that human behavior is best explained by transactions (reciprocal relationships) and interactions (cause and effect relationships) between persons and their environments. Like Stern, he believes it is important to understand the environment as it is perceived by the individual and also the difference between individuals' perceptions of themselves in relation to their situations. According to Walsh (1973), Pervin's model rests on three assumptions: (a) Large discrepancies between perceived real and ideal selves are painful and unpleasant; (b) individuals are attracted to objects that they perceive will move them toward their ideal selves; and (c) "similarity in regard to objects of importance to the individual is desirable where the individual has a low actual-self/ideal-self discrepancy and undesirable where the individual has a high actual-self/ideal-self discrepancy" (p. 158).

Clark and Trow's (1966) typology of student subcultures provides an example of the subcultural approach to describing college students' environments, which assumes that students not only share certain attitudes and behaviors, but that the students in a given subculture interact with each other, thus further shaping the behavior of the individual. By studying students along the following two dimensions (i.e., the degree to which they identify with ideas and the degree to which they identify with their college), Clark and Trow found four subcultures of students: (a) academic—serious students who identify with both ideas and their college; (b) collegiate—students loyal to their college, but not interested in, and perhaps even resistant to, intellectual activities; (c) nonconformist—a residual category of diverse students who share an involvement with ideas; and (d) vocational—interested only in training for their careers, these students do not identify with either ideas or their college.

Katchadourian and Boli (1985) arrive at somewhat similar categories in their study of Stanford students. Using scales of intellectualism and careerism, they found students tended to cluster into four types, which they called (a) strivers (high on both intellectualism and careerism), (b) intellectuals (high intellectualism, low careerism), (c) careerists (low intellectualism, high careerism), and (d) unconnected (low on both scales).

Bronfenbrenner's (1979) concept of "ecological transition" would appear to have particular relevance to orientation professionals. New students are clearly in ecological transition, entering a new ecological environment in which they experience both a new role and a new setting. According to Banning (1989), if the "sending environment" (i.e., a traditional-aged first-year student's home, school, community) differs too greatly from the "receiving environment" (i.e., the collegiate environment), the new student may find the transition too stressful and may fail to adjust, grow, and develop. As Banning suggests,

> Once the student arrives on the campus, the fit between student and institution may well determine whether the collegiate environment is going to have a positive impact (retention) or a negative impact (attrition). . . [T]he nature of the ecological transition and the resulting ecological congruence are critical to freshman success. To determine the "fit" suggested by these concepts, the environmental variables of site, demographics, and programs appear to be both useful and important tools. (Banning, 1989, p. 58)

Rendón's (1994) research on the transitional needs of nontraditional students from diverse backgrounds has raised awareness of the importance of validation in the success of students who have serious doubts about their ability to succeed in college. She found that validation, "an enabling, confirming and supportive process initiated by in- and out-of-class agents that foster academic and interpersonal development" (p. 44), enhances students' self-worth and helps them feel more confident in their ability to succeed. Most relevant to orientation professionals, she found that "[v]alidation is the most effective when offered early on in the student's college experience, during the first year of college and during the first weeks of class" (p. 45).

> "... 'educational environments are most powerful when they offer students three fundamental conditions: a sense of security and inclusion, mechanisms for involvement, and an experience of community.'"

As they design and construct their programs and services, orientation professionals also would be well served to consider the conditions necessary for favorable educational environments identified by Strange and Banning (2001). According to them, "educational environments are most powerful when they offer students three fundamental conditions: a sense of security and inclusion, mechanisms for involvement, and an experience of community" (p. xiii).

From Theory to Orientation Practice

Faced with this perhaps bewildering array of theories, the orientation professional might be inclined to disregard theory-based practice as unrealistic or unwieldy. The gap between theory and practice has been widely discussed, and student development researchers and theorizers are urged regularly to make their work more relevant to practitioners. Likewise, practitioners are urged to "obtain and internalize an in-depth knowledge of college student development" (Rodgers, 1989b, p. 118). Student affairs professionals have also been encouraged to know their students and their characteristics, to apply theory as they evaluate programs or plan new ones, to share what they know about their students with their students, and to build their personal theories to explain events around them (Brown & Barr, 1990).

But knowledge of theory alone is not sufficient (Evans et al., 1998; Rodgers, 1989a). Orientation professionals must also know how to apply theory. To aid in this, Upcraft (1993) summarized and adapted to the language of orientation an 11-step practice-to-theory-to-practice model developed by Wells and Knefelkamp.

1. *Identify pragmatic concerns.* What problems or issues need to be addressed?
2. *Determine orientation program goals.* What specific outcomes (information, attitudes, skills) are desired?
3. *Examine which theories may be helpful.* Which theory clusters or specific theories are related to the desired goals? For example, if learning information and attitude formation are the central goals of an orientation program, then the cognitive-structural cluster may be most useful. Or, if social integration is paramount, then perhaps a combination of psychosocial and person-environment interactionist models might be most illuminating.
4. *Analyze student characteristics from the perspective of each theoretical cluster.* Which theory or theory cluster seems to fit the students involved best? How might it help in both formally and informally viewing those students? For example, if the student population is largely returning adults, Schlossberg's concepts of marginality and mattering might prove more useful than those theories developed on studies of traditional-aged students.
5. *Analyze environmental characteristics from the perspective of each theoretical cluster.* Which theory or theory cluster seems to fit the environment best? How might it serve as a "filter" for viewing students in the environment? For example, Tinto's model or Bronfenbrenner's theory might be useful in understanding student behavior in stressful, competitive circumstances.
6. *Analyze the source of developmental challenge and support in the context of both student and environmental characteristics.* What are the specific sources of challenge and support? What is the optimum balance for these students in this environment? Seek to ensure that balance.
7. *Re-analyze orientation program goals and modify, if necessary.* Assess to discover if the students are "ready" to learn all that is planned at orientation and if the goals should be modified.
8. *Design the orientation program using methods that will facilitate the accomplishment of the intended outcomes.* For example, if a goal of an orientation program is to improve students' academic self-esteem (a complex and deep-seated personal trait) in the college environment, then a long-term program, as opposed to a onetime event, is more likely to be successful.
9. *Implement the orientation program.*

10. *Evaluate the program.* Has it accomplished its goals? Have students acquired the new knowledge, developed the new skills, and adopted the new attitudes intended? Are the staff and the students satisfied? Develop suggestions for the future.
11. *Redesign the orientation program if necessary.*

To this 11-step process, Upcraft (1993) added a 12th:

12. *Revise or confirm the theory on the basis of its practical application.* After a fair trial of several interventions based on the theory, it may become obvious that it is the theory, not the practice (orientation program), that should be revised.

Thus, Upcraft (1993) suggested that a "practice to theory to practice to theory" model would be most appropriate. In such a process, orientation professionals could contribute in significant ways to the body of theory that guides their practice. After all, if we expect informed practice, should we not expect and contribute to informed theory?

Summary

We have argued that knowledge and application of theory to practice is one aspect of professionalism. To promote intentional learning outcomes for students, an intuitive approach is insufficient; informed practice is necessary. By presenting examples of a range of theories, practitioners can delve more deeply into the scholarship on students and ground orientation programs in that theoretical foundation. This will enhance effectiveness in working with students, faculty, and student affairs colleagues.

This overview of student development theories is by no means comprehensive, and our brief descriptions of these theories, by necessity, lack the kind of depth required to apply the theories in practice effectively. We encourage readers to go to the original sources, spend some time with the ideas they find there, and consider those ideas in the context of their campus environments and student populations.

References

American Council on Education. (1937). *The student personnel point of view.* Washington, DC: Author.

American Council on Education. (1949). *The student personnel point of view.* Washington, DC: Author.

Astin, A. W. (1984). Student involvement: A developmental theory for higher education. *Journal of College Student Personnel, 25,* 297-308.

Astin, A. W. (1985). *Achieving educational excellence: A critical assessment of priorities and practices in higher education.* San Francisco: Jossey-Bass.

Astin, A. W. (1996). *Involvement in learning* revisited: Lessons we have learned. *Journal of College Student Development, 37,* 123-134.

Banning, J. H. (1989). Impact of college environments on freshman students. In M. L. Upcraft, J. N. Gardner, & Associates, *The freshman year experience: Helping students survive and succeed in college* (pp. 53-62). San Francisco: Jossey-Bass.

Barker, R. G. (1968). *Ecological psychology: Concepts and methods for studying the environment on human behavior.* Stanford, CA: Stanford University Press.

Baxter Magolda, M. B. (1992). *Knowing and reasoning in college: Gender-related patterns in students' intellectual development.* San Francisco: Jossey-Bass.

Baxter Magolda, M. B. (2001). *Making their own way.* Herndon, VA: Stylus.

Belenky, M. F., Clinchy, B. M., Goldberger, N. R., & Tarule, J. M. (1986). *Women's ways of knowing: The development of self, voice, and mind.* New York: Basic Books.

Blocker, D. H. (1977). The counselor's impact on learning environments. *Personnel and Guidance Journal, 55,* 352-355.

Blocker, D. H. (1978). Campus learning environments and the ecology of student development. In J. H. Banning (Ed.), *Campus ecology: A perspective for student affairs* (pp. 17-23). Cincinnati, OH: National Association of Student Personnel Administrators.

Braxton, J. M. (2000). Reinvigorating theory and research on the departure puzzle. In J. M. Braxton (Ed.), *Reworking the student departure puzzle* (pp. 257-274). Nashville, TN: Vanderbilt University Press.

Bronfenbrenner, U. (1979). *The ecology of human development.* Cambridge, MA: Harvard University Press.

Brown, R. D., & Barr, M. J. (1990). Student development: Yesterday, today, and tomorrow. In L. V. Moore (Ed.), *Evolving theoretical perspectives on students* (New Directions for Student Services No. 51) (pp. 83-92). San Francisco: Jossey-Bass.

Cass, V. C. (1979). Homosexuality identity formation: A theoretical model. *Journal of Homosexuality, 4*(3), 219-235.

Cass, V. C. (1984). Homosexuality identity formation: Testing a theoretical model. *Journal of Sex Research, 20,* 143-167.

Chickering, A. W. (1969). *Education and identity.* San Francisco: Jossey-Bass.

Chickering, A. W., & Reisser, L. (1993). *Education and identity* (2nd ed.) San Francisco: Jossey Bass.

Clark, B. R., & Trow, M. (1966). The organizational context. In T. M. Newcomb & E. Wilson (Eds.), *College peer groups: Problems and prospects for research* (pp. 17-70). Chicago: Aldine.

Creamer, D. G. (1990). Progress toward intentional student development. In D. G. Creamer & Associates, *College student development: Theory and practice for the 1990s* (pp. 3-8). Washington, DC: American College Personnel Association.

Creamer, D. G., & Associates. (1990). *College student development: Theory and practice for the 1990s.* Washington, DC: American College Personnel Association.

Cross, K. P. (1971). *Beyond the open door: New students to higher education.* San Francisco: Jossey-Bass.

Cross, K. P. (1981). *Adults as learners: Increasing participation and facilitating learning.* San Francisco: Jossey-Bass.

Dannells, M. (1997). *From discipline to development: Rethinking student conduct in higher education.* (ASHE-ERIC Higher Education Report, Vol. 25, No. 2). Washington DC: The George Washington University School of Education and Human Development.

D'Augelli, A. R. (1994). Identity development and sexual orientation: Toward a model of lesbian, gay and bisexual development. In E. J. Trickett, R. J. Watts, & D. Birman (Eds.). *Human diversity: Perspectives on people in context* (pp. 312-333). San Francisco: Jossey-Bass.

Erikson, E. H. (1950). *Childhood and society.* New York: Norton.

Erikson, E. H. (1968). *Identity: Youth and crisis.* New York: Norton.

Evans, N. J., & Broido, E. M. (1999). Coming out in college: Negotiation, meaning making, challenges, supports. *Journal of College Student Development, 40,* 658-668.

Evans, N. J., Forney, D. S., & Guido-DiBrito, F. (1998). *Student development in college.* San Francisco: Jossey-Bass.

Evans, N., & Levine, H. (1990). Perspectives on sexual orientation. In L. V. Moore (Ed.), *Evolving theoretical perspectives on students* (New Directions for Student Services No. 51) (pp. 49-58). San Francisco: Jossey-Bass.

Fowler, J. W. (1981). *Stages of faith.* San Francisco: Harper & Row.

Gilligan, C. (1982). *In a different voice: Psychology theory and women's development.* Cambridge, MA: Harvard University Press.

Heath, R. (1964). *The reasonable adventurer.* Pittsburgh: University of Pittsburgh Press.

Helms, J. E. (Ed.) (1990). *Black and white racial identity: Theory, research, and practice.* New York: Greenwood.

Holland, J. L. (1966). *The psychology of vocational choice: A theory of personality types and model environments.* Waltham, MA: Blaisdell.

Holland, J. L. (1985). *Making vocational choices: A theory of vocational personalities and work environments.* Englewood Cliffs, NJ: Prentice-Hall.

Huebner, L. A. (1989). Interaction of student and campus. In U. Delworth, G. R. Hanson, & Associates, *Student services: A handbook for the profession* (2nd ed., pp. 165-208). San Francisco: Jossey-Bass.

Jones, S. R. (1997). Voices of identity and difference: A qualitative exploration of the multiple dimensions of identity development in women college students. *Journal of College Student Development, 38,* 376-386.

Jones, S. R., & McEwen, M. K. (2000). A conceptual model of multiple dimensions of identity. *Journal of College Student Development, 41,* 405-414.

Josselson, R. (1987). *Finding herself: Pathways to identity development in women.* San Francisco: Jossey-Bass.

Josselson, R. (1996). *Revising herself: The story of women's identity from college to midlife.* New York: Oxford University Press.

Katchadourian, H. A., & Boli, J. (1985). *Careerism and intellectualism among college students.* San Francisco: Jossey-Bass.

Kiersey, D., & Bates, M. (1978). *Please understand me: Character and temperament types* (3rd ed.). Del Mar, CA: Prometheus Nemesis.

King, P. M. (1978). William Perry's theory of intellectual and ethical development. In L. Knefelkamp, C. Widick, & C. A. Parker (Eds.), *Applying new developmental findings* (New Directions for Student Services No. 4) (pp. 35-51). San Francisco: Jossey-Bass.

King, P. M., & Kitchener, K. S. (1994). *Developing reflective judgment.* San Francisco: Jossey-Bass.

Knefelkamp, L., Widick, C., & Parker, C. A. (1978). Editor's notes: Why bother with theory? In L. Knefelkamp, C. Widick, & C. A. Parker (Eds.), *Applying new developmental findings.* New Directions for Student Services, No. 4 (pp. vii-xvi). San Francisco: Jossey-Bass.

Kohlberg, L. (1971). Stages of moral development as a basis for moral education. In C. M. Beck, B. S. Crittenden, & E. V. Sullivan (Eds.), *Moral education* (pp. 23-92). Toronto: University of Toronto Press.

Kolb, D. A. (1976). *Learning styles inventory technical manual.* Boston: McBer.

Kolb, D. A. (1984). *Experiential learning: Experience as the source of learning development.* Englewood Cliffs, NJ: Prentice-Hall.

Lewin, K. (1936). *Principles of topological psychology.* New York: McGraw-Hill.

Love, P. (2002). Comparing spiritual development and cognitive development. *Journal of College Student Development, 43,* 357-373.

McEwen, M. K. (1996). The nature and uses of theory. In S. R. Komives, D. B. Woodard, & Associates, *Student services: A handbook for the profession* (3rd ed., pp. 147-163). San Francisco: Jossey Bass.

Moore, L. V. (Ed.). (1990). *Evolving theoretical perspectives on students* (New Directions for Student Services No. 51). San Francisco: Jossey-Bass.

Moos, R. H. (1976). *The human context: Environmental determinants of behavior.* New York: Wiley-Interscience.

Murray, H. A. (1938). *Explorations in personality.* New York: Oxford University Press.

Myers, I. B. (1980). *Gifts differing.* Palo Alto, CA: Consulting Psychologists Press.

Myers, I. B., & McCaulley, M. H. (1985). *Manual: A guide to the development and use of the Myers-Briggs Type Indicator.* Palo Alto, CA: Consulting Psychologists Press.

Pascarella, E. T. (1985). College environmental influences on learning and cognitive development: A critical review and synthesis. In J. Smart (Ed.), *Higher education: Handbook of theory and research: Vol. 1* (pp. 1-61). New York: Agathon.

Pascarella, E. T., & Terenzini, P. T. (1991). *How college affects students.* San Francisco: Jossey-Bass.

Perry, W. G., Jr. (1970). *Forms of intellectual and ethical development in the college years.* New York: Holt, Rinehart, & Winston.

Pervin, L. A. (1968). Performance and satisfaction as a function of individual-environment fit. *Psychological Bulletin, 69*(1), 56-68.

Rendón, L. I. (1994). Validating culturally diverse students: Toward a new model of learning and student development. *Innovative Higher Education, 19*, 33-51.

Rodgers, R. F. (1989a). Recent theories and research underlying student development. In D. G. Creamer (Ed), *College student development: Theory and practice for the 1990's.* Washington DC: American College Personnel Association.

Rodgers, R. F. (1989b). Student development. In U. Delworth, G. R. Hanson, & Associates, *Student services: A handbook for the profession* (2nd ed., pp. 117-164). San Francisco: Jossey-Bass.

Sanford, N. (1962). *The American college.* New York: Wiley.

Sanford, N. (1966). *Self and society.* New York: Atherton.

Sanford, N. (1967). *Where colleges fail.* San Francisco: Jossey-Bass.

Sanlo, R. L. (2000). The LGBT campus resource center director: The new profession in student affairs. *NASPA Journal, 37*, 485-495.

Schlossberg, N. K. (1984). *Counseling adults in transition.* New York: Springer.

Schlossberg, N. K., Lynch, A. Q., & Chickering, A. W. (1989). *Improving higher education environments for adults.* San Francisco: Jossey-Bass.

Schlossberg, N. K., Waters, E. B., & Goodman, J. (1995). *Counseling adults in transition* (2nd ed.). New York: Springer.

Stern, G. G. (1970). *People in context: Measuring person-environment congruence in education and industry.* New York: Wiley.

Strange, C. C. (1994). The evolution and status of an essential idea. *Journal of College Student Development, 35*, 399-412.

Strange, C. C., & Banning, J. H. (2001). Educating by design: Creating campus learning environments that work. San Francisco: Jossey-Bass.

Tinto, V. (1993). *Leaving college: Rethinking the causes and cures of student attrition* (2nd ed.). Chicago: University of Chicago Press.

Trickett, E. J., Watts, R. J., & Birman, D. (Eds.). (1994). *Human diversity: Perspectives on people in context.* San Francisco: Jossey-Bass.

Upcraft, M. L. (1989). Understanding student development: Insights from theory. In M. L. Upcraft, J. N. Gardner, & Associates, *The freshman year experience: Helping students survive and succeed in college* (pp. 40-52). San Francisco: Jossey-Bass.

Upcraft, M. L. (1993). Translating theory to practice. In Margaret J. Barr & Associates, *A handbook for student affairs administration.* San Francisco: Jossey Bass.

Upcraft, M. L., & Moore, L. V. (1990a). Evolving theoretical perspectives of student development. In M. J. Barr, M. L. Upcraft, & Associates, *New futures for student affairs* (pp. 41-68). San Francisco: Jossey-Bass.

Upcraft, M. L., & Moore, L. V. (1990b). Theory in student affairs: Evolving perspectives. In L. V. Moore (Ed.), *Evolving theoretical perspectives on students* (New Directions for Student Services No. 51) (pp. 3-23). San Francisco: Jossey-Bass.

Wall, V. A., & Evans, N. K. (2000). *Toward acceptance: Sexual orientation on campus.* Lanham MD: University Press of America.

Walsh, W. B. (1973). *Theories of person-environment interaction: Implications for the college student* (Monograph 10). Iowa City, IA: American College Testing Program.

Weidman, J. (1989). Undergraduate socialization: A conceptual approach. In J. Smart (Ed.), *Higher education: Handbook of theory and research: Vol. 5.* New York: Agathon.

Witkin, H. A. (1962). *Psychological differentiation.* New York: Wiley & Sons.

Witkin, H. A. (1976). Cognitive style in academic performance and in teacher-student relations. In S. Messick & Associates, *Individuality in learning* (pp. 38-72). San Francisco: Jossey-Bass.

20 Years of Trends and Issues in Orientation Programs

Gerry Strumpf, Greg Sharer, and Matthew Wawrzynski*

This chapter explores the trends that have shaped the field of orientation during the past 20 years. As campus demographics have changed, orientation professionals have been challenged by a variety of agendas facing institutions of higher education across the country. Additionally, the authors discuss the evolution of orientation programs and the challenges that will face orientation professionals in the future.

Historical Context

The history of orientation programs in the United States is almost as old as higher education itself. Harvard faculty saw the value of establishing a support system early in a student's education and was the first institution to formalize a system by which experienced students assisted new students in their transition to the institution (Upcraft, Gardner, & Associates, 1989). In addition to a personalized support system, students also experienced certain rites of passage, which, in today's vernacular, might be considered hazing. Clearly this system was not without its flaws, but it was the beginning of the formalization of orientation as a process for supporting students in their transition to the higher education community.

During the 19th century, faculty involvement and interest in students increased. Harvard institutionalized student-faculty contact by assigning faculty responsibilities outside the classroom. One of these responsibilities was the orientation of new students to the academic community. In the years that followed, other colleges adopted this approach and took an interest in those problems specific to first-year students (Upcraft, Gardner, & Associates, 1989). Following World War II, the college population began to change, due in large part to government action. The President's Commission on Higher Education (Truman Commission), the Serviceman's Readjustment Act of 1944 (G.I. Bill), the National Defense Education Act of 1958, the Higher Education Act of 1965 (with the 1972 amendments), and action by the Warren Court created access to higher education for some groups of students who had never had the opportunity to attend college (Barr & Upcraft, 1990).

This increase in enrollment and student diversity posed issues that institutions had not previously considered. Current orientation programs reflect institutional responses to the changing student populations in higher education. Women, students of color, international students, students with disabilities, first-generation college students, and nontraditional students clearly changed the focus of orientation programs across the country. Orientation programs have evolved from their roots in individualized faculty attention to programs that attempt to address a multitude of important issues while meeting the needs of a diverse student population. Clearly, orientation programs will continue to grow and change as they meet future needs.

*Matthew Wawrzynski joins Gerry Strumpf and Greg Sharer as they update "Trends and Issues in Orientation Programs" from the first edition.

Chapter Three

Summary of Major Trends in Orientation 1980 to 2000

The purpose of this section is to report, analyze, and interpret a number of the major trends in orientation from 1980 to 2000. The data from the *National Orientation Directors Association Data Bank* was used for the analysis. The *NODA Data Bank* is a compilation of responses from member institutions of the National Orientation Directors Association. It is designed to provide information on a variety of topics related to orientation programming and services and reflects an attempt to examine trends over time and assemble data of more current interest.

The Percentage of Students and Parents Attending Orientation Has Increased.

A comparative analysis of data from the past 20 years reveals that the percentage of first-year students, transfers, and parents attending orientation has risen. In 1980, 81% of first-year students attended orientation as compared to 86% in 2000 (Figure 1). The number of transfer students attending orientation has increased from 55% in 1980 to 63% in 2000. More parents and family members are also participating in orientation programs. In 1980, the average number of parents attending orientation for institutions with more that 15,000 students was 40%. By the year 2000, the average had increased to 51%.

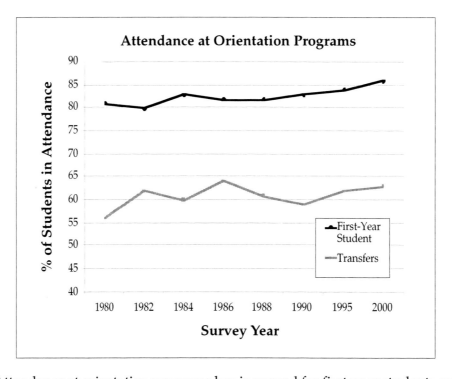

Figure 1. Attendance at orientation programs has increased for first-year students and transfers.

Why are students and parents attending orientation in larger numbers? Perhaps this increase is due to a change in the way institutions view orientation. Increasingly, orientation programs have moved away from a "fun and games" mentality to a more serious introduction to the academic community (Upcraft et al., 1989). Moreover, institutions now view the orientation process as a viable retention activity (El-Khawas, 1995). Colleges and universities are taking steps to encourage student and parent attendance by formalizing and marketing orientation programs with a more serious academic tone.

One way institutions have done this is by using academic advising as an impetus to encourage attendance at orientation. Though not mandatory at a majority of colleges, orientation programs appear to be the standard means of delivering academic advising prior to enrollment (Strumpf, 1990).

The Majority of Institutions Include Academic Advising During Orientation.

While a majority of institutions include academic advising during orientation, the number of institutions providing this has decreased moderately over the past two decades. In 1982, 90% of students received advising during orientation as compared to 86% in the year 2000 (Figure 2). In part, this finding may be attributed to the lower number of institutions responding to the survey, which went online for the first time in 2000.

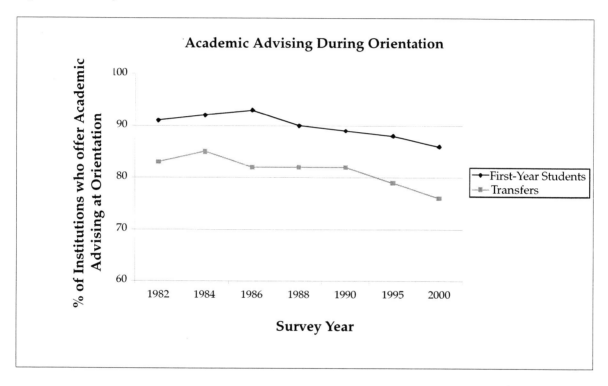

Figure 2. The percentage of orientation programs including academic advising has decreased slightly.

In spite of the apparent decrease in academic advising opportunities, this remains an important component of orientation programs. Stewart, Russell, and Wright (1997) posit that the first stage in the development of a strong retention program is a comprehensive orientation program for new students coupled with academic advising. Research indicates that when advising is a component of orientation, student retention rates are higher. By including academic advising during orientation, students may be more comfortable seeking out that important service during their first semester in institutions where academic advising is not mandatory. Some institutions also report that students who use academic advising services persist at a higher rate than those who do not (Barefoot, Warnock, Dickinson, Richardson, & Roberts, 1998). Because more first-year students are coming to college academically underprepared (Sax, Astin, Korn, & Mahoney, 1999), good academic advising becomes essential. Placing students into classes where they will be able to perform well, especially in mathematics and English, is a critical component of these early advising contacts.

The timing of academic advising may also be driven by students' strong vocational interests and consumerism. As students become more interested in vocational choices earlier in their college careers, their desire to obtain academic advising during orientation increases. Evidence of this vocationalism and consumerism can be seen in the shifting objectives for obtaining a college education. In the 1960s, first-year college students identified developing a meaningful philosophy of life as the primary reason to attend college. During the next 30 years, becoming well-off financially gained prominence as the primary objective for seeking higher education among first-year college students (Astin, Parrott, Korn, & Sax, 1997). Now more than ever before, students have adopted a consumer mentality in regard to their education and expect to receive services from the institution that will help them achieve their academic goals. Hence, the inclusion of advising in orientation may help students develop their academic and career plans earlier, giving them greater focus as they begin their college careers.

The Number of Orientation Courses Offered by Institutions Has Increased.

The number of institutions that offer ongoing orientation courses increased significantly from 1980 to 2000. In 1980, 13% of institutions reported that they had an ongoing orientation course, as compared to 72% in 2000 (Figure 3). This trend is consistent with the growing interest in the first-year experience and with the research reported in Chapter 12 of this monograph. Responses in the *NODA Data Bank* (Strumpf, 1990; Strumpf & Wawrzynski, 2000) suggest that institutions across the country are responding to the importance of orientation as an ongoing process. The primary mission of orientation, as stated by the Council for Advancement of Standards (Miller, 1999), is to ease the transition of new students into the community. This important mission, combined with the critical issue of retention now facing institutions of higher education, has generated a great deal of interest in the role of orientation as a retention activity. In fact, according to the 1995 issue of *Campus Trends*, 82% of colleges and universities have "taken steps to improve the freshman year" (El-Khawas, 1995, p. 7). One of the most successful vehicles for helping students in this transition is the first-year student seminar (El-Khawas, 1995), one of the most widely assessed courses in higher education (Barefoot, 1993). Chapter 12 reviews the outcomes related to the first-year seminar.

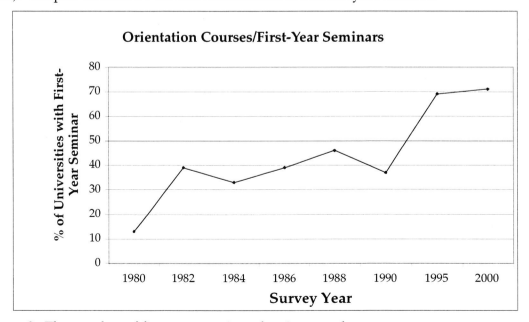

Figure 3. The number of first-year seminars has increased.

Fees Associated With Orientation Programs Have Increased.

Like the cost of most things during the past 20 years, the cost of orientation programs has risen. In 1980, the average cost for a two-day orientation program was $23 per participant. In 2000, the average cost for a two-day orientation program was $72 per participant (Figure 4). Typically the cost for the program covers meals, testing materials, printing, mailing, staff salaries, room rentals, on-campus transportation, and funds to operate the orientation office.

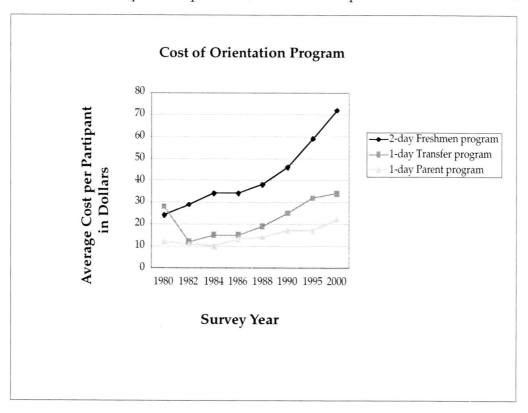

Figure 4. The cost for orientation programs of all types has increased.

Future Trends

The trends in orientation programs during the past 20 years suggest that orientation programs may be adapting to changing student populations and institutional demands. What can orientation professionals expect in the future as higher education becomes an increasingly digitized environment? What are the implications for orientation programs? One thing has remained constant: Orientation professionals continue to deal with competing agendas and limited resources, making planning for change essential.

Barr and Upcraft (1990) outlined broad trends in higher education that are directly related to societal trends. More than a decade later, these trends still have implications for student affairs and specifically for orientation professionals and orientation programs.

Assessment

The area of learning outcomes has received increasing attention in the last few years and will continue to have a profound effect on higher education in the future. The Council for the

Advancement of Standards in Higher Education has been developing standards for professional practice since 1979. The first sets of standards for student orientation were printed in 1986, and were revised in the 1997 CAS Blue Book (see Appendix for the most recent standards). In 1990, the *NODA data bank* first asked respondents if their institutions conducted a self-study using the CAS standards; 20% of the institutions responded affirmatively. In 2000, that percentage had increased to 29 (Strumpf & Wawrzynski, 2000).

Enrollment Trends

After years of declining enrollments in the 1980s, many campuses are experiencing double-digit increases (United States Department of Education, 2000). As a result, the demographic picture has changed the face of higher education in America. No longer are campuses dealing only with traditional-aged students of one race and gender. Institutions have experienced a growth in the population of female, ethnic minority, part-time, and older students (U.S. Department of Education, 2000).

Orientation programs must address the needs of this changing population. Many of the standard operating procedures may have been appropriate for the traditional 18-year-old population, but will they be appropriate for present or future populations? Should first-year non-traditional students be expected to attend a two-day summer orientation program? Are programs being developed for family members, as opposed to just parents? Are orientations being designed for distance learners? Should on-campus orientations be replaced with virtual orientations, making use of computer technology? Are orientation leaders reflecting the changes in the current demographic picture? Is information helpful to single parents or Latino students or other special student populations provided? Are students able to find the kind of support they need to be academically successful? Are programs being offered in the evenings for working students? Institutions need to evaluate the content of workshops and information sessions to assure their relevancy and appropriateness to the current new student population. Chapter 7 provides an in-depth discussion of the kinds of issues institutions must consider in relation to changing enrollments.

Impact of Technology

While there was no specific question in the *NODA Data Bank* regarding technology, the impact of technology cannot go unnoticed. Institutions of higher education are now educating students who have grown up with computers. Computer fluency and the ethical use of computers are issues addressed during many orientation programs. Some institutions are also developing web-based orientation programs for new students. Chapter 13 discusses the current impact of technology on orientation. In the future, the *NODA Data Bank* will collect data on these critical issues.

Social Trends

"Institutions cannot ignore the likelihood of conflict as campuses become more diverse and as old assumptions and privileges are challenged."

The current demographics bring inevitable changes in the social issues facing students and institutions. Institutions cannot ignore the likelihood of conflict as campuses become more diverse and as old assumptions and privileges are challenged (Hurtado, Milem, Clayton-Pederson, & Allen, 1999). In most institutions of higher education, students will be exposed to heterogeneity from the moment they enroll. An orientation program that does not address issues such as race, gender, religion, and sexual orientation may be committing a disservice to the entire community. Programs should address the needs of all students, both traditional and nontraditional. Activities designed to educate the entire community accentuate the institution's commitment to embracing diversity and creating an accepting environment where individual differences are celebrated (Smith, 1989) and where students of all backgrounds can thrive. In fact, Chang (1996) noted that encouraging ongoing discussions about diversity is beneficial to all students.

Astin (1993) has documented the important role that peer-peer and faculty-student interactions play in influencing achievement, growth, and development among undergraduates. Additionally, students will benefit greatly if they learn to communicate with peers and faculty from other cultures, because they will gain an understanding and appreciation for pluralism through such communication. As with problems of attrition, an institution should not look to orientation as the sole solution to intercultural conflict; rather, it should be seen as one step in a comprehensive educational process (Boyer, 1987).

Other complex societal problems such as substance abuse, crime, sexually transmitted diseases, sexism, homophobia, and physical and mental health will continue to be a part of college communities. If one of the goals of orientation is to prepare students for entry into a community of higher learning, they must be informed of relevant issues. The manner in which the information is communicated is critical.

> *"In addition to exposing students to current issues, an orientation program should be able to clearly portray and explain the institution's position on social issues."*

Students enter college at varying levels of social preparedness. Orientation professionals must be sensitive to students' readiness when addressing difficult issues. Sessions that allow students to process their thoughts and feelings are often appropriate forums. It is also essential that the staff conducting the sessions be well-trained. For example, when the topic of diversity is addressed at the University of Maryland, College Park, orientation advisers perform skits and then break into small groups to discuss "Life at Maryland." The small groups are successful because orientation advisers have been trained in ways to create a safe environment for discussing sensitive topics.

In addition to exposing students to current issues, an orientation program should be able to clearly portray and explain the institution's position on social issues. By helping a student understand the institution's social and behavioral expectations, campus regulations and policies will not be violated due to a lack of information.

Summary

Predicting the future is a very uncertain endeavor. Clearly, retention will continue to be a major force in the development of orientation programs across the country. A move to recapture an environment that responds to the individual needs of students will continue to have a profound effect on orientation. With a fair amount of certitude, we can predict that funding for orientation programs will continue to be a concern, especially as costs continue to rise. Demographic changes in our institutions of higher education, similar to those found in society at large, are also likely. Simply *reacting* to change will not ensure that orientation programs meet their goals or serve the needs of students and institutions. Assessment, planning, and ultimately implementing new and creative programs must take place to serve the changing populations of students and their families arriving on campus. Additionally, the entire field of technologically advanced orientation programs is beginning to develop and provides an appropriate vehicle to enhance the transition of new students into the academic community.

References

Astin, A. W. (1993). *What matters in college? Four critical years revisited.* San Francisco: Jossey-Bass.

Astin, A. W., Parrott, S. A., Korn, W. S., & Sax, L. J. (1997). *The American freshman: Thirty year trends.* Los Angeles: University of California, Higher Education Research Institute.

Barefoot, B., Warnock, C. L., Dickinson, M. P., Richardson, S. E., & Roberts, M. R. (Eds.). (1998). *Exploring the evidence: Reporting outcomes of first-year seminars, Vol. 2.* (Monograph No. 25). Columbia, SC: University of South Carolina, National Resource Center for The First-Year Experience and Students in Transtion.

Barefoot, B. (1993). *Exploring the evidence: Reporting outcomes of freshman seminars* (Monograph No. 11). Columbia, SC: University of South Carolina, National Resource Center for The Freshman Year Experience.

Barr, M. J., & Upcraft, M. L. (1990). *New futures for student affairs: Building a vision for professional leadership and practice.* San Francisco: Jossey-Bass.

Boyer, E. L. (1987). *College: The undergraduate experience in America.* New York: Harper & Row.

Chang, M. (1996). Racial diversity in higher education: Does a racially mixed student population affect educational outcomes? (Doctoral dissertation, University of California at Los Angeles, 1996). (University Microfilms No. AAT 9626812).

El Khawas, E. (1995). *Campus trends.* Washington, DC: American Council on Education.

Hurtado, S., Milem, J., Clayton-Pedersen, A., & Allen, W. (1999). *Enacting diverse learning environments: Improving the climate for racial/ethnic diversity in higher education.* (ASHE-ERIC Higher Education Report Volume 26, No. 8). Washington, DC: The George Washington University, Graduate School of Education and Human Development.

Miller, T. (Ed.) (1999). *The CAS book of professional standards for higher education 1999.* Washington, DC: Council for the Advancement of Standards in Higher Education.

Sax, L. J., Astin, A. W., Korn, W. S., & Mahoney, K. M. (1999). *The American freshman: National norms for Fall 1999.* Los Angeles: Higher Education Research Institute, UCLA.

Smith, D. G. (1989). *The challenge of diversity: Involvement or alienation in the academy.* (ASHE-ERIC Higher Education Report No. 5). Washington, DC: The George Washington University, Graduate School of Education and Human Development.

Stewart, G. L., Russell, R. B., & Wright, D., (1997). The comprehensive role of student affairs in African-American student retention. *Journal of College Admission, 154,* 6-11.

Strumpf, G. B. (1990). *NODA data bank.* College Park, MD: National Orientation Directors Association.

Strumpf, G. B., & Wawrzynski, M. R. (2000). *NODA data bank.* College Park, MD: National Orientation Directors Association.

Upcraft, M. L., Gardner, J., & Associates. (1989). *The freshman year experience.* San Francisco: Jossey-Bass.

U.S. Department of Education. (2000). National Center for Education Statistics. Washington, DC: Author. Retrieved on July 26, 2002 from http://www.nces.ed.gov/edstats

Components of a Comprehensive Orientation Program

Rebecca F. Smith and Richard K. Brackin

A comprehensive orientation program is designed to facilitate the smooth transition of students into the academic atmosphere of the college or university. Moreover, it is the first formal step in the transition process for students and includes opportunities to enhance both academic and personal development. The best orientation experiences occur when the whole campus is committed to the process and result from the collaborative efforts of students, senior administrators, faculty, and a broad spectrum of student affairs and educational support staff. Successful programs are tailored to fit the individual needs of matriculating students on a given campus. Rather than provide a blueprint for the design of orientation programs, this chapter offers questions, conditions, and factors which institutions must consider as they design the transition process for new students.

The Importance of Institutional Mission in Determining Program Goals

The recruitment, orientation, academic advising, and retention of new students must be viewed as an institutional commitment rather than as isolated departmental tasks. Tinto (1990) calls on institutions to be committed to the welfare of students and "to serve the goals of their intellectual and social development" (p. 41). One way colleges and universities honor these commitments is by providing orientation programs. Not only does orientation demonstrate the institution's commitment to its students, it also serves as "a means for the institution to convey [its] academic and social expectations" (Nadler, Miller, & Casebere, 1998, p. 27). Ultimately, orientation programs strive to integrate the institutional mission and the personal growth of entering students.

The Council for the Advancement of Standards (CAS) in Higher Education has designated 18 goals applicable to orientation programs regardless of the size or objective of the institution. No matter what individual program goals are, the mission of student orientation must be to "facilitate the transition of new students into the institution; prepare new students for the institution's educational opportunities; and initiate the integration of new students into the intellectual, cultural, and social climate of the institution" (Council for the Advancement of Standards, 2001, p. 222). If "orientation is the first formal exposure of many students to their new academic and social environment and serves to set the tone for many of their experiences to come" (Mann, 1998, p. 20), it is imperative that orientation programs have a defined purpose and be incorporated into the institutional mission. Rather than a series of disjointed programs, orientation must become a deliberate and coherent institutional process in which issues and questions are addressed in a timely fashion (Lenning, Sauer, & Beal, 1980).

To determine the components of a comprehensive orientation program, one begins by asking three basic questions:

1. What is the nature and mission of the institution?
2. What is the mission of the orientation program?
3. What orientation program content will accomplish this mission?

Chapter Four

Kuh (1996) expands this list of questions for institutions and orientation directors who are committed to the notion of "seamless learning environments," suggesting they must grapple with the following:

1. What is the relationship between orientation and the institution's mission?
2. What is the obligation of orientation to the institution?
3. What is the institution's obligation to orientation?
4. What is the obligation of orientation to new students?
5. Should the philosophy of orientation be to encourage students to do whatever they think best or should the institution delineate what constitutes acceptable behavior in this academic community?
6. If orientation should be reinvented, how should it be structured so that newcomers are introduced to the resources they need to be successful academically and socially? (p. 136)

Taken together, these two sets of questions can serve as guidelines for developing the orientation program's goals and objectives and for aligning them with the institutional mission.

The Mission of Orientation and its Value to the Institution

As stated above, the primary goal of orientation is the adjustment and success of entering students. Upcraft and Farnsworth (1984) define orientation as "any effort on the part of the institution to help entering students make the transition from their previous environment to the collegiate environment and to enhance their success in college" (p. 17). Orientation is an intentional set of programs that integrate entering students into a new environment. Further, it can be a systematic approach to addressing entering students' needs in all areas of adjustment to college life. Finally, the goal of orientation program delivery is the personalization of the program—its ability to respond to individual student needs.

Just as the orientation program must serve the larger institutional mission, the development of a viable orientation program depends on the institution's commitment to the orientation program's mission. Common understanding of this mission by faculty, staff, students, and administrators will provide a cooperative framework for delivering an effective orientation program. Active involvement by faculty, staff, administrators, and students is a prime factor in creating a community environment where entering students want to belong, perform, and contribute. Concentrated efforts should be made to affirm that the entering student is a member of the campus community.

> *"Just as the orientation program must serve the larger institutional mission, the development of a viable orientation program depends on the institution's commitment to the orientation program's mission."*

One way to ensure wide-ranging support for orientation is to educate campus constituent groups on the role they play in student success and persistence. Nadler et al. (1998) state that "orientation programs play a pivotal role in student success" (p. 27), and such programs are a significant part of a multifaceted approach to retention (Titley, 1985). For example, Beal and Noel (1980) found orientation to be the third most effective retention activity overall. More recent research corroborates this finding, suggesting that " . . . orientation programs can have a tremendous impact on both academic and social integration into the institution and thereby provide the foundation for improvement in student retention" (Mullendore, 1998, p. 5). The role of orientation in retention and the institutional mission might be defined best on an activity continuum. The recruitment of students would be on one end of the continuum and commencement of graduates on the other end. Integrated along the continuum are increased faculty involvement and enhanced service delivery. Orientation is a major activity on the continuum that provides entering students with the opportunity to interact closely with faculty and to develop lifelong learning skills. Therefore, orientation plays a critical role in the entering students' adjustment and transition to a new environment.

Orientation Program Content

Orientation programs vary greatly depending on the nature, size, staffing, clientele, and purpose of the program at each institution. Upcraft and Farnsworth (1984), however, highlight four general areas that orientation programs should address on all campuses: (a) the academic environment, (b) personal adjustment issues and the social environment, (c) the needs of parents and families, and (d) the characteristics and needs of new students.

Academic Environment

The primary emphasis of orientation programs should be on students' adjustment to the academic environment. Entering students must be provided information concerning academic policies, procedures, requirements, and programs. They must also have an opportunity to assess their own academic abilities. Further, orientation programs must focus on academic issues, which may be of greatest concern to entering students (Brady, 1978; Brinkerhoff & Sullivan, 1982; Higginson, Moore, & White, 1981). The *National Orientation Directors Association Data Bank* (Strumpf, & Wawrzynski, 2000) reported that orientation professionals on all size campuses rated academic structure, requirements, and grades almost as equally important as campus activities, clubs, and events for inclusion in orientation programs. However, as early as 1981, Higginson et al. reported that first-year students indicated their top three priorities were academic concerns (course scheduling, choice of major, and sources of academic information) followed by campus activities. Arnold and Kuh (1999) concur with research that indicates that " . . . the lives of traditional-age residential students focus on the people and activities of their campus. Friendships and academic success are at the center" of importance to students (p. 20). Thus, addressing academic issues in orientation helps answer student questions and calm anxieties, and providing information on specific academic survival strategies is a useful tool for promoting successful student learning (Hadlock, 2000).

Personal Adjustment and Social Environment

Orientation programs and services should also assist students with their personal adjustment to the social environment (Upcraft & Farnsworth, 1984). These programs must include experiences that enable new students to anticipate and understand the values and behavioral norms of their new social setting and the institution's expectations of them as members of their new community. An environment should be created that minimizes anxiety, promotes positive attitudes, and stimulates self-awareness. Personal developmental issues that students encounter in college should also be addressed. The orientation program must provide information about the support services available to assist students with personal development issues. From the initial point of contact, the institution must ensure that the entering student is integrated into the social and academic communities of the institution. Orientation programs can help students develop and refine the interpersonal and intellectual skills to become socially adjusted citizens within the learning community.

Parents and Families

Orientation programs should provide parents and family members with educational information and services to increase awareness of possible changes the student may experience during the transition to the institution (Upcraft & Farnsworth, 1984). The family, as the primary support group, plays an important role in the life of each student. It is essential to provide information to family members to help them understand the intellectual and social development of the entering student. Chapter 11 describes programs designed to facilitate family and parent orientation in greater detail.

Addressing Institutional Needs

Orientation programs and services should provide the institution with a better understanding of its entering students (Upcraft & Farnsworth, 1984). One way to accomplish this is by giving entering students and faculty opportunities to discuss institutional expectations and perceptions of the campus as well as their respective views of the social and intellectual climate of the campus. A faculty-student mentoring program often proves to be an important part of the support system needed for learning. Further, faculty and student mentors can provide the institution with an important perspective on students' needs and concerns. Therefore, orientation programs provide opportunities for entering students to develop realistic academic and personal goals, to locate student support services and resources, and to meet faculty and peer mentors. In addition, orientation programs can help families understand the student's intellectual and social transition to a new environment.

Academic Program Content

Orientation programs tend to be seen either as a final step in the admissions process or the first step in students' adjustment to their new environment. In fact, orientation may be viewed as an ongoing process of personal, intellectual, and academic development. This process begins with the first contact between the prospective student and the admissions staff and continues throughout the undergraduate years, culminating for many with graduation and for others with interruption of the academic experience. A significant responsibility of the orientation staff is to set the stage for academic success once the student matriculates (Young, Backer, & Rogers, 1989).

Certainly a high priority of any orientation program is to give students opportunities to begin to meet their personal and professional goals. The focus of many orientation programs, therefore, has moved from enhancing social interaction and giving information about the campus and the community to providing relevant counseling and sound academic advising for each individual student (Hadlock, 2000; Pascarella, Terenzini, & Wolfle, 1986). In order for an orientation program to be a significant step in the developmental process of new students, both traditional and nontraditional, it must include opportunities for interaction not only with other students who have similar interests, needs, and experiences, but also with professional staff and faculty who have expertise in areas of students' expressed interests and needs (Dayton, 1989). Retention studies indicate that quality student interaction with individual teaching faculty and with peers is the most important factor in student satisfaction (Pascarella & Terenzini, 1978, 1991). In addition, Astin (1993) states that an undergraduate peer group is one of the most influential factors affecting student growth and development. An effective way to introduce the new students to support personnel is to use the staff for small group facilitation within orientation. Ultimately, this will give the faculty and staff the opportunity to show concern for new student success. Additionally, it allows university employees to assist students and facilitate the initial phase of creating a positive institution and student fit (Mann, 1998). The small group sessions can also help students meet peers and form early social relationships.

Some faculty believe that orientation is the time to tell new students of the glories of certain academic programs, but, in fact, orientation is really a time to listen to students. By the time a student arrives for orientation, it can be assumed that the student has established some level of com-

> *"Some faculty believe that orientation is the time to tell new students of the glories of certain academic programs, but, in fact, orientation is really a time to listen to students."*

mitment to the institution and to curricular goals. Although it is important that requirements and performance expectations be articulated for new students, the primary role of the faculty advisor is to listen to the needs expressed by each student and to help that student weigh his or her options and make decisions to meet their self-recognized goals (Priest & Milne, 1991).

The collegiate atmosphere encourages students to assess their interests, values, and abilities (Frost, 1991). These assessments, sometimes made during orientation, lead students through the sequential decision-making process that links them to an academic major. This process is designed to help students discover and consider academic and career options and to make informed choices about educational programs, courses, and career goals. Barefoot (2000) suggests that first-year programs should link curricular and co-curricular activities, increase academic expectations for new students, and assist students who need additional academic preparation as they navigate this decision-making process. The orientation program staff, including faculty advisors, must collaborate with individual students in the learning process as they frame further questions, gather new data, identify changing values and needs, and recognize that initial choices may be interim decisions.

For example, Astin (1977) maintained that more than half of those students who enter college with an identified major change that initial commitment. In certain academic areas the rate of change is as high as two thirds (e.g., pre-medicine, prelaw, social work). More recent data from at least one large university indicate that 26% of students changed their major within one year of enrolling (from 2000 to 2001) and that 48% changed within two years of enrolling (from 1999 to 2001) (M. Williford, personal communication, September 9, 2002).

Academic majors and curricula that lead to degrees are based on a wide variety of requirements and range from highly sequential professional programs in engineering, the fine arts (e.g., music, theatre, dance), education, and the hard sciences to less-sequential programs like general studies. To advise students effectively, orientation program staff must be familiar with institution-wide requirements, individual college requirements, major department requirements, and special curricular requirements. They must also be able to clarify those requirements in a supportive and nonthreatening atmosphere.

The orientation staff also must listen for indications of anxiety and insecurity and offer nurturing reassurance in regard to initial academic decisions. The staff can also help students identify their needs and identify resources for meeting those needs. Thus, commitments to a course of study may change as students gain academic experience. Staff members should reassure incoming students that support personnel including career counselors, academic advisers, teaching faculty, residence hall staff, and others are available to assist with these decisions and transitions (Pascarella et al. 1986).

As orientation leaders, upperclass students establish an instant rapport and credibility with new students and can play an important role in a new student's academic orientation to the institution. Mann (1998) suggests that "upperclass students are . . . effective in setting expectations for the new students [and] in conveying the differences between high school and college in the areas of academics, studying, and assuming responsibility for one's actions, and in passing on school traditions" (p. 18).

Helping new students develop strong academic skills and habits should become an immediate goal of the transition process if such behaviors are not already in place. Essential academic skills include reading, note-taking, writing, proofreading, listening, and asking questions. Attending every scheduled class and keeping appointments with faculty are habits that must be established at the outset if students are to expect success. All these ideas and more need to be articulated regularly and frequently throughout the orientation process.

Program Content and Design

When institutional commitment has been assured and the needs of target populations have been assessed, the content of the orientation program can be developed. The *CAS Standards and Guidelines for Student Orientation Programs* (CAS, 2001; see Appendix) identifies a number of areas important to student learning and development that should be addressed in orientation programs. These include

- ◆ Intellectual growth
- ◆ Communication skills
- ◆ Self-awareness/self-knowledge
- ◆ Self-esteem
- ◆ Values clarification
- ◆ Career decision making
- ◆ Leadership development
- ◆ Health and physical fitness
- ◆ Interpersonal relationships
- ◆ Ability to work both independently and collaboratively
- ◆ Social responsibility
- ◆ Decisions about lifestyle
- ◆ Social responsibility
- ◆ Aesthetic and cultural diversity
- ◆ Personal goal setting

Orientation programs at colleges and universities around the country were surveyed to determine topic areas that are addressed specifically during orientation. The *National Orientation Directors Association Data Bank* (Strumpf, & Wawrzynski, 2000) reported the frequency of institutional responses for each topic by institutional size (Table 1). Three academic areas are identified as having increased presence in orientation programs during the last several years: (a) academic issues, (b) faculty involvement, and (c) common readings for entering students. Table 2 provides the percentage of institutions reporting such offerings in 2000.

What issues do entering students want addressed during orientation? Higginson et al. (1981) asked 2,566 first-year students to rank their perception of their needs at orientation. Students identified the following issues in order of importance

- ◆ Course scheduling
- ◆ Major
- ◆ Sources for academic information

◆ Learning about activities and resources for meeting student needs the first week on campus
◆ Housing
◆ Money
◆ Extracurricular activities
◆ Social

These responses indicate that entering students desire information about academic issues and personal/social concerns during a comprehensive orientation program. The current structure of orientation programs on many campuses seems to satisfy these needs, but institutions should continually seek feedback from new students about those topics they perceive to be most important during the orientation period.

Program Delivery and Assessment

Delivery of an orientation program depends on the institutional response to a series of questions:

1. What is the commitment from faculty, students, staff, and administrators to the orientation program?
2. What is the institution's commitment to budget and staffing?
3. How much time is necessary to accomplish the mission of orientation?
4. What are the institutional and student needs?
5. How much coordination is needed with various departments in the campus and local communities?
6. What have evaluations and assessments of previous programs revealed?

Obviously the structure and needs of a particular institution must be assessed before deciding on a specific orientation program format or combination of formats. Systematic evaluation of an orientation program provides staff members constructive data to help determine whether orientation activities are accomplishing their main purposes. It also allows participating departments and staff to share in the ownership of the program and ultimately serves to strengthen the orientation process. Continuing assessment of orientation programs is also necessary to meet the specific needs of the increasingly diverse population of entering students including those who are nontraditional, commuters, of international origin, attending part-time, racially or ethnically diverse, military veterans, and academically gifted or those students who have disabilities or who have transferred to the institution. Orientation also might include programs for parents and spouses of students, new graduate students, new faculty or administrators, as well as readmitted and currently enrolled students. Once the target audiences are determined and their needs assessed, effective orientation programs can be developed for either limited or general populations.

The CAS standards mandate that orientation programs address, identify, assist, and promote a wide variety of concepts and activities. To accomplish these mandates, the institution must consider a number of questions:

1. When will the orientation program(s) be provided and what format(s) will work best? A two-day summer program? A week-long fall program? A three-hour evening program? Which format will allow enough time to accomplish your goals?
2. Is the program required or voluntary? If voluntary, can the institution justify providing orientation for only some of its new students?

Table 1.
Topics Most Frequently Addressed During Orientation (N = 278)

Topic Area	Institutions with fewer than 5,000 students (small)	
	Percentage of Institutions Responding	Rank Order
Campus activities/clubs/events	91	1
Social activities	91	1
Residence hall living	89	2
Meeting with dean/faculty/academic administrators	84	3
Academic structure/requirements/grades	81	4
	Institutions with 5,000 to 15,000 students (medium)	
Campus activities/clubs/events	96	1
Academic structure/requirements/grades	92	2
Class scheduling	89	3
Business matters (financial aid, tuition, fees, etc.)	86	4
Meeting with deans/faculty/academic administrators	83	5
	Institutions with more than 15,000 students (large)	
Campus activities/clubs/events	98	1
Academic structure/requirements/grades	90	2
Business matters (financial aid, tuition, fees).	85	3
Class scheduling	85	3
Residence hall living	83	4

Source: Strumpf, G., & Wawrzynski, M. R. (Eds.). (2000). *National Orientation Directors Association Data Bank*. College Park, MD: University of Maryland, NODA.

Table 2.
Academic Content in Orientation Programs by Institutional Size

Topic	Percentage of Reporting Institutions		
	Small (< 5,000 students)	Medium (5,000 – 15,000 students)	Large (> 15,000 students)
Time devoted to academic matters	41	52	52
Faculty involvement in orientation program	46	35	40
Common book/required reading for new students	23	12	9

Source: Strumpf, G., & Wawrzynski, M.R. (Eds.). (2000). *National Orientation Directors Association Data Bank.* College Park, MD: University of Maryland, NODA.

3. Do the components of the program combine into a purposeful and coherent whole? Is the schedule student-centered or institution-centered? What do new students know, what can they do, and how do they feel when they have completed the program? How will the program's impact be assessed?
4. What institutional requirements govern orientation, and how do these requirements enhance or detract from the success of your program? For example, are students required to take a battery of placement tests or complete myriad surveys during orientation? If so, how much program time is allocated to these activities relative to other activities? (Smith, 1998)

For example, the *NODA Handbook* (Gohn, 1978) offers a list of relevant factors that institutions should consider before determining a program format:

1. Type of student body (e.g., social and economic background, intellectual abilities, background of parents)
2. Size and location of campus
3. Availability of campus facilities
4. Advising and registration procedures
5. Availability of administrators, faculty, staff, and student leaders
6. Finances
7. Relationship to and commitment of other university departments
8. Size of student body
9. Geographic makeup of student body
10. Other planned campus programs
11. Availability of student records
12. Academic calendar

It is necessary to determine the specific needs of the diverse population of entering students, availability of key campus administrators, and feasibility of using campus facilities before making decisions about the format or content of orientation programs.

After determining the structure of the orientation program, the next step is to develop the program content in an organized, coherent manner. Austin (1988) identified six broad categories for orientation sessions and activities (Figure 1).

Academic Information	*General Information*	*Logistical Concerns*
◆ academic structure, guidelines, regulations ◆ class scheduling ◆ meeting faculty and deans ◆ study skills information ◆ exposure to live or simulated class	◆ campus tours ◆ international policies/ regulations ◆ description of services available ◆ campus history, traditions	◆ financial aid, business matters ◆ registering a car ◆ getting an ID card/ library card ◆ purchasing books
Social/Interpersonal Development ◆ information on campus activities clubs, and events ◆ social activities ◆ get acquainted exercises ◆ group/team building exercises	*Testing/Assessments* ◆ placement tests ◆ attitudinal tests ◆ career/personality tests ◆ demographic survey	*Transitional Programming* ◆ special workshops on subjects such as career development, cultural diversity, substance abuse awareness, personal safety, roommates, aquaintance rape, commuting ◆ workshops on affective issues such as leaving home, changing relationships, fears and anxieties

Figure 1: *Categories of orientation activities and sessions (Austin, 1988).*

Format of Orientation Program

What are the ways in which orientation programs can be presented? Orientation programs may be delivered using one approach or a combination of approaches.

Brief Summer Programs

Summer orientation programs can range from one to three days prior to the beginning of school. These programs allow the entering student and family members an opportunity to become acquainted with and adjusted to the campus community and relieve anxieties. Such programs also provide concentrated, personal attention to students and families and serve as a positive retention tool. Summer programs tend to be expensive for the student and family. They also require extra time and effort from faculty, staff, student leaders, and administrators and may need to be duplicated in the fall for those students unable to attend during the summer or who are admitted later.

Fall Programs

Fall orientation programs are generally held prior to the beginning of classes and may last for a week on many campuses. This program format is inexpensive for both the institution and the student, has increased relevance for the student, and provides more natural timing for becoming a part of the new environment. In addition, this format provides natural integration for faculty, staff, and student leaders and eliminates the need to provide programs during the summer and fall. Fall program weeks, however, tend to place less emphasis on academic advising, compete with other campus activities, and are less personalized. Due to the number of participants, this program format is more often used by smaller colleges than by larger, more comprehensive institutions.

Orientation Course

Orientation courses are designed specifically for first-year students. They are implemented to "improve the likelihood of academic and social integration and overall satisfaction with the college experience through the development of close student/student and student/faculty relationships" (Barefoot, 1992, p. 2). Barefoot (2000) also suggests that "a significant number of first-year programs, including first-year seminars . . . are intentionally designed to provide students the interaction with peers necessary for group bonding and affiliation." (p. 15). The advantages of an orientation course frequently include improved retention rates and grade point averages, an increased sense of belonging to the campus community as indicated by campus involvement, and increased out-of-class contact with faculty and staff. It is essential that continuous orientation be integrated into the total education community and that it encompass the institutional mission.

Winter Term/Spring Semester Orientation

Entering students admitted during the academic year are also in need of specific assistance. Orientation programs for these students are designed with the same focus as summer programs. The orientation is held immediately prior to the beginning of a new term or semester and is designed to provide transition assistance to new students as well as to meet the logistical and information needs of students entering mid-year.

Summer Bridge Programs

Many institutions have developed "summer bridge," "summer start," "links," or "headstart" programs to ensure that entering students who are at academic risk have the opportunity to acquire the academic skills needed to succeed and learn while in college. Such programs are designed to integrate entering students into the regular academic curriculum by helping students overcome learning deficiencies. This early intervention enables the student to grow and develop during subsequent years in college.

Institutional Commitment to the Orientation Process

As mentioned earlier, institutional commitment to the mission and goals of the orientation program is vital. It is not possible for one person or group—whether a department, a dean of students, or an orientation steering committee—to develop an effective orientation process or a successful orientation program. The positive support of the entire campus community, from the president to the grounds-keeping staff, is necessary if an honest, facilitative atmosphere is to be established. This does not mean that every member of the campus community will have direct programmatic responsibility. It *does mean* that every member of the faculty, administration, and support staff will be attuned to the importance of the process as well as to the specifically identified program and will contribute to the achievement of the goals of a sound orientation program.

The president and chief academic officer as well as the chief student affairs officer must set the tone for the entire campus community. The quality of the program as reflected by evaluations from new students and parents can be improved when senior administrators are visible and participating. In addition, positive participation in the program by the president, the provost, the dean of students, and the deans of the academic colleges sets an example for other staff. Deans tend to be more willing to participate when they know that the president will deliver the official campus welcome. Faculty are willing to prepare for and participate with students and parents when they see deans participating as well. The food service and housekeeping staffs also tend to be more amenable to presenting a positive image when they feel that they are part of a team. Achieving team spirit across the campus community does not just happen by accident; rather, it is achieved by establishing an atmosphere of cooperation and feelings of ownership among service personnel. Such an attitude strengthens the reputation of the institution and enhances the entire campus community. Orientation directors spend the largest percentage of their time and effort in educating, engaging, and coordinating the many individuals who play critical roles in the orientation program. Therefore, the orientation director must be a well-qualified professional educator and administrator who knows and understands both the academic and the social development needs of entering students. The director also must have the administrative skills needed to develop comprehensive and effective orientation programs.

Creating a campus wide commitment to quality orientation takes time and energy from each member of the senior administration as well as from the head of each academic and nonacademic department. It is the responsibility of each leader to articulate the individual departmental role in meeting the goals of the orientation program. Individual department goals for helping students make a smooth transition to college might include

- Providing accessible academic advising from faculty
- Highlighting the availability of good libraries and ample study space
- Making counseling and career planning available from the outset
- Providing adequate, comfortable living space
- Offering programs to enhance time management and study skills
- Hiring challenging instructors
- Fostering an atmosphere in which intellectual growth and development are encouraged
- Providing opportunities to test personal values in a non-judgmental atmosphere
- Presenting a courteous and helpful staff to new students and their families
- Providing good food attractively served
- Providing clean, attractive hallways, bathrooms, and classrooms

The orientation committee needs to have responsibility for providing a comfortable, nurturing, challenging, and rewarding atmosphere as well as a sense of ownership for enhancing the intellectual, spiritual, and academic development of each student on the campus. In addition to the officer who is identified as director of the program, the orientation committee needs representation from every constituency in the campus community. Besides developing goals and guidelines for the program, the orientation committee is the primary means by which orientation policies and plans are articulated to each constituency. Ownership of, and commitment to, the orientation program by the campus community at large begins with this committee.

By sharing the notion that developing a campus of satisfied students begins with a positive orientation experience, the orientation committee can make significant progress toward developing a program that is challenging and responsive to each individual student. The result is that satisfied students stay longer, have lower attrition rates, higher graduation rates, and a greater overall sense of satisfaction with the quality of their academic preparation (Pascarella, 1980). Additionally, according to Mullendore (1998) orientation professionals need to understand that " . . . retention is everyone's business, and that orientation is a critical component in student persistence" (p. 1). Increased retention and student satisfaction ultimately lead to both academic and fiscal success for any college or university community.

If senior level administrators see the significant positive effects of orientation on first-year persistence and if they recognize the fiscal impact of improved retention, it is hoped that they also will see the importance of appropriate budgetary support for orientation. Providing support for a quality orientation process seems like good pedagogy as well as good business.

Summary

A comprehensive orientation program focuses on meeting the individual needs of the many student groups seeking both academic success and the opportunity to meet professional goals. An effective orientation program assesses the needs of new students, designs program goals to address those anticipated needs, and involves professional staff, student leaders, and faculty members to deliver accurate information and thoughtful, sensitive advising. A seamless orientation program requires a widely-distributed investment of time and energy by the entire campus community as well as commitment of significant financial support.

References

Arnold, K., & Kuh, G. D. (1999). What matters in undergraduate education? Mental models, student learning, and student affairs. In E. J. Whitt (Ed.), *Student learning as student affairs work: Responding to our imperative* (NASPA Monograph Series Vol. 23) (pp. 11-34). Washington, DC: National Association of Student Personnel Administrators.

Astin, A. W. (1977). *Four critical years.* San Francisco: Jossey-Bass.

Astin, A. W. (1993). *What matters in college? Four critical years revisited.* San Francisco: Jossey-Bass.

Austin, D. (1988). Building an orientation program from the ground. *Campus Activities Programming, 21,* 41-45.

Barefoot, B. (2000). The first-year experience: Are we making it any better? *About Campus, 4*(6), 12-18.

Barefoot, B. (1992, Fall). The first-year life jacket. *The Keystone, 1.* Belmont, CA: Wadsworth Publishing.

Beal, P. E., & Noel, L. (1980). *What works in student retention.* Iowa City: American College Testing Program and National Center for Higher Education Management Systems.

Brady, S. M. (1978). Academic advising: A study of faculty goals and student needs. *Dissertation Abstracts International, 39,* 145A-146A.

Brinkerhoff, D. B., & Sullivan, D. E. (1982). Concerns of new students: A pretest-posttest evaluation of orientation. *Journal of College Student Personnel, 23,* 384-390.

Council for the Advancement of Standards (CAS) in Higher Education. (2001). *CAS standards and guidelines for student support services/development programs.* Washington, DC: Author.

Dayton, L. (1989, July). *Toward the future vitality of student development services: Traverse City five years later.* Chapter 3. Summary Report of the Sixth Annual Leadership Colloquium, Traverse City, Michigan.

Frost, S. H. (1991). *Academic advising for student success: A system of shared responsibility.* (ASHE-ERIC Higher Education Report No. 3). Washington, DC: The George Washington University School of Education and Human Development.

Gohn, L. A. (1978). Program development. In A. G. Matthews (Ed.), *Handbook for orientation directors.* Iowa City: National Orientation Directors Association.

Hadlock, H. L. (2000). Orientation programs: A synopsis of their significance. *The Journal of College Orientation and Transition, 7*(2), 27-32.

Higginson, L. C., Moore L. V., & White, E. R. (1981). A new role for orientation: Getting down to academics. *NASPA Journal, 19,* 21-28.

Kuh, G. D. (1996). Guiding principles for creating seamless learning environments for undergraduates. *Journal of College Student Development, 37*(2), 135-148.

Lenning, O. T., Sauer, K., & Beal, P. E. (1980). *Student retention strategies.* (ASHE-ERIC Higher Education Research Report No. 8). Washington, DC: The George Washington University School of Education and Human Development.

Mann, B. A. (1998). Retention principles for new student orientation programs. *Journal of College Orientation and Transitions, 6*(1), 15-20.

Mullendore, R. H. (1998). Orientation as a component of institutional retention efforts. In R. H. Mullendore (Ed.), *NODA orientation planning manual.* Bloomington, IN: National Orientation Directors Association.

Nadler, D. P., Miller, M. T., & Casebere, J. (1998). Student satisfaction with orientation: Toward a framework for program effectiveness. *Journal of College Orientation and Transition, 6*(1), 27-35.

Pascarella, E. T. (1980). Student-faculty informal contact and college outcomes. *Review of Educational Research, 50*(4), 545-595.

Pascarella, E. T., & Terenzini, P. T. (1978). Student-faculty informal relationships and freshman year educational outcomes. *The Journal of Educational Research, 73,* 183-189.

Pascarella, E. T., & Terenzini, P. T. (1991). *How college affects students.* San Francisco: Jossey-Bass.

Pascarella, E. T., Terenzini, P. T., & Wolfle, L. M. (1986). Orientation to college and freshman year persistence/withdrawal decisions. *Journal of Higher Education, 57,* 155-173.

Priest, D., & Milne, J. (1991). A next step in student retention: Academic advising. *Journal for Higher Education Management, 6*(2), 35-41.

Smith, R. F. (1998). Planning standards-based orientation programs. In R. H. Mullendore (Ed.), *NODA orientation planning manual.* Bloomington, IN: National Orientation Directors Association.

Strumpf, G., & Wawrzynski, M.R. (Ed.). (2000). *National Orientation Directors Association data bank.* College Park, MD: University of Maryland, National Orientation Directors Association.

Tinto, V. (1990). Principles of effective retention. *Journal of the Freshman Year Experience, 2*(1), 35-48.

Titley, B. S. (1985). Orientation programs. In L. Noel, R. Levitz, & D. Saluri (Eds.), *Increasing student retention.* San Francisco: Jossey-Bass.

Upcraft, M. L., & Farnsworth, W. M. (1984). Orientation programs and activities. In M. L. Upcraft (Ed.), Orienting students to college. (New Directions for Student Services No. 25) (pp. 27-38). San Francisco: Jossey-Bass.

Young, R. B., Backer, R., & Rogers, G. (1989). The impact of early advising and scheduling on freshman success. *Journal of College Student Develoment, 30*(4), 309-312.

Orientation as a Catalyst for Student Success: Effective Retention Through Academic and Social Integration

Updated by Jim Zakely*

Updated by Jim Zakely*

Well-designed orientation programs are an effective way to help students integrate socially and academically into an unfamiliar college or university environment, especially when those programs incorporate quality academic advising components. Because of their role in academic and social integration, orientation programs may exert a positive effect on student retention from the first to second college year. Such programs may also be associated with higher graduation rates (Cuyjet & Newman, 1999; Donald, 1997; Dunphy, Miller, Woodruff, & Nelson, 1987; Fidler & Hunter, 1989; Grites, 2001; Kuh, 2001; Kuh, Schuh, Whitt, & Associates, 1991; Robinson, Burns, & Gaw 1996; Schuh & Whitt, 1999; Tinto, 2000).

Evidence from the research cited above suggests that students who participate in orientation are more likely to persist and graduate at significantly higher rates than non-participants. However, as Pascarella and Terenzini (1991) point out, nearly all of these studies fail to take into account the voluntary nature of most orientation programs and the possibility that students who choose to participate in orientation activities may already (prior to matriculation, that is) have higher educational aspirations, be more motivated and self-directed learners, and have a higher level of commitment to particular institutions. Thus, the connection between orientation and student persistence and degree completion may be only indirect (Pascarella, Terenzini, & Wolfle, 1986). What we can conclude from all of the research on orientation is that successful orientation programs have a positive influence on first-year social and academic integration, and that, furthermore, social and academic integration have a significant effect on student persistence and educational attainment. Orientation is, therefore, a catalyst, precipitating a chain of events that will help students understand and participate fully—and ideally, thrive—in their new academic and social environments (Tinto, 1987).

Academic Integration

The integration of students into the academic environment is a critical component of new students' academic lives because it nurtures their hope for and expectation of graduating. Encompassed in that anticipated graduation are all the hopes and dreams of students' families, their friends, and the institution itself. Orientation fosters the first steps toward making those dreams a reality.

None of these dreams can be realized unless students are in good standing with the institution. Every relationship between the students and the school (e.g., financial aid, participation in sports, living on campus, membership in clubs and organizations, and work on campus) is predicated on the student's continued successful academic progress. Hence, "the most important goal of orientation is to help freshmen succeed academically" (Perigo & Upcraft, 1989, p. 83).

---

* Jim Zakely returns to update and revise the chapter he co-authored with Louis Fox, Roger Morris, and Michaelann Jundt in the first edition.

Chapter Five

Most orientation programs do provide a forum for academic integration to occur (Nadler, 1992). Unfortunately that tendency may be on the decline. Biannually, the National Orientation Directors Association (NODA) surveys its membership. The survey takes a "snapshot" of orientation programs and practices in the United States and Canada. In 1991, 93% of institutions responding to the survey reported that their orientation programs covered "academic structures," 88% involved "class scheduling," and 100% of the programs surveyed incorporated academic advising into the orientation program (Strumpf, 1991). The most recent survey showed a 7% drop (to 86%) in programs covering "academic structures," a 6% decrease (to 82%) in "class scheduling," and a 14% decrease (to 86%) in the number of programs providing academic advising during orientation (Strumpf & Wawrzynski, 2000).

At the same time, there has been an increase of 11% (from 73% to 84%) in the programs covering "residence hall living," a 7% increase in "social activities" (from 75% to 82%), a 14% increase (from 47% to 61%) in "alcohol awareness programs," and a 16% rise (from 43% to 69%) in the number of programs covering "date rape/sexual assault" issues (Strumpf, 1991; Strumpf & Wawrzynski, 2000). Such data suggest that institutions have de-emphasized the academic components of their programs in favor of more emphasis on social issues, although the reason for this change in focus remains unclear.

The apparent decline of academic components in orientation programs is especially troubling because competent advising is central to successful academic integration. Students must receive timely and accurate information in order to make informed choices about courses and major selection, and they need assistance from trained faculty and staff advisers to do so. The advising process is the first time that students' perceptions of their abilities, skills, and interests are met head-on by the demands and realities of the institution (Grites, 2001), and it is the only process that involves virtually every other aspect of the institution—e.g., administration, faculty, and student services (Glennen & Vowell, 1995). Although it is one of the most common components of orientation programs, Boyer (1987) "... found advising to be one of the weakest links in the undergraduate experience" (p. 51). Almost 15 years later Kuh (2001) reports that "the area in which students tend to be the least satisfied is academic advising ..." (p. 282). Thus, in spite of its importance, students may receive inadequate advising during the orientation process and throughout their academic careers.

> "Such data suggest that institutions have de-emphasized the academic components of their programs in favor of more emphasis on social issues, although the reason for this change in focus remains unclear."

Inadequate advising during orientation may happen, in part, because of the division within institutions between offices of student affairs and offices of academic affairs and the subsequent division of responsibilities for orienting new students to campus and managing their academic experiences. Fewer than 10% of orientation professionals report to academic affairs, while more than 65% of orientation programs use faculty advising models. In addition, 30% of programs use professional staff advisers who presumably report to academic officers (Strumpf & Wawrzynski, 2000). While we do not mean to suggest that this division of labor automatically leads to a lack of commitment to academic issues during orientation, it certainly suggests a difference in commitment, training, and focus between those who run orientation programs and those who deliver the academic message within that program.

The challenge for orientation professionals is to develop programs that use the skills of the orientation professional and of faculty to help students make a smooth transition into their new academic environments, but developing a viable partnership with academic affairs is often a difficult task. Two factors complicate collaborations on issues related to academics in the orientation program. The first has to do with the relationship with and knowledge about students held by faculty, staff, and administrators. Kuh (2001) reports that "many faculty members ignore what students do outside the classroom or how students' personal lives affect their learning. Most student-affairs professionals have little first-hand information about (and too often little interest in) what happens inside the classroom and how students' academic experiences affect their lives outside the classroom" (p. 295). Misunderstandings about the reality of student life make it difficult for academics and student affairs staff members to communicate with each other about the critical academic issues that need to be covered in the orientation program.

A second factor complicating academic and student affairs partnerships in orientation programming is misperceptions or a lack of knowledge about the differences in academic and student affairs functions and the campus work environment. For example, the academic and professional experience of student affairs professionals has often given them little insight into the academic life of institutions. Faculty issues such as promotion and tenure review; the balance among teaching, advising, institutional service, and scholarly activity; and the ebb and flow of the faculty member's academic year (i.e., term breaks and summer contracts) are issues of which student services professionals often lack awareness or understanding. In many cases, student services staff dismiss faculty as being uninterested in and unavailable to students.

At the same time, many faculty members also have little understanding or appreciation of student development theory, the nature and purpose of student services, program and budget development, and the ebb and flow of the academic year for student services professionals. In the worst cases, faculty members tend to lump student services professionals in with administrators—the president, vice presidents, and others "who do not teach."

In order to bridge this gap, student services professionals need to learn more about the academic culture of the institution. Training programs should expose them to the academic processes mentioned above, the history of the institution, and issues and challenges currently faced by the institution. If possible, student services professionals should read the minutes of the faculty senates on their campuses and spend time listening to the concerns of their faculty colleagues. Boyer's (1990) *Scholarship Reconsidered* can be extremely useful in understanding the roles that faculty members play in colleges and universities (Glassick, Huber, & Maeroff, 1997).

At the same time, faculty could also benefit by learning more about student services. Student affairs professionals can assist by making faculty aware of relevant, current issues in the leading journals addressing student development. Reading books such as *The Freshman Year Experience* (Upcraft & Gardner, 1989), *The Professional Student Affairs Administrator* (Winston, Creamer, Miller, & Associates, 2001), and *Student Services: A Handbook for the Profession* (Komives & Woodard, 1996) or attending relevant professional meetings can be enlightening for faculty members and may help them develop new approaches to teaching undergraduate courses, especially those that involve first-year students.

Factors Involved in Academic Integration

Levitz and Noel (1989) identified many factors critical to the success of first-year students. Researchers such as Tinto (1987, 1993) have called attention to the necessity of orientation programs addressing academic issues in a way that helps students make a successful academic transition. These factors are important for academic integration to occur and should be included and addressed in the design of the academic component of summer and continuing orientation programs.

Academic preparedness. Students need to be given accurate and timely assessments of their skills and placed at the appropriate level in courses such as math, English, and foreign languages. Usually this information is available as a part of the admissions process (SAT/ACT scores) or through placement tests, often administered during orientation programs. Institutions should undertake correlation studies to determine whether placement tests and placement levels correspond to student success in these courses. Other course work such as the College Level Examination Program (CLEP) and advanced placement scores also need to be evaluated. If admission criteria are not sufficient to make these recommendations, then internal tests need to be developed. In addition, advisers should have clearly stated options for those students who do not have the necessary minimal skills in particular academic proficiency areas. Placing students in classes that are either above or below their ability can set them up for failure: The former scenario leads to frustration; the latter leads to boredom.

Limited or unrealistic expectations. Students need to understand what their institutions expect of them—academically and socially—and then set realistic goals for themselves. While most orientation programs provide programming around social expectations and opportunities, too few provide an emphasis on academic expectations.

Students are seldom exposed to the fact that academic rigor and standards of a college are very different from those of high school. Strategies that worked for students in high school no longer work in the college setting. The pace and rigor of a 10- to 15-week course are very different from those of a nine-month course.

Orientation programs must make new students aware of the academic requirements of the institution. They must also provide information on how to balance the demands of social, personal, and academic concerns. Caring professionals who provide programming based in student development theory are of little value to a student who fails to meet graduation requirements.

Career confusion. Many students enter college with uncertain career goals and with questions about what academic major(s) to pursue. Students not only need to know that this career confusion is normal, but they also need to know what resources are available to help them decide on appropriate and realistic career goals. Students should also meet with academic advisers who can help them integrate their career goals with the specific curricula they plan to follow, both in their general education courses and in their major coursework.

Advising. An important step in helping students make a smooth academic transition is the assistance of qualified advisers (Frost, 1991; Kramer & Spencer, 1989). Advisers should know a student's academic background, the course requirements of academic programs students plan to pursue, and the campus resources available to assist students. Advisers should be familiar with those courses and instructors that challenge students while providing a supportive environment that allows students to be successful.

Advisers should also be familiar with and sensitive to the different types of students present at their institutions, particularly those students who are at risk of dropping out or who may face particularly difficult periods of adjustment in the academic environment. Special consideration should be given to the academic needs of special or marginally admitted students, students with disabilities, and transfer students.

As mentioned earlier, faculty advising is the most prevalent model used in orientation programs. The advantage of this model is that it mirrors the traditional advising model that exists on most college campuses. Ideally, the faculty member who serves as the adviser for a student during orientation will continue in that role through that student's first year. Outstanding faculty who teach first-year courses can make excellent advisers because of the opportunity they have for continued contact both in and out of the classroom.

Many faculty are not on contract during the summer months and therefore are not available. The cost of extending contracts so that faculty are available for summer advising may be prohibitive. Those faculty who are on summer contract are often teaching, and their schedules may not match with the advising times in

"Advisers should be familiar with those courses and instructors that challenge students while providing a supportive environment that allows students to be successful."

orientation. In addition, advising is, unfortunately, not considered in the faculty reward system on many campuses and is, consequently, not eagerly pursued by the faculty on those campuses. In a national survey of faculty, only 25% rated academic advising as being very or fairly important in achieving tenure (Boyer, 1990). Thus, the faculty advising model may not be feasible for all institutions.

> *"Peer advisers can relate easily with new students, particularly with traditional-aged first-year students, and are able to convey the appropriate information in the undergraduate vernacular."*

An alternative to a faculty advising model is the use of peer advisers. Often peers can use their intimate knowledge of the institution to assist students in very concrete ways. Peer staffs are also less expensive to hire and have flexible summer schedules. To be successful, however, peer advisers need extensive training and closer supervision than faculty. While the investment in peer training and development is great, the potential benefits of using peer advisers are numerous. Peer advisers can relate easily with new students, particularly with traditional-aged first-year students, and are able to convey the appropriate information in the undergraduate vernacular (Gordon, 1992; Reinarz, 2000).

Social Integration

In addition to academic and intellectual growth during their college years, students experience significant social and personal change. For a traditional 18-year-old first-year student, autonomy—personal and academic—is the theme behind social and intellectual integration. Students going off to college have never chosen an academic major or planned their career path to the extent they will as an undergraduate. Students who have lived at home with their parents and siblings all their lives will join fellow young adults in living groups without "adult supervision." Students will encounter many different types of people and ideas in college and will be challenged to define their opinions and values. With this new autonomy students confront many new issues, trying to balance new freedoms and responsibilities, including those surrounding the definition of their identities and the exploration of intimate relationships.

Searching for and developing identity is at the center of the social integration undertaken during the college years. Beginning life at college allows a student the opportunity to look at old behaviors in a different light. Students will question some of the norms and values that may have been accepted in their family or previous environment. Independence from family, a new environment, and new intellectual challenges all contribute to a student's definition of self. Coburn and Treeger (1988) explain the development of identity this way: "Colleges and universities offer a time-out, a breather after the period of childhood and before the commitments of adulthood. During this time, students may explore, take risks, test and 'try on' new ways of being, and make mistakes without drastic consequences" (p. 15).

Intimacy—including both friendships and romantic relationships—also plays an important role in the social integration that students experience. In initiating potential relationships, students have to consider what they want and how to find it. They must also determine the impact that "getting close" will have on maintaining their own sense of identity. Sexual expectations and sexual orientation may be questioned for the first time, and the need to make decisions about long-term commitments will be the inevitable result of some relationships. Orientation can provide opportunities for students to meet and learn about each other. Getting to know other new students can help first-years ease into the initial period of social exploration and change.

Orientation professionals are faced with the challenge of addressing many difficult issues in order to help students with their social integration. In 1989, a needs assessment was conducted that specifically looked at how orientation programs were addressing alcohol and substance abuse, multiculturalism, campus and personal safety, and personal relationships (National Orientation Directors Association, 1989). The assessment concluded the following: (a) most institutions have difficulty addressing these issues in their orientation programs and are looking for ways to do so; (b) these issues involve behavioral change, which is difficult to instill in a two- or three-day program; and (c) structured programs regarding these issues are usually not well-received. Frequently, students report that they have "been given this information" in high school and resent being told how to behave now that they are "adults." Nevertheless, orientation professionals conducting the study concluded that, in order to make an impact, these issues need to be considered when designing an orientation program and integrated throughout campus life.

The model and timing of "issue programs" vary. A variety of teaching and learning strategies need to be used, including handouts and brochures, discussions, panels, films and videos, lecture, small group discussions, and role-playing. Student orientation leaders can present the information, or bring in individuals who can relate to new students' experiences. In addressing substance abuse, personal safety, and personal relationships, orientation programs should include a combination of printed literature, information regarding campus resources, and creative programming.

Colleges and universities need to promote recognition, understanding, and appreciation of other cultures through student, faculty, and staff programs that highlight multiculturalism. We must develop orientation programs for all new members of the community, not just new students. In addition to the activities that an office of minority affairs might initiate, multiculturalism must be addressed throughout the entire orientation program. For example, the University of Wisconsin–Green Bay produces a "Good Morning Live" program that covers sensitive issues such as alcohol

"Peers can effectively deliver important social information while sharing personal experiences and teaching campus norms to new students, because they are honest and direct and have no hidden academic or administrative agenda."

use and abuse; sexuality, sexual health, and sexual harassment; and racism. The program is updated each year to reflect current issues and ideas. Similarly, Virginia Tech has developed a four-day program, "Paws Preview," through which students are exposed to diversity training and multicultural issues.

An important consideration impacting social integration is a student's prior experiences and environments. Peers and family influence the campus and community resources that a student needs and uses. An 18-year-old first-year student will probably depend primarily on peers, while a 30-year-old returning student with a spouse and children will have family as his or her first priority. In planning orientation programs, these differences need to be constantly considered.

Because students must deal with so many new issues when starting college, it is crucial that information about campus resources be presented during orientation in a pertinent, lively, and honest way. Peers can effectively deliver important social information while sharing personal experiences and teaching campus norms to new students, because they are honest and direct and have no hidden academic or administrative agenda (Ender & Newton, 2000; Ender & Winston, 1984).

The most successful presentations also allow for small group experiences, where a level of intimacy and trust can develop. Participatory activities and programs should be encouraged, and various forms of media should be used. Often a variety of methods can be effective, such as following a skit with a panel presentation or small group discussion.

The use of skits or role playing can also be a successful method to identify campus resources. In the process, the orientation participants are exposed to characters, played by the student orientation leaders, who express typical concerns in starting college. Will I have any friends? Will I be accepted if I have a different sexual orientation than my roommate? Will I survive academically? These and other issues are addressed in these unique, student-initiated productions.

Every method possible should be used to teach new students about opportunities and programs available at the institution. New students must be given the tools needed to become integrated into campus life and to be successful both socially and academically. Because new students often suffer from "information overload" during their transition, formal and informal strategies should be created to address students' concerns and questions as they become accustomed to their new environments.

Extended orientation throughout the first term, such as first-year courses or seminars, creates opportunities for students to deal with issues and find out about campus resources within the context of their academic coursework and their new environments. A side benefit of using faculty and student affairs staff to teach new student seminars is a greater understanding by both of the issues that students face in and out of the classroom, as well as a greater understanding of each of their roles in helping or hindering students in meeting the challenges of the first year. According to Donald (1997), "Programs designed for first-year students can focus attention on learning, may save many students from a negative learning experience," and create a sense of renewal among faculty (p. 122). First-year seminars also appear to have a positive effect on increasing graduation rates and student satisfaction (Donald, 1997). For a more in-depth discussion of first-year seminars, see Chapter 12 in this monograph.

The college experience can be like a roller coaster ride. Some of the twists and turns and ups and downs make new students feel like they are going too fast or they are losing control. The challenge for those creating orientation programs is to demonstrate to students that they are still on track as they experience those feelings. The up-and-down nature of college life is inevitable. Orientation can give students the tools to cope with change and find help when it is needed. This crucial aspect of social integration begins at orientation.

The Balancing Act

Successful students balance their lives. They make time for academics, extracurricular activities or work, and family and friends. Introducing these components during orientation—and beginning to teach students how to balance them—is one of the best services provided by orientation programs. According to Pascarella and Terenzini (1991), to be effective (in early socialization of students) orientation "should facilitate academic adjustment and initial social integration, thereby increasing the likelihood of persistence and degree completion" (p. 419).

Kuh and his colleagues have studied data from more than 51,000 students nationwide who have completed the College Student Experiences Questionnaire (CSEQ). The questionnaire asks students to indicate their participation in various collegiate behaviors and evaluate their progress (gains) in areas of academic and personal development. Through extensive analysis student "types" were developed based on predominate behaviors, (e.g., recreator, socializer, grind, individualist). The study suggests that "placing too much emphasis on a single activity … produces at best only average (and more frequently below-average) gains" (Kuh, 2001, p. 291). For this reason, orientation programs should address a range of academic and social issues.

Students need basic academic skills. How do I know what is expected in a class? Where can I get help with writing papers? What are finals like? Professors can give students a picture of what it is like inside a classroom—how much reading and writing they can look forward to, standards of academic honesty, the different daily demands of a science or humanities class. Academic advisers, whether they are faculty or professional staff, can help students determine what disciplines interest them, and how their major can lead to a career. Advisers can also lead students to academic resources such as writing centers, study skills courses, and computer and language labs.

Students must be introduced to campus resources and ways of coping with problems. Who can I talk to if I have problems with my roommate? Where can I go if I get sick? College students do not go to class and study in a vacuum. Outside pressures—new friendships and relationships, homesickness, family expectations, poor eating habits, and little sleep—make it more difficult to concentrate on the academic subjects.

Students should have the opportunity to discuss some of the issues they will face on campus. What kinds of people go to school here? How do I make friends? What are parties like? What about dating? The transition to college involves academic and social integration. Students who know what to expect socially feel more confident and secure. Students who have thought about the issues they may have to face should be able to respond to new situations responsibly.

Most important, students need to learn how to balance their different responsibilities, expectations, and activities. How can I manage my time with three classes and a part-time job? How do I balance family desires for my major and career with my own? What can I be involved in besides classes? Can I have a social life and still be a successful student? Orientation can begin to teach students about balance. Since many different workshops and tours are offered during a typical orientation session or welcome week and because students can't do it all, they have to decide which topics and activities interest them. They are also exposed to all kinds of information—academic requirements and options, procedures for registration and financial aid, various campus resources, and many different opportunities for involvement. Students must juggle all this information and prioritize their needs.

Student orientation leaders and other student leaders are the key to showing new students how to balance the academic and social life of an institution. The leaders' personal experiences serve as models for new students, often replacing their previous ideas about how successful college students look and act. When student leaders talk about choosing classes, searching for a major, studying for an essay exam, joining a sports team, or finding information on sexually transmitted diseases, new students listen to what they say. New students see that the orientation leaders are successful students, experienced in maneuvering through bureaucracy, adept at surviving numerous demands on their time and energy, and committed to the intellectual, cultural, and social life of the college or university.

"Astin's (1985) student involvement theory emphasizes that students are more likely to continue working toward their degree when they are engaged in the academic and community life of a college or university."

Students are more likely to attain their degree when they are involved with their fellow students and with faculty (Astin, 1993). Orientation leaders can effectively conduct an entire orientation program. Student staff can handle logistics (checking students in, giving directions, leading students to meals and appointments) as well as developing and facilitating the workshops, tours, and advising discussions that form the backbone of the program. In this model, new students come to see their orientation leaders as mentors and role models and feel comfortable asking about academics, activities, and campus social life. Faculty should be involved in orientation programs as academic advisers or as guest speakers, discussing academic responsibilities and their expectations of students. Some of the best connections between faculty and students are made informally, so inviting professors to participate in academic discussions or to join the group for a meal is effective.

Astin's (1985) student involvement theory emphasizes that students are more likely to continue working toward their degree when they are engaged in the academic and community life of a college or university. Students can build their involvement with a college or university upon the foundation laid during an orientation program. Orientation teaches skills that can be honed in first-year seminars, in extended orientation courses, and within academic departments. Orientation also encourages extra-curricular involvement that can be built on by special academic programs (e.g., honors programs, freshman interest groups), student government and clubs, living groups, public service opportunities, and campus events and activities. These sorts of curricular and co-curricular learning environments give students a sense of common purpose, while counteracting feelings of isolation (Astin, 1985). Orientation serves as a student's first learning community, setting the tone for future academic pursuits and connections within the academic community.

Continuing research concerning the outcomes of learning communities has sustained the value of early involvement and shared communities for new students. Curricular learning communities such as freshman interest groups (FIGs), new student seminars, and residential academic communities (e.g., living-learning centers) can all have a positive effect on students. Tinto (2000) indicates that learning communities provide shared knowledge (students take the same courses together), shared knowing (students work together to construct knowledge, forming academic and social connections), and shared responsibility (at some level students become active in helping each other gain knowledge). As such, shared learning experiences do "more than simply cement friendships; they serve to bridge the academic-social divide that typically plagues student life" (Tinto, 2000, p. 86).

Students do not experience their collegiate careers as distinct parts, but rather as an integrated whole. As Kuh (1991) reminds us:

> Indeed it is difficult to determine what students learn in the classes and what they learn through out-of-class experiences. In fact, the demarcation between activities undertaken in the classroom, laboratory, library, residence hall or on-campus job that promote learning and personal development is not always clear. (p. 7)

For this reason, academic and social integration is crucial to a student's success.

References

Astin, A. W. (1985). *Achieving academic excellence.* San Francisco: Jossey-Bass.

Astin, A. W. (1993). *What matters in college? Four critical years revisited.* San Francisco: Jossey-Bass.

Boyer, E. L. (1987). *College: The undergraduate experience in America.* New York: Harper & Row.

Boyer, E. L. (1990). *Scholarship reconsidered: Priorities of the professoriate.* Princeton, NJ: The Carnegie Foundation for the Advancement of Teaching.

Coburn, K. L., & Treeger, M. L. (1988). *Letting go: A parent's guide to today's college experience.* Bethesda, MD: Adler & Adler.

Cuyjet, M., & Newman L. (1999). Learning and development from theory to practice. In F. Stage, L. Watson, & M. Terrell (Eds.), *Enhancing student learning: Setting the campus context.* Lanham, MD: University Press of America.

Donald, J. (1997). *Improving the environment for learning: Academic leaders talk about what works.* San Francisco: Jossey-Bass

Dunphy, L., Miller, T., Woodruff, T., & Nelson, J. (1987). Exemplary retention strategies for the freshman year. In M. Stodt & W. Klepper (Eds.), *Increasing retention: Academic and student affairs administrators in partnership.* San Francisco: Jossey-Bass.

Ender, S., & Newton, F. (2000). *Students helping students.* San Francisco: Jossey-Bass.

Ender, S., & Winston, R., Jr. (Eds.). (1984). *Students as paraprofessional staff.* (New Directions for Student Services No. 27). San Francisco: Jossey-Bass.

Fidler, P., & Hunter, M. S. (1989). How seminars enhance student success. In M. L. Upcraft & J. N. Gardner (Eds.), *The freshman year experience: Helping students survive and succeed in college* (pp. 216-237). San Francisco: Jossey-Bass.

Frost, S. H. (1991). *Academic advising for student success: A system of shared responsibility.* (ASHE-ERIC Higher Education Report No. 3). Washington, DC: Association for the Study of Higher Education.

Glassick, C., Huber, M., & Maeroff, G. (1997). *Scholarship assessed: Evaluation of the professoriate.* San Francisco: Jossey-Bass.

Glennen, R., & Vowell, F. (Eds.). (1995). *Academic advising as a comprehensive campus process* (NACADA Monograph Series No. 2). Provo, UT: Brigham Young University Press.

Gordon, V. (1992). *Handbook of academic advising.* Westport, CT: Greenwood Press.

Grites, T. (2001). Developmental academic advising model. In V. Farmer & W. Barham (Eds.), *Selected models of developmental education programs in higher education.* New York: University Press of America

Komives, S. R., Woodward, D. G., Jr., & Associates. (1996). *Student services: A handbook for the profession,* (3rd ed.). San Francisco: Jossey-Bass.

Kuh, G. (2001). College students today: Why we can't leave serendipity to chance. In P. Altbach, P. Gumport, & B. Johnstone (Eds.), *In defense of American higher education.* Baltimore, MD: Johns Hopkins University Press.

Kuh, G., Schuh, J., Whitt, E., & Associates (1991). *Involving colleges: Successful approaches to fostering student learning and development outside the classroom.* San Francisco: Jossey-Bass.

Kramer, G. L., & Spencer, R. W. (1989). Academic advising. In M. L. Upcraft & J. N. Gardner (Eds.), *The freshman year experience: Helping students survive and succeed in college.* San Francisco: Jossey-Bass.

Levitz, R., & Noel, L. (1989). Connecting students to institutions: Keys to retention and success. In M. L. Upcraft & J. N. Gardner (Eds.), *The freshman year experience: Helping students survive and succeed in college* (pp. 65-81). San Francisco: Jossey-Bass.

Nadler, D. P. (Ed.). (1992). *Orientation director's manual.* Statesboro, GA: National Orientation Directors Association.

National Orientation Directors Association. (1989, October). *Needs assessment survey of membership* [Unpublished data].

Pascarella, E., & Terenzini, P. (1991). *How college affects students.* San Francisco: Jossey-Bass.

Pascarella, E., Terenzini, P., & Wolfle, L. (1986). Orientation to college and freshman year persistence/withdrawal decisions. *Journal of Higher Education, 57,* 155-175.

Perigo, D. J., & Upcraft, M. L. (1989). Orientation programs. In M. L. Upcraft & J. N. Gardner (Eds.), *The freshman year experience: Helping students survive and succeed in college* (pp. 82-94). San Francisco: Jossey-Bass.

Reinarz, A. (2000). Delivering academic advising. In V. Gordon, W. Habley, & Associates (Eds.), *Academic advising: A comprehensive handbook.* San Francisco: Jossey-Bass.

Robinson, D., Burns, C., & Gaw, K. (1996). Orientation programs: A foundation for student learning and success. In S. Ender, F. Newton, & R. Caple (Eds.), *Contributing to learning: The role of student affairs.* (New Directions for Student Services No. 75). San Francisco: Jossey-Bass.

Schuh, J., & Whitt E. (1999). *Creating successful partnerships between academic and student affairs.* (New Directions for Student Services No. 87). San Francisco: Jossey-Bass.

Strumpf, G. (Ed.). (1991). *National Orientation Directors Association data bank.* University of Maryland, College Park: National Orientation Directors Association.

Strumpf, G., & Wawrzynski, M. R. (Eds.). (2000). *National Orientation Directors Association data bank.* University of Maryland, College Park: National Orientation Directors Association.

Tinto, V. (1987). *Leaving college: Rethinking the causes and cures of student attrition.* Chicago: University of Chicago Press.

Tinto, V. (1993). *Leaving college: Rethinking the causes and cures of student attrition* (2nd ed.). Chicago: University of Chicago Press.

Tinto, V. (2000). Linking learning and leaving. In J. Braxton (Ed), *Reworking the Student Development Puzzle.* Nashville: Vanderbilt University Press.

Upcraft, M. L., & Gardner, J. N. (Eds.). (1989). *The freshman year experience: Helping students survive and succeed in college.* San Francisco: Jossey-Bass.

Winston, R., Creamer, D., Miller, T., & Associates (2001). *The professional student affairs administrator: Educator, leader, and manager.* New York: Brunner-Routledge.

Chapter Six

Organization and Administration of Orientation Programs

Jimmy W. Abraham, Bryan G. Nesbit, and Jeanine A. Ward-Roof*

The increasing emphasis on retaining students has heightened the attention paid to orientation, and several researchers have identified a relationship between comprehensive orientation programs and improved retention. Pascarella, Terenzini, and Wolfle (1986) argue that orientation has "relatively substantial and significant effects on both social integration during college . . . and subsequent commitment to the institution attended" (pp. 169-170). The orientation experience has a positive impact on first-year persistence by "facilitating a student's initial ability to cope with a new set of social challenges in an unfamiliar environment" (Pascarella et al., 1986, pp. 169-170). Forrest's (1982) study of 44 institutions confirms the link between comprehensive pre-college orientation and academic advising programs and student persistence and graduation.

But as Mann (1998) notes, the potential of orientation programs to aid in student retention may be compromised by an unclear and frequently narrow view of their purpose and goals: "New student orientation programs are too often viewed as either a testing and registration activity in the enrollment of students, or as the time when students participate in 'fun and games, to the exclusion of academic concerns" (p.15). On the other hand, Nadler, Miller, and Casebere (1998) note that ". . . [orientation programs] have been traditionally built and structured around the functional attribute of what academic or study skills can be transferred to new students and generally what is expected of new students in terms of performance, behavior, and so forth" (p. 30-31). Successful orientation programs, Mann suggests, balance a wide range of student and institutional goals. Further, excellence in orientation programming is the result of a successful collaboration of strong organizational skills and considerable human and financial resources. When attempting to build a strong program, orientation professionals are challenged by the initial process of integrating students to their new college environment, the availability of resources, and the assessment of program outcomes.

This chapter discusses general standards for orientation and provides information on the institutional home of orientation, staffing, and fiscal management. The authors review professional standards for orientation programs and offer recommendations on key issues related to program management.

Orientation Programs and Institutional Hierarchy

Traditionally, orientation has been viewed overwhelmingly as a student affairs function. In recent years, an increasing emphasis on enrollment management and student retention has led to a renewed interest in orientation, causing the location

---

* In the first edition, Richard H. Mullendore and Jimmy Abraham collaborated on this chapter. Abraham is joined by Bryan Nesbit and Jeanine Ward-Roof in updating and revising this chapter.

of administrative responsibility for orientation programs to be examined. This section reviews the orientation function and the administrative placement of orientation and offers recommendations regarding reporting lines for the program.

The Orientation Function

The Council for the Advancement of Standards (CAS) in Higher Education (1998) identified 13 indispensable standards of best practice for orientation programs. Among other things, well-designed orientation programs

- Assist new students in understanding the purposes of higher education
- Assist new students in understanding their responsibilities within the educational setting
- Provide new students with information about academic policies, procedures, requirements, and programs sufficient to make well-reasoned and well-informed choices
- Inform new students about the availability of services and programs
- Provide intentional opportunities for new students to interact with faculty, staff, and continuing students
- Provide relevant orientation information to the new students' primary support groups (pp. 222-223)

To meet these standards, orientation professionals must harness and direct numerous resources throughout the institution, but they must also remain cognizant of the ways in which institution type, mission, size, and student population create special demands for the orientation program. These standards should be adapted to meet the unique needs of the institution, students, and other participants who are involved in the orientation process.

In addition to the standards, CAS promotes a three-part mission for student orientation programs including (a) the preparation of new students for the educational opportunities that await them at the institution; (b) the integration of new students into the social, intellectual, and cultural atmosphere of the institution; and (c) the oversight of the overall process of a new student's transition into the institution (CAS, 1998). Further, CAS identifies essential qualities of orientation programs, including intentionality, coherence, theoretical basis for practice, focus on the development and demographic characteristics of new students, and responsiveness to individual needs. Taken together, the goals and characteristics suggest that an orientation program should help students with their academic success and their personal adjustment to college, help families of new students understand the adjustment students must make, and help the college or university learn about its entering students (Perigo & Upcraft, 1989).

Thus, professional standards of practice outline the current expectations of those who supervise the orientation function. Leaders who understand the importance of these expectations and meet them will have a profound impact on the experiences of new students. This impact will ultimately have a strong influence on student retention. In fact, the orientation mission and goals listed above closely parallel those of a successful retention program. Like orientation programs, other effective retention efforts

commonly stress the manner in which their actions serve to integrate individuals into the mainstream of the social and intellectual life of the institution and into the communities of people who make up that life. They consciously reach out and make contact with students in order to establish personal bonds among students and between students, faculty and staff members of the institution. (Tinto, 1990, p. 36)

In addition, orientation programs connect new students with faculty, which can have a great impact on retention. As Tinto (1990) reminds us, "interaction with faculty, especially outside the classroom is the single strongest predictor of student voluntary persistence" (p. 36). In Chapter 4, Smith and Brackin discuss faculty involvement in orientation.

Administrative Home of Orientation Programs

An analysis of the *National Orientation Directors Association (NODA) Data Bank* (Strumpf & Wawrzynski, 2000) shows that orientation functions are performed by a variety of campus units including orientation offices, counseling centers, deans of students, student activities offices, undergraduate studies programs, admissions offices, academic units, student development offices, and enrollment management offices. Thus, there is no consensus among institutions of higher education regarding which office should be responsible for the orientation function. The CAS Standards (1998) suggest that "the size, nature, and complexity of the institution should guide the administrative scope and structure of the orientation program" (p. 223). For example, half of the large institutions (more than 15,000 students) surveyed reported that orientation programs are the responsibility of an orientation office and are the primary job responsibility for one individual (50%) (Strumpf & Wawrzynski, 2000). These figures have been steadily increasing over the last two decades; however, between 1990 and 1995, increases stopped and the category of orientation function as a primary job responsibility of an individual has fallen by 1% as Table 1 shows. A comparison of reporting lines indicates that orientation is primarily a student affairs function, with approximately 62% of orientation professionals reporting to the chief student affairs officer or a subordinate (Strumpf, 2000).

Table 1.
Orientation Function Within Large Institutions (> 15,000 students), 1982 to 1997

Orientation Function	Survey Year		
	1982	1990	1995-1997
Performed by Orientation Office	39%	49%	50%
Primary Job Responsibility of an Individual	23%	48%	47%

Note. Data from NODA Databank (Strumpf, 1990, 1996).

Orientation is the primary job responsibility of an individual in nearly one third of mid-sized (5,000 to 15,000 students) institutions. However, in small (less than 5,000 students) institutions, 97% of individuals responsible for orientation perform this function in addition to other responsibilities. Table 2 shows the lines of reporting for orientation programs at small and mid-sized institutions. As in large institutions, orientation is primarily assigned to the student affairs area.

Cawthon and Ward-Roof (1999) also examined the management of orientation within the institutional hierarchy. They conducted a survey of orientation professionals via the National

Table 2.
Reporting Lines for Orientation Function in Mid-sized & Small Institutions

	Percentage of Institutions	
Reporting Line	Mid-Sized	Small
Chief Student Affairs Officer or Subordinate	56%	72%
Chief Academic Affairs Officer or Subordinate	10%	5%

Note. Data from 2000 NODA Databank

Orientation Directors Association listserv. More than half (59%) of the respondents were associated with mid-sized institutions (5,000 to 10,000 students), while close to one third (32%) were at large institutions (more than 15,000 students). For institutions of all sizes, most orientation professionals (76%) report to the division of student affairs, while only 12% report to academic affairs. An overwhelming 95% of all respondents stated that orientation was only one of their responsibilities. Of those reporting multiple job functions, 22.5% indicated that orientation duties consisted of 75 to 100% of their responsibilities.

These data indicate that the responsibility for orientation programs is primarily in the area of student affairs in institutions of all sizes. A relatively small number of institutions (2%, according to the 1995-97 and 2000 *NODA Data Banks*) indicate that orientation is performed through the enrollment management office. A review of past data from the *NODA Data Banks* shows an increase in "other" or unspecified reporting lines for orientation programs. Currently, in 15% of mid-sized institutions, 14% of small institutions, and 10% of large institutions, orientation staff report to an "other" institutional unit. Some of these variant reporting lines may be accounted for by decentralized orientation activities, which may or may not be attached to an institution-wide orientation program. In some institutions, students receive orientation to a specific academic program, department, or college rather than to the institution as a whole.

Recommendations for the Placement of the Orientation Function

The orientation function should report through the division of student affairs or have significant input from student affairs staff. Student affairs professionals constantly work within and beyond division lines. They are trained to understand how an institution functions, know what services are available, and possess significant knowledge of student development theory and practice—all important in designing and implementing an orientation program that will achieve the desired outcomes. Student affairs professionals are often in the best position to recruit, select, train, and evaluate student orientation leaders. In addition, student affairs professionals often have an appropriate conceptualization of the value of both academic and social integration into the college or university.

In some institutions, it may be appropriate that the orientation staff report to the office of enrollment management, which may or may not be within the division of student affairs. In those institutions where enrollment management is outside student affairs, Bean and Hossler (1990) recommend that there be, at the very least, a student affairs liaison officer, who is responsible for seeing that the many student affairs activities support the enrollment management strategy for the college or university. In particular, this person should help develop (or at some institutions have responsibility for) orientation, co-curricular programs, retention programs (like student skills centers), placement and alumni recruitment. (p. 229)

Whether in a direct coordination role or a liaison role, it is important that the orientation function be connected to both the student affairs division and the institution's enrollment management efforts and that collaborative efforts include all facets of the institution, including academic affairs.

Institutions that currently provide only decentralized, program-specific orientations should also provide a college- or university-wide orientation program. Decentralized programs may not meet the needs of students who are undecided about a major or those who will change majors. These programs may be helpful in the academic integration of students but may not adequately educate students about college or university services, activities, policies, and procedures, including important social integration components.

Orientation Staff Members and Program Characteristics

Perhaps the most important aspect in establishing an effective orientation program is the staff. These individuals bring to the program professionalism, passion, and energy. They are ultimately responsible for coordinating the activities that take place during the program. They serve on the front line, fielding a multitude of questions from students and families. In this way, they serve as key "public relations agents" for the institution.

> *"Because orientation can be both an institution-and community-wide program, the orientation professional must be a competent individual who is respected within and beyond the institution."*

Professional and Support Staff

Many institutional and human variables must be considered when staffing an orientation program. While some institutions have an individual who is solely responsible for orientation, it is more common for professionals to have other job responsibilities. Because of their multiple responsibilities, orientation professionals must be able to perform a multitude of tasks, but they must also be able to delegate responsibility successfully. As orientation professionals well know, attention to hundreds of details is essential in establishing a quality program. It is important that these individuals be able to motivate not only those who work for them, but other people on campus and in the community as well. Because orientation can be both an institution-and community-wide program, the orientation professional must be a competent individual who is respected within and beyond the institution.

The orientation professional also must enjoy working directly with students. Few administrative positions provide the opportunity for the constant, positive student contact afforded to the orientation professional. This person works year-round with the student orientation leaders and during events with all of the enthusiastic, but sometimes anxious, new students. Appropriate graduate school training or an appropriate combination of education and experience working with students should be a prerequisite for the orientation position.

Support staff. Few orientation professionals would even consider putting together a program without quality support staff, but in many institutions support staff members are not given the credit due to them. They are the ones whom students meet first, the first voice on the telephone, and often the first to give an impression of the college or university. These individuals, above all, must enjoy working with people—students, parents, faculty, and staff. They must be knowledgeable and patient, and they must understand that they set the tone for the office and the institution.

Support staff must be appropriately trained in all skills areas including office and program management. In today's competitive market for students, quality service must be provided by all staff. Consumers want timely and accurate responses when they ask for information about orientation or when they are waiting for confirmation. It is important that support staff be empowered to make decisions when necessary and made to feel a part of the orientation team.

Recommendations for Staffing

The CAS Standards (1998) recommend that the orientation program staff be adequate in terms of size and qualifications to accomplish its mission and goals. Moreover, it should be led by professional staff members holding graduate degrees in a related field or who have a comparable degree of education and professional work experience. Sixteen percent of orientation professionals hold bachelor's degrees, 76% hold master's degrees, and 9% hold doctorates (Strumpf & Wawrzynski, 2000). Cawthon and Ward-Roof (1999) found a similar pattern among NODA's electronic mailing list respondents: 16% have bachelor's degrees, 77% have master's degrees, and only 4% have doctorates. Though these percentages seem to be somewhat in line with the educational levels mandated by the CAS standards, the orientation function is often performed by an entry-level professional. Mullendore (1992) writes of the diverse skills required: "the orientation professional must be extremely proficient in coordination, negotiation, supervision, and public relations in order to effectively meander through the institutional milieu and implement a meaningful and successful program or a series of programs" (p. 43).

The orientation professional should not be at entry-level unless previous experiences or current supervision can provide the necessary knowledge and skills to perform this vital function successfully. The individual responsible for orientation must know and be able to work comfortably with virtually every component and constituency within and beyond the institution in order to provide effective orientation programs. Relationships with the academic advising units, departments, colleges and schools, business offices, campus police, physical plant, residence life, dining services, local businesses, and others are critical to a successful and comprehensive orientation. To summarize this point, Greenlaw, Anliker, and Barker (1997) state that collaboration across the campus is imperative. Orientation professionals must be able to recruit, select, and train student staff; manage a budget; and plan and implement a complex series of programs. An individual with experience in orientation planning and execution will be more likely than a new professional to possess the skills necessary to direct a successful, comprehensive orientation program.

Institutional Considerations

Obviously, programs must reflect the characteristics and needs of their target populations. Although first-year and transfer students share many needs in common, they also have some very unique ones. Similarly, residential and commuter students will also differ in their needs. Institutional admission policies, which will determine the composition of the student body, will also drive the content and delivery of orientation programs. Campuses which serve nontraditional students will have different program foci than those attracting traditional students. The history, mission, and goals of the college or university must be considered, as well as the goals of individual departments, divisions, schools, and colleges within the institution.

After the mission and goals of the institution are clearly articulated and understood, it is appropriate to consider the type or types of orientation program(s) that an institution wants to implement. There are many types of orientation programs, and careful consideration must be given to the kind of program initiated at each institution. Administratively, an institution needs to look at its facilities when developing an orientation program. For example, will students and families be housed on campus? How many can be accommodated in university housing? How many people can the campus dining facility serve? Often, there are other summer programs that conflict with orientation program needs. These and other considerations lead some institutions to offer only a fall program, which brings students in for orientation anywhere from two weeks to two days before the fall semester begins. Some institutions do a combination of both summer and fall programs in which students come in for a few days in the summer and return for a few days prior to the beginning of school. In addition, many schools have an ongoing orientation program whereby they continue the process throughout the first semester or year. In institutions with fewer than 5,000 students, the majority of programs are held for three days preceding the beginning of the semester (Strumpf & Wawrzynski, 2000). For institutions with 5,000 to 15,000 students, 51% bring their students in for two days during the summer, while 52% of the institutions with an enrollment of 15,000 or more use this model (Strumpf & Wawrzynski, 2000).

"As competition for students, in particular top scholars, increases and as parents, spouses, and others become more involved in the college selection process, orientation programs for these groups become more important. Family members need to have an opportunity to interact with faculty, students, and staff; to tour the campus; and to receive answers to the many questions they have."

Other factors, such as the make-up of the entering student population, should be considered when planning an orientation program. Institutions across the country offer special programs for the following special student populations in conjunction with orientation: academically disadvantaged students; students with disabilities; graduate, honors, or academically talented students; international students; minority students; nontraditional students; scholarship athletes; and veterans. Chapter 7 in this monograph describes some of the issues orientation professionals should consider when planning programs for or inclusive of these student groups.

Orientation professionals should also consider parents and family members of incoming students in their planning. The parent/family program can be an integral part of the orientation process. As competition for students, in particular top scholars, increases and as parents, spouses, and others become more involved in the college selection process, orientation programs for these groups become more important. Family members need to have an opportunity to interact with faculty, students, and staff; to tour the campus; and to receive answers to the many questions they have. Parents in particular must feel comfortable with and knowledgeable about the institution that their student has chosen. They should also have the opportunity to ask some questions without their student present. At many colleges and universities, family and student programs are held concurrently, with separate sessions for parents/families and students. Chapter 11 discusses these issues in greater depth.

Two-year college orientation programs often include a different range of activities than four-year schools typically provide. In contrast to the social and issues-related programs of four-year schools, two-year colleges emphasize counseling and academic placement. Two-year colleges are realizing how important a successful orientation program is to student recruitment as well as retention. For a more extensive discussion of community and two-year college orientation programs, see Chapter 10 of this monograph.

Administration, Staff, and Faculty

It goes without saying that the orientation program does not occur in isolation. It is a college- or university-wide effort, and the involvement of faculty and staff is critical to its success. As noted earlier, interaction with faculty outside the classroom is a powerful retention agent. As orientation professionals, it is important to try to get those faculty and staff who want to be a part of the program and who understand the goals and objectives to become involved. This will provide a better working relationship and ensure a positive first impression for the students, parents, and other groups whom faculty and staff meet during the orientation program.

An orientation professional, after being at an institution for some time, will often identify specific faculty and staff members to make presentations during the orientation program. For instance, a common activity on many campuses is an icebreaker exercise held at the beginning of the orientation program. If a faculty member or campus administrator with high energy and excellent communication skills can lead this type of activity, his or her efforts will be greatly appreciated by the students.

Because scheduling classes is an important component of the orientation process at most institutions, academic advising is frequently included. Weekend programs are held on many campuses, and faculty members and professional academic advisers often give up a weekend to be a part of this process with students. It is extremely important that these individuals, especially those who receive no extra compensation, are thanked for making this special effort. Most faculty members want to be of assistance; many went into the teaching profession to be of service to students, so they understand the importance of the orientation program. As noted by Mullendore, Biller, and Busby in Chapter 14 of this monograph, most institutions conduct evaluations of the orientation program, and the results need to be shared with the college or university community, including both faculty and staff members.

The importance of faculty involvement in the life of students is stressed by Pope (2001) in an examination of the overall relationship between faculty and student affairs. Faculty benefit student affairs functions in three areas: (a) conveying academic expectations, (b) serving as role models outside of the classroom, and (c) integrating "academic curriculum into student activities that can potentially provide unique and beneficial learning experiences" (p. 7). If faculty are to have the positive effects listed above, orientation professionals must examine avenues for incorporating these key individuals into the orientation framework.

Selection and Training of Student Orientation Leaders

The selection and training of student orientation leaders are keys to a successful orientation program. The importance of a fair and comprehensive selection process on each campus should not be ignored. Basic guidelines include determining what qualities a student orientation leader should possess, developing a selection procedure that will help identify these qualities, implementing the selection process, and conducting an evaluation of the selection process to determine its effectiveness. Student staff selection usually consists of an application and interviews, both group and personal. Efforts must be made to attract and recruit a diverse group of students for these critical leadership positions. Former orientation leaders should also be used, as they can provide valuable insights, and their involvement in the process should be welcomed and encouraged.

On most campuses, the orientation leader is highly respected, which means that the number of applicants often exceeds the number of openings. Besides the usual routine of hanging posters and announcing the deadline in the school paper, via e-mail, and on radio or television, many institutions use former orientation leaders who are still on campus to help recruit new leaders. During or following the application process, it is important to hold an informational meeting to introduce, in as much detail as possible, what will take place for the students in interviews and while they are orientation leaders. Information on salary (if it is a paid position), the length of the orientation program, dates, and the expectations associated with the position should be communicated during the information meeting. Orientation professionals should develop a selection timetable, and candidates should know when they will find out about their selection or non-selection. Many orientation professionals would agree that clarifying expectations up front can help build a very successful orientation team and prevent some problems from occurring. Such information will also help students be fully committed to the selection process and to the orientation program.

After student applicants understand the position, the program requirements, the orientation professional's expectations, and their responsibilities, then the interview process can begin. Some institutions use group interviews, some use individual interviews, some use interviews with faculty and staff, and some provide interviews with former orientation leaders. Many institutions observe both written and verbal communication skills through a variety of experiences.

A critical element in the selection process is identifying those individuals with true leadership potential. Posner and Rosenberger (1997) state that "[i]n selection, attention should be paid to whether potential OAs (orientation advisers) understand and appreciate the leadership aspects of the position. Similarly, their appreciation of and capacity for using particular leadership skills might be examined ..." (p. 54). Critical traits required of an orientation student staff member include excellent communication skills, superb time management, a diligent work ethic, integrity, and the ability to work with a diverse group of students and parents. The influence that orientation leaders will

> *"One of the most critical parts of a successful orientation program is ensuring that the staff members are trained properly and thoroughly."*

have on new first-year students and transfer students should never be underestimated. These student leaders, who often times are the first contact new students have with a college or university, will make the difference in creating excitement or discouragement in the hearts and minds of these new students. The student orientation leaders hold a captive audience of new students who will quickly discern the level of leadership skills they possess. Thus, leadership training is a critical element in any orientation leader educational program.

When the staff has been selected, the training process should begin as soon as possible in order to capitalize on the excitement generated by selection. For each program there are basic steps which may be used as guidelines, including (a) assessing the training needs of the student orientation leaders and other staff, (b) designing the appropriate training program based on these needs, (c) conducting the training, and (d) evaluating the training to determine its effectiveness. When designing the training program, several factors should be considered, including the time commitment, facilities needed, and equipment and materials required. It may be appropriate for the orientation professional to work with an orientation advisory committee, comprising students, faculty, and administrators, particularly if the needs of all the groups are to be addressed.

One of the most critical parts of a successful orientation program is ensuring that the staff members are trained properly and thoroughly. Many institutions accomplish this training by offering a class for orientation leaders. Of those that offer a class, some give academic credit while for others it is a required component of the training process. Because there is no way that one individual, the orientation professional, can meet with the hundreds or thousands of people that come to orientation programs during the summer or the fall, developing a comprehensive training program for orientation leaders is imperative. The student orientation leaders are the ones who will be "in the trenches," sharing information and responding to questions. Training should include discussions or hands-on experiences dealing with the following: (a) appropriate ways to communicate information to prospective students and their families, (b) college or university services and the process for making referrals, (c) team-building, and (d) the value of supporting one another. Orientation leaders should also have the opportunity to meet with deans, department heads, vice presidents, and even the president.

The student orientation leaders must know the standards and values of the orientation program, and they must see those standards and values throughout the entire orientation experience. With careful thought, the orientation professional will be able to select and train a staff that will understand this and make the institution very proud.

Funding Orientation Programs

In the current era of growing constraints on program funding in higher education, funded programs will be those that have engaged in planning and have implemented assessment strategies linking program planning to program effectiveness and outcomes, especially retention. These programs will also link planning and assessment processes to the larger institutional budgentary review procedure. Orientation programs, perceived by some as "fun and games," may be placed in a defensive posture budgetarily if a solid case for support is not made.

Orientation Program Expenses

Funding needs vary considerably from institution to institution depending on the size of the school, length and timing of the orientation program, housing and dining service needs, comprehensiveness of the program, size of the professional and student staff, and other factors. The CAS standards clearly articulate a need for adequate funding to carry out the mission and goals of the orientation program. Expenses associated with orientation programs include the following:

Staff salaries. Typical staff in an orientation program may include a program director, student orientation leaders, clerical support, and other employees. As outlined in the CAS Standards, salary and benefits for orientation professionals and support staff should be comparable to similar positions within the institution or within the geographic region and to similar positions at comparable institutions. Paraprofessional staff should also receive fair compensation. If the position is voluntary, their services should be adequately recognized and otherwise rewarded.

Operating expenses. Operating expenses for an orientation program might include capital expenditures on furnishings and equipment, but they will also include more routine expenses like telephone services, printing, postage, and office supplies. The CAS Standards recommend that money for the orientation program be "allocated on a permanent basis" and that it be adequate to accomplish the mission and goals of the program (CAS, 1998, p. 24). Further, all expenses should be linked to the program's mission and goals, whether they are determined as part of a normal planning cycle or identified in response to unexpected occurrences.

Because institutions often see orientation as an extension of their recruitment efforts, expenses related to printing and postage can be extremely high. Further, it demands that orientation brochures and other materials sent to incoming students are professional in their appearance and format. Materials also must be sent to all admitted students—often thousands more than will actually enroll. Decisions must also be made about whether to send materials bulk rate or first class and the amount of follow-up correspondence to be sent. Some institutions provide a toll-free telephone service or e-mail address to respond to student and family queries. Such services carry their own expenses, but they also require adequate staff to answer the phone and respond to e-mail in a timely way. Each decision influences costs associated with the program.

Other routine orientation-related expenses include nametags, pencils, folders for participants, directional signs, evaluation forms, and general supplies. Other program costs include media or technical support for audiovisual presentations, entertainment (e.g., disk jockeys, bands, games, transportation), and paraphernalia (t-shirts or other giveaways). Campus facility costs can include room rentals, and setup and clean-up charges. Areas of tremendous expense for many programs include overnight housing, meals, and for institutions with large campuses, transportation of students and parents throughout the program. Some of these costs may be underwritten by fees charged directly to participants.

Training and development. The CAS Standards recommend that orientation programs provide "appropriate professional development opportunities" (CAS, 1998, p. 223). Expenses associated with professional development include membership in professional organizations, subscriptions to relevant periodicals, participation in external meetings, and training opportunities. Additionally, student orientation leaders generally receive considerable training, which can be expensive, especially if travel costs to regional meetings are associated with the training program.

Individuals overseeing orientation programs may also want to provide uniforms for their student leaders and professional staff for orientation sessions. Uniforms allow orientation staff members to appear professional, promoting the image of the program and the institution. Often, orientation professionals can negotiate special pricing with local vendors, bookstores, or marketing companies to provide matching clothing for student and professional staff. In addition to portraying a professional appearance, staff members can be easily recognized by the hundreds of new students and parents (as well as being recognizable to student and professional staff) when assistance is needed.

Not only do student orientation programs require funding, programs for parents, family, spouses, and others have become extremely sophisticated in their design and implementation and involve considerable expenses. This list and discussion is not meant to be exhaustive. Every program is unique and has costs specific to that program.

Methods of Funding

Many individuals assume that orientation programs are funded predominantly through institutional general funds. This is often not the case; program budgets must frequently incorporate multiple sources of funding. Fortunately, many sources of funding are available to the orientation professional. Such sources may include funds from the state, registration fees from students and parents, university student activity fees, donations, rentals, contributions, concessions, and other types of sales. Despite the wide range of funding available, the CAS Standards argue that institutional funding is required for minimal program operation, as such funding demonstrates institutional support for orientation programs. However, orientation professionals must employ a variety of methods for securing the funding necessary to direct a quality, comprehensive orientation program.

The CAS Standards (1998) recommend that money from the college's or university's general fund should be allocated to underwrite orientation expenses. This standard is strongly supported by orientation professionals. Many programs may cease to exist, especially in times of decreased state funding, if the institution does not understand their importance. This support must begin with the president and be conveyed to everyone working within the institution and to the local community.

One of the advantages of directing an orientation program is the opportunity to interact with a multitude of internal and external constituencies. Within those interactions are excellent opportunities to supplement traditional funding sources for orientation programs. The list of funding options below is not exhaustive. However, it will provide creative ideas for orientation professionals seeking alternative methods of funding their programs.

Institutional budget/general funds. As noted in the CAS standards, institutional commitment of resources to orientation is imperative. These funds do more than any other source to indicate the value of the program to the institution. At the very least, wherever possible, professional and clerical staff salaries should be covered by these funds, in addition to basic program support, including supplies, equipment, furnishings, and room rental charges.

Student, user, or matriculation fees. Many institutions rely heavily on student fee income for support of several campus programs including orientation. Use of general student fees is acceptable, but user or matriculation fees are more appropriate because of the definable nature of the population served. User fees are generally tied directly to program expenses and are meant to recoup specific program costs such as room, board, t-shirts, and student staff salaries. This type of fee is paid only by those students who actually participate in the program and is often collected by the orientation office. (Whenever possible, fees should be collected through an institutional billing process). A matriculation fee is a set fee charged to all new students whether or not they participate in orientation, and the funds are collected in the billing process and may be allocated to orientation and other programs.

Internal donations/contributions. Several funding sources exist on campus that can provide tremendous financial support for the program and visibility for the donor. The office of the chancellor or president is a good source for a sponsorship of an orientation event such as a student/parent/faculty/administration reception or picnic. An organized parents' council or alumni council is another excellent source for funding for a parent handbook or a reception during the program. The student government association is often a willing contributor, especially if it is allowed to sponsor an event and if the association president is allowed to provide a student welcome during a general session. Individual colleges and schools may also be willing contributors to the program, which will allow exposure to undecided students and parents while showing support for student orientation leaders who are currently majoring in these academic areas. As more and more universities privatize their campus bookstores, these corporate entities are very eager to have their name publicized to new students. Other groups seeking visibility with new students (and who are often willing to pay for it) include ROTC, student activities organizations, and Greek organizations.

> *"Orientation professionals should gather extensive knowledge about budgeting, fund raising, and cost containment."*

External donations and contributions. Colleges and universities have considerable economic impact on the communities in which they are located. Many businesses specifically target and depend on the student population, and they are eager to identify new customers. Orientation staff can capitalize on this phenomenon to the benefit of both businesses and the orientation budget. For programs that attract large numbers of students from great distances, deals can be made (for tickets or cash) with airline companies. Internet service providers seeking the student market may contribute large donations in exchange for their name on the orientation t-shirt. Cellular telephone companies eager to attract new customers may be willing contributors to orientation programs and the publicity that follows. Banks can sponsor receptions and have representatives on hand to help students and parents open accounts. Orientation professionals should exercise caution in allowing credit card companies to sponsor events, especially if they do so in exchange for the right to distribute applications to students. The mission of the orientation program should be to provide students with the tools they need to make a successful transition to college, not to contribute to the continuing increase in credit card debt among students.

Fast food outlets are often willing to feed large numbers of students for free. For example, they can provide continental breakfast items at orientation check-in. Soft drink companies will often set up booths and keep them supplied throughout a program or series of programs. The opportunities for local businesses are endless; however, orientation professionals may want to restrict the types of goods and services promoted to students. For example, businesses should be not be allowed to advertise alcohol, drink specials, or other products contradictory to the institutional mission during an orientation program. In addition, it is wise to secure the approval of the institution's development or advancement office before approaching specific local businesses.

Advertising. Opportunities to generate revenue for orientation programs through advertising exist internally and externally. A special orientation issue of the school paper can be produced with advertising revenues (beyond actual printing costs) designated for orientation. This process allows the newspaper staff to showcase the paper, seek assistance for future issues, and provide a service and funds for orientation. Externally, local companies are often willing to provide materials for free (e.g., local maps), to advertise on orientation materials (e.g., packets), or to provide necessary services at no cost (e.g., city bus transportation).

Fundraising. Campus student organizations often rely on fundraising efforts to survive or to meet the matching revenue requirements established by their student government associations. Student orientation leaders can join together to become a registered student organization, thus allowing them the privilege of campus fundraising. Bake sales, car washes, and raffles can generate needed funds for training and especially for travel to regional orientation conferences.

Grants. Though external grants are often overlooked as sources of funding, they can be sought from agencies, foundations, corporations, and associations to provide programming in a variety of subject areas that involve educating new students or to assist with evaluation and assessment.

Cost-cutting measures. Another way to generate revenue is to cut costs. Orientation professionals should gather extensive knowledge about budgeting, fund raising, and cost containment. One way of keeping costs low is to exercise sound fiscal management and to reduce operating costs. Although it may be very easy to maintain relationships with the same vendors year after year, orientation professionals should constantly seek out quality goods for use in orientation programs while containing costs. In addition to supplementing the institution's funding by implementing the above ideas and keeping costs low through appropriate budgeting practices, orientation professionals may consider using graduate and undergraduate interns or practicum students to staff their programs.

Building and Maintaining Budget Support

As already noted, institutional funding rarely covers all of the expenses associated with orientation programs, but orientation typically yields a good return on the investment made by institutions. The value of orientation to the institutional bottom line should continually be stressed to the campus community, especially to those who have some responsibility for allocation of resources. As Forrest notes, "probably the most important move an institution can make to increase student persistence to graduation is to ensure that students receive the guidance they need at the beginning of the journey through college to graduation" (1982, p. 44). Orientation programs provide such guidance for students. In fact, Tinto urges institutions to allocate scarce retention resources to those programs that ensure, from the very outset of contact with the institution, that entering students are integrated into the social and academic communities of the college and acquire the skills and knowledge needed to become successful learners in those communities. (Tinto, 1990, p. 44)

Forrest and Tinto provide a powerful message regarding institutional funding for orientation programs—that their role in helping students persist to graduation is vital for the financial health of the institution. A properly administered orientation program focuses as much, if not more, on the academic transition students face as it does on the personal and social transition. Unfortunately, the social events and activities (which are important and do occur) are often more visible to the broader academic community.

However, orientation professionals may occasionally find themselves in a defensive posture as they attempt to make a case for budget support. In order to build or maintain budget support for a comprehensive orientation program, it is critical that representatives from throughout the campus be involved in its planning, implementation, and evaluation, so that they "all understand how important orientation is to freshman success, and provide appropriate support through participation and contribution of resources" (Perigo & Upcraft, 1989, p. 84). This involvement can make allies of enemies and broaden the base of support. To ensure this support, it is recommended that the orientation professional develop an orientation advisory group, composed of faculty, staff, students, and representatives of central administration (Perigo & Upcraft, 1989).

This advisory group would be instrumental in designing, implementing, and assessing the orientation program. The implementation and review processes should involve a large number of individuals from throughout the institution such as the aforementioned orientation advisory committee. Such a process can establish program credibility. Second, group involvement is necessary for the planning of the orientation program. Smith and Brackin (Chapter 4) list and explain the rationale for a variety of components that should be included in orientation. The orientation advisory committee can be especially helpful in the development of a program, and the members can serve as ambassadors to articulate the academic nature of the program as well as the need for personal and social experiences. Third, the orientation program must be evaluated by participants and others and the results distributed widely throughout the institution. The committee can help design the evaluations and the dissemination of the results.

Representatives to this group should be carefully selected in order to ensure both a broad base of support and political and economic clout. The literature is clear regarding the need to support new student experiences, and orientation is a key experience. The related budgetary process, however, is often difficult, and orientation staff must be constantly prepared to state and restate their case.

To establish an appropriate reporting relationship within the university administrative framework as well as develop programming excellence, orientation programs should undergo a CAS self-assessment: "Putting the standards into place can also assist in program planning, staff development, self-study for reaccreditation, educating the campus community, and political maneuverability" (Mullendore, 1992, p. 43).

Summary

This chapter has provided insights regarding the relationship between orientation and retention, described the administrative placement of orientation within the institutional hierarchy, discussed a multitude of considerations that must be addressed in staffing orientation, and advised readers on strategies for building and maintaining budgetary support for orientation programs.

Orientation has recently received increased attention and scrutiny due to research indicating that comprehensive orientation and advising programs positively influence student retention. At the same time, the CAS standards have provided a credible vehicle for comparing, assessing, and improving orientation efforts. With an established administrative framework, a self-evaluation and the implementation of recommendations, placement of competent and qualified professional staff, budgetary management, and most important, a dedicated and energetic team of student orientation leaders, individuals charged with the planning and implementation of orientation programs will reap the rewards, both intrinsic and external, of excellence in new student programming.

References

Bean, J. P., & Hossler, D. (1990). Tailoring enrollment management to institutional needs: Advice to campus leaders. In D. Hossler & J. P. Bean (Eds.), *The strategic management of college enrollments*. San Francisco: Jossey-Bass.

Cawthon, T. W., & Ward-Roof, J. (1999). A survey on the skills necessary for effective orientation professionals. *Journal of College Orientation and Transition, 56*(2), *15-19.*

Council for the Advancement of Standards (CAS) in Higher Education. (1998). *CAS student orientation standards and guidelines self-assessment guide.* Washington, DC: Author.

Forrest, A. (1982). *Increasing student competence and persistence: The best case for general education.* Iowa City: The American College Testing Program (ACT), National Center for the Advancement of Educational Practices.

Greenlaw, H. S., Anliker, M. E., & Barker, A. J. (1997). Orientation: A student affairs function? *NASPA Journal, 34*(4), 303-313.

Mann, B. A. (1998). Retention principles for new student orientation programs. *Journal of College Orientation and Transition, 6*(1), 15-20.

Mullendore, R. H. (1992). Standards-based programming in orientation. In D. Nadler (Ed.), *Orientation Director's Manual.* Statesboro, GA: National Orientation Directors Association.

Nadler, D. P., Miller, M. T., & Casebere, J. (1998). Student satisfaction with orientation: Toward a framework for program effectiveness, *Journal of College Orientation and Transition, 6*(1), 27-35.

Pascarella, E. T., Terenzini, P. T., & Wolfle, L. M. (1986). Orientation to college and freshman year persistence/withdrawal decisions. *Journal of Higher Education, 57*, 155-174.

Perigo, D. J., & Upcraft, M. L. (1989). Orientation programs. In M. L. Upcraft & J. N. Gardner (Eds.), *The freshman year experience: Helping students survive and succeed in college* (pp. 82-94). San Francisco: Jossey-Bass.

Pope, M. (2001). Faculty involvement in student affairs: Legitimate claim or latest fade? *Journal of College Orientation and Transition, 8*(2), 7-12.

Posner, B. Z., & Rosenberger J. (1997). Effective orientation advisors are also leaders. *NASPA Journal, 35*(1), 46-56.

Strumpf, G. B. (Ed.). (1990). *National Orientation Directors Association data bank.* College Park, MD: National Orientation Directors Association.

Strumpf, G. B. (Ed.). (1996). *National Orientation Directors Association data bank.* College Park, MD: National Orientation Directors Association.

Strumpf, G. B. & Wawrzynski, M. R. (Eds.). (2000). *National Orientation Directors Association data bank.* College Park, MD: National Orientation Directors Association.

Tinto, V. (1990). Principles of effective retention. *Journal of The Freshman Year Experience, 2*(1), 35-48.

Methods for Orienting Diverse Populations

Bonita C. Jacobs and Brian S. Bowen*

The college student population is increasingly diverse. At the same time, institutions are placing a greater emphasis on student retention and student success. Thus, if orientation professionals are to provide programs that enable students to make effective transitions to their institutions, they must first understand the diverse populations on their campuses. This chapter identifies special populations of students who are increasingly found on today's college campuses and discusses approaches for responding to their unique needs through individualized orientation programs.

The Need for Special Programming in Orientation

At one time, orientation was planned primarily with the traditional-aged, full-time, residential undergraduate in mind. In recent years, however, the demographics on college campuses in the United States have changed. These changes, in turn, have altered orientation programming. Fluctuating economic conditions, federally funded student aid programs, the maturation of the baby-boomers, the change in gender role expectations, the replacement of an industrial society with an information society, the GI Bill, the Civil Rights Act of 1964, the Americans with Disabilities Act of 1990, the Individuals with Disabilities Education Acts of 1990 and 1997, and Section 504 of the 1973 Rehabilitation Act have all had an impact on the number and type of students entering college.

The "traditional" college student is becoming increasingly rare on American campuses. Nationwide, only 20% of college students are 23 years old and younger, attending full-time, and living on-campus (Spitzer, 2000). Approximately 40% of beginning first-year students commute or live off campus (Cook, 2000), and 27% are students of color (Digest of Education Statistics, 1999). College populations now include such diverse groups as international students, graduate students, transfer students, student athletes, academically disadvantaged students, veterans, students with disabilities, gay/lesbian/bisexual/transgender students, and honors students. These changes are reflected in the composition of college classrooms, which are "more diverse, both ethnically and with respect to age. More than 45% of all college students can be termed 'nontraditional' because they are over 25 years of age" (Spitzer, 2000, p. 82).

The Council for Advancement of Standards (CAS) in Higher Education (Miller, 2001) states that orientation "must nurture environments where similarities and differences among people are recognized and honored" (pp. 224-225), a mandate that assigns particular responsibility for attending to the transitional needs of diverse populations. Programs must be selected based on the documented evidence of the developmental needs of students (Jacobs, 1988); awareness of these various needs is crucial for an orientation program to maximize

---

* Bonita Jacobs is joined by Brian Bowen in updating and revising her chapter "Orienting Diverse Populations" that appeared in the first edition.

opportunities for successful student transitions. Declining enrollments spawned a new emphasis on student transition, retention, and satisfaction, and orientation is the natural pacesetter for an institution's commitment to student success.

Getting students off to a good start, both academically and socially, is important for improving student retention, and orientation should be a crucial component of every enrollment management program that is serious about student success. Yet, the most dazzling of programs, the sharpest of speakers, the most detailed agenda, or the strongest of academic resources cannot ensure student success without an understanding of and appreciation for the diverse backgrounds of our students. Individualized orientation programs provide the mechanism for transmitting to students the institution's concern that each one of them, regardless of background, succeeds academically, learns leadership skills, develops interpersonal skills, makes positive lifestyle choices, and graduates. Understanding who our students are and adjusting to their unique needs have become perhaps the most challenging items on the orientation agenda. Furthermore, each institution has a different student composition, and the orientation professional must be cognizant of the campus student profile in order to facilitate effective programs.

Student Subpopulations

Students from diverse populations cannot be categorized together. Each group will have unique problems and will be at risk for different reasons. The goal of the orientation professional should be to help students feel they "fit" the institution. This section identifies a series of diverse student populations and explains why each might need particular attention during the orientation period in order to ease that fit between student and institution. Some suggestions for the types of programs needed to address these issues are also offered.

Students of Color

According to the Digest of Educational Statistics (1999), the presence of students of color on American college campuses is increasing.

♦ Higher education's pool of non-White students has increased from 16% in 1976 to 27% in 1997.
♦ While college attendance by Black students has fluctuated, it rose from 9.6% in 1976 to 11% in 1997.
♦ The rate of college attendance for Hispanic youths increased from 4% in 1976 to 9% in 1997.
♦ While Asian and Pacific Islanders only make up 4% of the U.S. population, their rate of college attendance has tripled, from 2% in 1976 to 6% in 1997.
♦ College attendance by American Indian students, currently at 1%, lags far behind Black and Hispanic attendance.

Although the number of ethnic minority students on campuses has increased, the graduation rate of minority students, with the exception of Asian students, is still lower than their White counterparts. Only 40% of Black students (Padilla, Trevino, Gonzalez, & Trevino, 1997) and 22% of Hispanic students (Devarics, 2000) graduate from a four-year college. To increase the graduation rate of minority students, universities must increase these students' satisfaction with college and their social support (Brown, 2000). Green (1990) suggests that institutions must proceed on two fronts if students of color are to persist to graduation: Those who "have had the most success with support services [including orientation] find that they assist minority students in both their academic and social adaptation to the institution" (p. 37). Brown (2000) reminds educators of the urgency of helping students of color succeed, noting that high college failure rates for students of color coupled with their increasing population may result in a majority of Americans being undereducated and relegated to a lower social status.

The *NODA Data Bank* (Strumpf & Wawrzynski, 2000) indicates that 47% of reporting institutions and 50% of institutions with more than 15,000 students provide some type of special programming for students of color. Programs for students of color often take the form of workshops offered in conjunction with the regular student orientation program, but they may also appear as separate and distinct programs in place of the traditional year-long con-

> *"The NODA Data Bank . . . indicates that 47% of reporting institutions and 50% of institutions with more than 15,000 students provide some type of special programming for students of color."*

tinuing orientation activity. Some useful and effective tools include using peer helpers, providing direct academic support services, openly addressing issues, and involving professional staff (Hughes, 1990; McPhee, 1990).

Gender Issues in Orientation

The enrollment rates of men and women in higher education have been unequal during the past 15 years. According to the Digest of Education Statistics (1999), from 1987 to 1997 enrollments of male students increased by 7%, while enrollments of women increased 17% during the same time period. Currently, women make up 55.5% of the student body on American college campuses. This increase may cause the male/female ratio to be so one-sided on some campuses that the smaller group might be considered a gender minority and experience feelings of marginalization. These students will need encouragement to become involved in campus activities, a factor that positively correlates with student retention (Nelson, Scott, & Bryan, 1984).

Miville and Sedlacek (1991) found evidence that women react differently than men when placed in predominantly male college environments, tending either to overachieve or to perform at mediocre levels. In addition, women in predominantly male institutions are often faced with "chilly" classroom climates, peer pressure for gender conformity, and a lack of female role models (Ehrhart & Sandler, 1990). Despite the increasing numbers of women students on campus, some of these issues persist within institutions of higher education where gender parity does not exist in faculty and administration or when pedagogies rely on a male-dominated model.

Perhaps of greater concern than the percentages of men and women on campus are the fundamentally different approaches to learning between men and women. Generally, "men are at higher risk academically and are in greater need of academic counseling and assistance than women are... [but] men seem to have a slightly better profile of learning styles and approaches than do women" (Miller, Finley, & McKinley, 1990, p. 153). Typically, women are more organized, more able to integrate new information, more intrinsically motivated, more strategic in their approach, and more sensitive to the expectations of instructors. Men are generally more able to learn by comprehension and evidence, more achievement motivated, and more inclined to a deep-process and deep-approach style of learning. Areas of concern for women include their tendency to rely on surface approaches to learning (e.g., skimming, memorizing unrelated facts), a more pronounced fear of failure, and their expression of fewer educational goals. Men experience difficulty most often because they have negative feelings about school and hold attitudes that validate "just getting by" (Miller et al., 1990).

When designing programs, the orientation professional must seek to emphasize the strengths associated with men's and women's learning styles and attitudes toward learning and to minimize their weaknesses. For example, the orientation professional might concentrate on affective concerns such as fear of failure and goal-setting behaviors when dealing with a group of women students, while stressing organization and time management skills when orienting a group of men. Regardless of the strategies and format employed, it is important to realize that students may face specific challenges because of their gender and that those challenges may be exacerbated if they find themselves in the minority in terms of gender.

Student Athletes

Athletes have a unique set of personal, social, academic, and athletic adjustments that must be addressed early in their college careers. Orientation and other support services must help ensure student athletes get off to a good start, a critical factor in their subsequent academic success (Willoughby, Willoughby, & Moses, 1991). One seeming contradiction lies in student athletes themselves: These students are generally highly motivated to succeed in their chosen sport, yet many of them lack such motivation in the classroom (Simons, Van Rheenen, & Covington, 1999). However, the orientation professional should be cautious in assuming that the student athlete is simply uninterested in academics. Simons et al. (1999) note,

> The maintenance of academic motivation and achievement is made more difficult because of the institutional demands of their sport. Student athletes are required to devote upwards of 25 hours per week when their sport is in season, miss numerous classes for university sanctioned athletic competitions, and deal with fatigue and injuries as a result of their athletic participation. These factors detract from the realistic likelihood of academic success, which in turn affects their academic motivation to succeed. (p. 151)

Understanding the difficulties faced by student athletes and providing the expertise needed to initiate them into the college environment is a particularly important role for the orientation professional. A number of factors put student athletes at greater risk for academic and social failure, including heightened visibility and the pressure of being in the public eye, underpreparedness for college, lack of career planning skills, feelings of isolation and lack of self-confidence outside of athletics, and extraordinary demands on time related to training, practice, and participation in sports. There are appropriate niches in college athletic programs where student services or orientation professionals can help athletes avoid the hazards of being athletes. Encouragement and support, academic support services, residential counselors, a personal development course, first-year testing to determine appropriate levels of remediation, study skills training, advising and registration, workshops, peer mentors, research and evaluation, group counseling, and a senior exit seminar are all useful tools for the student services professional in assisting the student athlete.

In addition, some differences between male and female athletes and between athletes in revenue-producing and nonrevenue-producing sports should be noted. Athletes in revenue-producing sports, such as football and men's basketball, generally do not

> *"A number of factors put student athletes at greater risk for academic and social failure, including heightened visibility and the pressure of being in the public eye, underpreparedeness for college, lack of career planning skills, feelings of isolation and lack of self-confidence outside of athletics, and extraordinary demands on time related to training, practice, and participation in sports."*

show the same level of motivation in academics as they do in athletics. Meanwhile, female athletes and nonrevenue-producing athletes generally demonstrate more academic motivation, as reflected in higher academic performance. It has been consistently shown that female athletes perform better academically than male athletes, and that nonrevenue-producing athletes perform at a higher level than revenue-producing athletes (Simons et al., 1999). Such differences in motivation and performance should be taken into account when designing orientation programs for student athletes, as some sports programs may demand a different range of interventions than others do.

International Students

The number of international students enrolled in U.S. colleges and universities is increasing. In 1997, 461,000 international students enrolled on U.S. campuses compared with 219,000 in 1976 (Digest of Educational Statistics, 1999). Performing well academically is "imperative [for international students]; failure is not an option for most of these young people because they feel enormous pressures from their families or their own governments to succeed in the disciplines in which they have been sent to study" (Wehrly, 1988, pp. 4-5).

Obviously, international students have much to offer a campus community; yet, language and cultural differences may heighten transitional problems including homesickness, adjustment problems, loneliness, and depression related to academics, finances, and separation from families (Wehrly, 1988). In order to make the orientation programs more meaningful to international students, information about admission procedures, academic survival, immigration policies, social involvement, and community norms should be provided. Other international students can often help address these issues. It is "particularly helpful to see someone from their home countries with whom they can talk about host institution expectations" (Nadler & Miller, 1999, p. 26).

Orientation programs for international students should be distinct from those provided to the general population and might need to be delayed for a few days into the semester to include late arrivals. International students who participate in peer programs have significantly higher academic performance and have lower drop-out rates than do non-participants (Westwood & Barker, 1990). For this reason, highlighting peer mentoring programs during the orientation process may be especially valuable for international students. Other issues which might be included in an orientation program for international students are a discussion of regulations such as insurance requirements and immigration responsibilities, an opportunity for international students to interact with American students, and tips on basic day-to-day living on an American college campus. Additionally, student service domains typically addressed during all other orientation programs (e.g., career counseling, health services, financial aid, and student employment) should be part of an international program as well.

Honors Students

Although honors students typically rank in the top 10% of their high school graduating classes and obtain superior scores on college admission exams, they often drop out of college despite their prior academic performance (Day, 1989). A number of factors may be involved in this, not least of which are adjustments to campus and individual self-esteem. Some honors students may have been able to ease through high school requirements with little effort and will need to improve study habits and skills, while others may need to develop more tolerance and acceptance of others. They often have perfectionist tendencies and high expectations and may need help dealing with anxiety, stress, overwork, and underconfidence (Day, 1989).

Thus, it is sometimes wise to consider honors students as a special population when planning orientation so that their unique motivations and resources might be given more in-depth consideration than with the general orientation program. Some of the issues to be incorporated into a program for honors students include (a) their potential to succeed in a number of areas, thus creating a need for increased career exploration; (b) pressures faced in a larger degree by honors students to choose career options based on opinions expressed by family members; (c) self-discovery and values clarification in order to narrow choices more effectively; and (d) information to avoid career stereotyping so that the honors student makes decisions based on his or her potential, values, and interests rather than on gender or ethnic roles (Gordon, 1983). The thoroughness required for such activities almost certainly requires the honors orientation to be an ongoing semester project, perhaps in cooperation with the director of the honors program.

Students With Disabilities

Students with disabilities form a diverse, multifaceted population, and a single-minded orientation program may shortchange one or more subpopulations since these students are different from one another in their backgrounds, concerns, and strengths. Thus, students with disabilities may be like the general student body in terms of their primary needs but have very specific, individual secondary needs.

Students with disabilities "face being treated differently and are often not expected to perform as well as their peers" (Nadler, 1992, p. 35). They are generally older, receive financial aid, and have lower family incomes (Hodges & Keller, 1999). Students with disabilities must at times compensate for deficiencies in secondary school preparation and, simultaneously, adjust to an environment unprepared to address their special needs.

The number of students who identify themselves as having disabilities has grown from 2.6% in 1978 to 9.2% in 1994 (Henderson, 1995). Four factors have contributed to this increase:

1. Services mandated by Section 504 of the Rehabilitation Act of 1973 now exist for those who qualify.
2. Because of the Individuals with Disabilities Education Acts of 1990 and 1997, students with disabilities receive better preparation in high school.
3. More people with disabilities are entering professions that require a postsecondary education.
4. The Americans with Disabilities Act of 1990 has increased the opportunities for adults in higher education (Hitchings, Horvath, Luzzo, Ristow, & Retish, 1998).

Among students with disabilities, the fastest-growing subgroup is that of students with learning disabilities. These students have "grown up" with Section 504 and are generally aware of their legal rights and are able to articulate their concerns. However, because the disability is not seen, it is sometimes more difficult to elicit support from faculty members, and students with learning disabilities are erroneously labeled "lazy" or "incapable." One of the most critical issues for students with learning disabilities is "understanding their specific learning styles and . . . recognizing compensatory strategies for dealing with the challenges of postsecondary education" (McGuire, Hall, & Litt, 1991, p. 101)

The increase in the numbers of students with disabilities (both learning disabilities and physical disabilities) has underscored the need for an effective, individualized approach to orientation on college campuses. Of course, one of the requisites of all orientation programs is sensitivity to the accommodations needed by students and parents attending the program. Participants should be invited to request assistance as needed, including sign-language interpreters for students or guests with hearing impairments, materials written in large-print or in Braille for students or guests with visual impairments, and room locations that are accessible to students or guests with mobility impairments. However, orientation for students with disabilities goes beyond these basic accommodations; it entails more than an absence of discrimination. The Higher Education Transition Model—a framework for facilitating college transition among students with disabilities—highlights specific objectives that should be met during the orientation process. Such objectives for students with disabilities include

1. Encouraging students to build a bond with the university as soon as possible through involvement in activities
2. Encouraging friendships among students with and without disabilities
3. Providing students with opportunities to review college literature
4. Providing campus tours and information
5. Preparing students to participate in campus life
6. Teaching students strategies for accessing the community, such as banking and shopping (Gartin, Rumrill, & Serebreni, 1996)

Commuting Students

The number of commuting students varies greatly across institutions. Thus, orientation programs must be specially designed at each campus to meet the needs of the students in attendance. The obvious challenge of providing an effective orientation program is to find a time and place that will encourage the support and participation of commuting students.

> *"Planning an orientation strategy for commuting students, particularly when considering the various types of students within the commuting population, may require adjusting the time when orientation is offered or the length of the sessions."*

In addition to living off campus, many commuting students are also nontraditional. They are more likely to have work, school, and family obligations and, consequently, may not have the time to devote to orientation programs (Pascarella & Terenzini, 1991). "Simply providing services and programs is not sufficient to ensure that an individual's or group's needs are met . . ., that they have a high-quality experience, and that they are treated equitably" (Jacoby, 2001, p. 3). Thus, services must be offered at times tailored to commuter students' lifestyles—normally evenings and weekends.

Commuter students may assume that the information provided at orientation is primarily important for younger, residential students. However, the importance of attending the orientation program must be emphasized to commuting students, especially because the "growing population of commuters has been identified as a particularly high risk for attrition" (Wolfe, 1993, p. 321). The lack of opportunity to be involved with informal contacts appears to be the reason that commuter students are at a greater risk of attrition (Wolfe, 1993). Thus, institutions must find a way to help commuter students feel like a valued part of the university community. Paying special attention to the needs and concerns of commuters during orientation may be one way to do this, because as Jacoby (2001) reminds us:

The institution must demonstrate respect for the worth of each individual and accord membership in the community….[A] student who feels like a second-class citizen would most likely not seek out within the campus community the kinds of risk-taking experiences that lead to personal growth. (p. 4)

Planning an orientation strategy for commuting students, particularly when considering the various types of students within the commuting population, may require adjusting the time when orientation is offered or the length of the sessions. Specific topics should be determined according to the campus profile of commuter students and their potential for difficulties in adjustment, either academically or socially, to the campus community.

Nontraditional Students

The number of nontraditional learners (students 25 years or older) enrolled in institutions of higher education increased from 28% in 1970 to 43% in 1997 (Digest of Educational Statistics, 1999). Additionally, while the enrollment rate of students under 25 years of age is increasing by 4% annually, the enrollment rate of nontraditional students is increasing by 16% annually (Levine & Cureton, 1998). However, nontraditional enrollments are beginning to level off: "From 1997 to 2000, the National Center for Educational Statistics projects a rise of 6 percent in enrollments of persons under 25 and an increase of 3 percent in the number 25 and over" (Digest of Educational Statistics, 1999).

Nontraditional students can be single, married, widowed, divorced, employed, unemployed, male, female, veterans, homemakers, parents, grandparents, part-time students, full-time students, first-year students, and transfers. Despite their diversity, adult learners also have numerous similarities: "Older students juggle their time amongst their classes, work, families, roles in the community, [and] there is often little time for campus involvement outside the classroom" (Graham & Long Gisi, 2000, p. 100). For example, one study found that nontraditional students did not participate in college organizations or activities due to lack of time (Graham & Long Gisi, 2000). Thus, "college faculty and officials interested in students' developmental gains could focus their attention on creating an overall campus ethos that supports learning and caring for students, rather than to simply look for ways for students to become more 'involved' in campus activities" (Graham & Long Gisi, 2000, p. 118). For a more in-depth discussion of orientation programs for nontraditional students, see Chapter 9 in this monograph.

Gay/Lesbian/Bisexual/Transgender Students

Gay, lesbian, bisexual, and transgender (GLBT) students often have a difficult time fitting into the mainstream of college life throughout their college careers, regardless of the types of institutions they attend. Unlike other student subpopulations, GLBT students "are an invisible population, often forgotten at best and summarily rejected at worst" (Wall & Evans, 2000, p. 643). However, GLBT students should be "viewed as minority populations and given the same consideration that students of color, older or returning students, and physically challenged students are given" (Malkin, 1992, pp. 49-50). Having an orientation program for GLBT students demonstrates their value to the university community and "underscore[s] the importance of student life through symbolic actions" (Kuh et al., 1991, p. 360). This population, however, is often not comfortable with self-identification upon entrance into college, and the orientation professional must realize that it is not always practical to organize events specifically for this population. Instead, all students should be given information about resource groups, including GLBT organizations; programs designed to educate and support students such as GLBT Awareness Week; and the names of support persons on campus, such as a list of GLBT "allies." As entering students become more comfortable with disclosure, programming for the GLBT population should already be in place for them. In the meantime, acceptance of GLBT students by the heterosexual population and self-acceptance for GLBT students are issues that should be addressed to the entire student population as part of the orientation agenda. Sexual orientation issues should certainly be included as part of the training for student orientation leaders (Sanlo, 2000).

Strategies for Orienting Diverse Populations

In surveying the various groups of students who may be participating in an orientation program, it becomes obvious that each orientation professional must determine the composition of new students entering the institution and assess their needs. The mission of the institution and the goals of orientation should be carefully reviewed in order to allocate often-scarce resources to the most-needed areas. There are several types of adjustments to orientation that best serve the various populations, and it is important to determine the most appropriate direction to take with each group. Following is a list of strategies for individualizing orientation programs for target groups.

Separate Programs

A separate orientation program for a specific group of students may be warranted if that student population is widely recognized to be more "at risk" than other student groups. For example, students of color may face particular difficulties in adjusting to and succeeding on a predominantly White campus. A special orientation program not only can provide greater detail on academic regulations, student development, and student affairs resources available to them, but also can help students of color become better acquainted with one another and build a much-needed peer support group.

International students can often benefit from a separate orientation program. Because international students must adjust to college at the same time they become adjusted to a new country and a new culture, they frequently have transition difficulties not found in other student groups. An orientation program for international students usually includes explanations of immigration policies, a list of locations to purchase ethnic foods, an overview of traffic laws, a review of resources for and policies governing housing between semesters, and other pragmatic issues not generally relevant to any other orientation group.

> "A separate orientation program for a specific group of students may be warranted if that student population is widely recognized to be more 'at risk' than other student groups."

Extended Programs

All student orientations should be extended, in some form, throughout the first year. However, some student groups may need to have an extended orientation program geared especially to their individual needs. Extended programs are ideally a year-long endeavor but may also be effective as workshops held in addition to the regular orientation program, usually immediately preceding or following the regular orientation program.

Since many of these extended programs are coordinated by offices other than the orientation office, it is important to note the importance of collaborative efforts. An example of a year-long orientation program found on many campuses, and one that is organized outside of orientation, is the program for the student athlete. Study halls, developmental programs, time-management seminars, gender issues, and lifestyle selections are appropriate topics for an extended orientation program for student athletes. It is important that the goals of the extended program be considered when planning the initial orientation program for these students.

Honors students are another group for which a special extended orientation is often scheduled. Seminars are sometimes a part of the honors program, and an assessment of their orientation needs and implementation of developmental programming are efficient ways to provide extended orientation for these students.

Other groups that would benefit from an extended orientation, either as a year-long activity or as an additional workshop, are those that tend to face new difficulties as the semesters progress or have particularly low retention rates. Nontraditional students, students with disabilities, and minority students are examples of groups that would benefit greatly from extended contact.

Schedule Revisions

Because student lifestyles are so varied, the orientation professional cannot have the luxury of assuming that typical working hours or even "typical orientation hours" are acceptable for all students. Students who work part-time or full-time, have families, or commute are obvious examples of those who need orientation schedule revisions. Nontraditional students do not fit the common mindset about students, and their orientation needs do not fit the most widely-used approach to orientation: one to five days and nights of packed orientation events.

Revisions in orientation and registration may take the form of night orientation, weekend orientation, or both, and might also include relocating orientation to an off-campus site more convenient for the participants. Often, because there is so much variation in the needs of married, working, or commuting students, one orientation "time" may not be enough. Some working students can only attend orientation during day hours, some only during evening hours, and some only during weekend hours. On campuses with a significant nontraditional population, child-care options must be explored and, if possible, made available on a gratis or cost basis. Time spent in orientation sessions must be streamlined as much as possible in order to cover all the necessary topics while also freeing participants to meet their outside time demands.

Another approach to orientation schedule revisions may be needed with international students. Since it is not uncommon for travel itineraries to delay the arrival of new international students until after the first day of classes, it may become necessary to delay orientation for international students or to offer an early orientation program followed by an orientation session for late arrivals.

Break-Away Sessions

There are a number of instances when break-away sessions (i.e., separating students with particular needs from the group-at-large or separating all participants into small groups based on interests or needs) during regular orientation may be appropriate for certain populations. For example, some campuses may feel that students with disabilities will benefit most from the regular sessions but also need a time to explore additional resources or to meet with specially trained academic advisors.

Another example of the valid use of breakaway sessions is for White students on a historically Black campus. Since these students have unique needs, but often do not see themselves as needing a special orientation program, a single break-away session might be helpful.

Almost any other special student group can benefit from a break-away session provided there is enough interest to persuade students to attend. It is a particularly productive approach for those student groups who have unique needs but who do not warrant (either because of lack of numbers or level of needs) a separate or extended program. The orientation professional must evaluate, however, whether a break-away session will cause unnecessary disruptions to the overall program. One approach is to have break-away sessions for all students and to include sessions for groups such as minority students, commuting students, and students with disabilities along with sessions on topics such as campus involvement, living in a residence hall, campus safety, and financial management. It is important, however, that multiple time slots be provided so that, for example, a commuting student is also able to attend the session on campus safety.

Summary

At one time, commuting students and nontraditional students were considered special students because of their uniqueness to a campus. The influx of these groups in record numbers has drawn attention to their importance, both in terms of student recruitment and retention and the overall personality of a campus.

Additionally, orientation programming has "grown up" to the extent that professionals are now observing and responding to the special needs found in diverse groups. Each group of students is unique and has individual adjustment needs, and orientation professionals are being asked to determine those needs and to individualize programs as much as possible. Some of the programmatic strategies, which might be employed to target a specific population, are separate programs, extended programs, schedule revisions, and break-away sessions. The orientation professional is charged with knowing about the diverse groups and with determining the appropriate orientation protocol for each group, thereby aiding each new student in his or her transition into the institution.

References

Brown, T. L. (2000). Gender differences in African American students' satisfaction with college. *Journal of College Student Development, 41*(5), p. 479-487.

Cook, L. P. (2000). Constructing comprehensive programs on the two-year campus. In M. J. Fabrich (Ed.), *Orientation planning manual* (pp. 19-25). Washington, DC: National Orientation Directors Association.

Day, A. L. (1989). Honors students. In M. L. Upcraft & J. N. Gardner (Eds.), *The freshman year experience* (pp. 352-362). San Francisco: Jossey-Bass.

Devarics, C. (2000). Hispanic-serving institutions make impressive strides. *Black Issues in Higher Education, 17*(9), 32-35.

Digest of Education Statistics. (1999). *Postsecondary education.* Retrieved June 30, 2002 from http://nces.ed.gov/pubs2000/digest99/chapter3.html.

Ehrhart, J. K., & Sandler, B. R. (1990). *Rx for success: Improving the climate for women in medical schools and teaching hospitals* (Research Report from the Project on the Status and Education of Women). Washington, DC: Association of American Colleges.

Gartin, B. C., Rumrill, P., & Serebreni, R. (1996). The higher education transition model: Guidelines for facilitating college transition among college-bound students with disabilities. *TEACHING Exceptional Children, 29*(1), 30-33.

Gordon, V. N. (1983). Meeting the career development needs of undecided honors students. *Journal of College Student Personnel, 24*(1), 82-83.

Graham, S. W., & Long Gisi, S. (2000). Adult undergraduate students: What role does college involvement play? *NASPA Journal, 38*(1), 99-121.

Green, M. F. (1990). *Minorities on campus: A handbook for enhancing diversity*. Washington, DC: American Council on Education.

Henderson, C. (1995*). College freshmen with disabilities: A statistical profile* [online]. Retrieved April 11, 2003 from http://www.ACENET.edu/Programs/HEALTH/Collegefresh.html

Hitchings, W. E., Horvath, M., Luzzo, D. A., Ristow, R. S., & Retish, P. (1998*)*. Identifying the career development needs of college students with disabilities. *Journal of College Student Development, 39*(1), 23-32.

Hodges, J. S., & Keller, M. J. (1999). Perceived influences on social integration by students with physical disabilities. *Journal of College Student Development, 40*(6), 678-686.

Hughes, E. M. (1990). A design for diversity: Proactive planning to reduce ethnic tensions and to enhance human resources. In R. W. Hively (Ed.), *The lurking evil: Racial and ethnic conflict on the college campus* (pp. 59-66). Washington, DC: American Council on Education.

Jacobs, B. (1988). Beyond policy: Ethical consideration in student development. In G.A. Antonelli, B. A. Mann, E. E. Meyer, Jr., T. H. Stafford, Jr., G. W. Stillion, L. S. White, & H. L. Wilson, Jr. (Eds.), *Student services: Responding to issues and challenges: The fifth compendium of papers by student services officers of the University of North Carolina* (pp. 145-152). Chapel Hill: The University of North Carolina General Administration.

Jacoby, B. (2001). The art of advocacy. *Commuter Perspectives 26*(3), 2-7.

Kuh, G. D., Schuh, J. H., Whitt, E. J., & Associates. (1991). *Involving colleges: successful approaches to fostering student learning and development outside the classroom.* San Francisco: Jossey-Bass.

Levine, A., & Cureton, J. (1998). *When hope and fear collide.* San Francisco, CA: Jossey-Bass.

Malkin, A. (1992). The lesbian student coming out on the college campus: Issues for the heterosexual student affairs professional. *The College Student Affairs Journal, 12*(1), 48-55.

McGuire, J. M., Hall, D., & Litt, A. V. (1991). A field-based study of the direct service needs of college students with learning disabilities. *Journal of College Student Development, 32*(2), 101-108.

McPhee, S. (1990). Addressing the attrition of minority students on predominantly white campuses: A pilot study. *The College Student Affairs Journal, 10*(1), 15-22.

Miller, T. K. (Ed.). (2001). Student orientation CAS standards and guidelines. *The book of professional standards for higher education* (pp. 221-225). Washington, DC: Council for the Advancement of Standards in Higher Education.

Miller, C. D., Finley, J., & McKinley, D. L., (1990). Learning approaches and motives: Male and female differences and implications for learning assistance programs. *Journal of College Student Development, 31*(2), 147-154.

Miville, M. L., & Sedlacek, W. E. (1991). Profile of potential persister and nonpersister university students. *The College Student Affairs Journal, 11*(1), 45-53.

Nadler, D. P. (Ed.). (1992). *The orientation director's manual.* Statesboro, GA: National Orientation Directors Association.

Nadler, D. P., & Miller, M. T. (1999). Designing transitional programs to meet the needs of the multi-ethnic first-year students. *Journal of College Orientation and Transition, 7*(2), 41-43.

Nelson, R. B., Scott, T. B., & Bryan, W. A. (1984). Precollege characteristics and early college experiences as predictors of freshman year persistence. *Journal of College Student Personnel, 25*(1), 50-54.

Padilla, R. V., Trevino, J., Gonzalez. K., & Trevino. J. (1997). Developing local models of minority student success in college. *Journal of College Student Development, 38*(4), 387-400.

Pascarella, E. T., & Terenzini, P. T. (1991). *How college affects students.* San Francisco: Jossey-Bass.

Sanlo, R. (2000). Lavender graduation: Acknowledging the lives and achievement of lesbian, gay, bisexual, and transgender college students. *Journal of College Student Development, 41*(6), 643-647.

Simons, H. D., Van Rheenen, D., & Covington, M. V. (1999). Academic motivation and the student athlete. *Journal of College Student Development, 40*(2), 151-162.

Spitzer, T. M. (2000). Predictors of college success: A comparison of traditional and nontraditional age students. *NASPA Journal, 38*(1), 82-98.

Strumpf, G., & Wawrzynski, M.R. (Eds.). (2000). *NODA data bank 2000*. College Park, MD: National Orientation Directors Association.

Wall, V., & Evans, N. J. (2000). *Toward acceptance: Sexual orientation issues on campus*. Lanham, MD: University Press of America.

Wehrly, B. (1988). Cultural diversity from an international perspective, Part 2. *Journal of Multicultural Counseling and Development, 30*(6), 567-569

Westwood, M. J., & Barker, M. (1990). Academic achievement and social adaptation among international students: A comparison groups study of the peer-pairing program. *International Journal of Intercultural Relations, 14*, 251-263.

Willoughy, L. M., Willoughby, D. S., & Moses, P. A. (1991, Fall). Mentors for beginning college student-athletes: A possible aid for academic success. *Academic Athletic Journal*, 1-12.

Wolfe, J. S. (1993). Institutional integration, academic success, and persistence of first-year commuter and resident students. *Journal of College Student Development 34*(3), 321-326.

Orienting Transfer Students

Jeanine A. Ward-Roof, Patricia Kashner, and Valerie Hodge

Chapter Eight

The number of students transferring among colleges and universities is continuing to increase (Baxter Magolda, Terenzini, & Hutchings, 1999). Further, Townsend (2001) notes that a significant segment of the college population has attended more than one college and that many of the students enrolled at four-year institutions have community college coursework on their transcripts. Kozeracki (2001) also found that thousands of students transfer every year. Thus, it is crucial to focus on this large and ever-growing population when exploring orientation and transition issues. This chapter describes the characteristics of transfer students in higher education and highlights effective programs and services that have been implemented to address the transfer transition. Moreover, this chapter identifies barriers to transfer and highlights programs and initiatives designed to reduce barriers and contribute to long-term student success and persistence.

Defining Transfer

Cuseo (1998) defines transfer "as the movement of a student from one post-secondary institution to another..." (p. 1). In 1991, an estimated 325,000 of the one million graduates of four-year institutions transferred before graduation (Cuseo, 1998). More recently, Eggleston and Laanan (2001) report that "at least one out of every five community college students transfer" (p. 87). A study of national transfer rates conducted by the Center for the Study of Community Colleges in Los Angeles found that 52% of students who entered higher education in 1995 completed 12 or more credits at a community college. One quarter of students who started at a community college in 1995 had transferred to a four-year, in-state institution four years later (ERIC Clearinghouse for Community Colleges, n.d.).

Although many orientation professionals believe that students transfer mainly from two-year or community college environments, that is not always the case, as there are many types of transfer students. Less commonly discussed types of transfer students are those who enroll in college classes during high school to accelerate their academic coursework and four-year college students who for reasons of convenience or cost take courses at local community colleges (ERIC Clearinghouse for Community Colleges, n.d.). Current literature defines various types of transfer students as vertical transfers—those who transfer from two-year to four-year institutions; horizontal transfers—those who move between four-year institutions; reverse transfers—those who transfer from four-year to two-year institutions; and multiple transfers—those who transfer from institution to institution (Cuseo, 1998; Daniel, 1998; Harrison, 1993; Laanan, 2003). This chapter focuses primarily on those transfer students characterized as vertical transfers; however, the information presented can be applicable to all types of transfer students.

Community College Transfer and Educational Success

One of the roles of the community college is the transfer function (Kim, 2001; Lannan, 2003). In addition, the community college campus can provide much of the initial coursework for the baccalaureate degree and may serve a large population of students who were unable or uninterested in gaining admission to a four-year college or university. Kim (2001) also notes that factors such as lower tuition costs, smaller class sizes, and faculty focused on teaching at two-year institutions attract many students who are eligible to attend four-year institutions.

> *"Compounding the problem of low minority transfer rates is the fact that ethnic and racial minority students who begin their education at a community college are less likely to earn bachelor's degrees than minority students who begin their degrees at four-year institutions."*

Community colleges in the United States enroll half of all first-time, first-year students and almost half of U.S. undergraduates each year (Cohen & Brawer, 1996; California Community Colleges, 1994; Parnell, 1986). That figure approaches 10 million students annually, half of whom are enrolled in courses for credit (Vaughan, 2000). As these numbers continue to rise, orientation professionals, as well as other higher education faculty and staff, must be prepared to help these students make successful transitions within and among higher education environments.

The critical need for transfer orientation programs is underscored by the fact that the entry point for higher education has a significant effect on subsequent educational attainment (Pascarella & Terenzini, 1991). One reason for this may be that students who begin their college careers in a community college traditionally have lower educational abilities (Cohen & Brawer, 1996). However, completion of an associate's degree may help ameliorate prior educational deficiencies. Laanan (2001) found that students who completed an associate's degree prior to transferring to a four-year institution had a higher rate of bachelor's degree completion than those without an associate's degree.

In terms of academic achievement, Cohen and Brawer (1982; 1996) found that community college transfer students achieved lower cumulative grade point averages and had higher attrition rates than the native students. More recently, Diaz (1992) examined 62 studies focusing on transfer students and found that in 79% of those studies, transfer students experienced transfer shock, defined as a drop in grade point average after transferring. In the transfer studies based on community college transfer students who experienced transfer shock, 67% recovered from the shock within a year. Laanan (2001) also found that the research suggested students who transferred from two- to four-year institutions experienced a variety of academic, social, and psychological adjustments due to the differing campus environments.

Ultimately, if orientation professionals are able to understand the characteristics, needs, and barriers faced by transfer students, they will be better prepared to design and implement programs and services that assist these students with a successful transition to campus and with persistence to graduation. The following demographic information offers insights about the transfer population and is intended to guide the work of orientation professionals.

The community college population is large and varied (Cohen & Brawer, 1996). In 1991, 47% of the ethnic minority students in higher education were enrolled in community colleges (Cohen & Brawer, 1996). The ERIC Clearinghouse for Community Colleges (n.d.) reports that 65% of today's community college students are part-time, 58% are women, and 67% are White. In terms of ethnicity, 12% of today's community college students are African American, 12% Hispanic, 6% Asian or Pacific Islander, and 1% Native American or Alaskan Natives (ERIC Clearinghouse for Community Colleges, n.d.).

Zamani (2001) found that only 20 to 25% of those enrolled in two-year institutions transferred to four-year institutions; furthermore, the rates of transfer among minority groups are alarmingly low. Thus, a large gap exists in the number of ethnic minority students who enroll in community colleges and those who transfer to four-year institutions. This gap has persisted during the past 20 years (Zamani, 2001). Compounding the problem of low minority transfer rates is the fact that ethnic and racial minority students who begin their education at a community college are less likely to earn bachelor's degrees than minority students who begin their degrees at four-year institutions (Zamani, 2001). Given the ethnic and racial diversity of community colleges, orientation professionals might expect that incoming transfer populations will display a similar diversity. Thus, many of the considerations discussed in Chapter 7 might also apply to transfer orientation programs.

Barriers to Transfer

According to Zamani (2001), the "transfer process increases educational opportunity and access beyond two-year institutions; however, paradoxically, it also immobilizes many students, as policies related to the movement of students beyond community colleges and four-year colleges/universities are inconsistent or nonexistent" (p. 17). Inconsistencies in or lack of policies governing the transfer process can be a significant barrier to making a successful transition to a new institution. For example, Cuseo (1998) identifies several types of barriers to transferring from two- to four-year institutions:

♦ *Curricular barriers.* These barriers cause confusion regarding which courses will transfer between two- and four-year institutions and may be precipitated by differing institutional missions, lack of identifiable transfer articulation agreements or processes, curriculum changes or inflexibility in the curriculum that does not allow for course transfer, and failure to adhere to articulation agreements by faculty and staff.

♦ *Financial aid barriers.* Frequently, institutions have limited or no funds available for transfer students in terms of scholarships or other aid.

♦ *Policy and procedural barriers.* Such barriers include requiring transfer students to pass standardized tests regardless of prior academic performance; offering registration to transfer students after all other students register, resulting in limited course availability; completing transcripts after the student is already enrolled in classes; and failing to admit community college transfers into academic honors.

Laanan (2003) suggests other barriers to student success are poor teaching, faculty discouragement to transfer, inability to find and use appropriate student services, and inadequate academic preparation. Anxiety may be another significant obstacle to success. Transfer students may experience increased anxiety based on the overall transfer experience, financial issues, and credit transfer (Lehning, 2000). In addition, increased stress may also be due to transition to a larger system or differences in culture, family dynamics, motivation, services, courses, and advising (Lehning, 2000). Although most students experience degrees of stress when moving to a campus environment, after some adjustment the general level of transition stress usually decreases; however, transfer students experience increased levels of and continued stress as they move from one campus environment to another. Thus, many transfer students may be academically well-prepared but unprepared for the psychological aspects of the transfer process (Kodama, 2002).

Removing Barriers to Transfer

Cuseo (1998) suggests several strategies for assisting transfer students, including those focused on the curriculum, academic advising, orientation, support programs, faculty involvement, and effective institutional research and assessment. Specific strategies include

- *Curricular issues.* Efforts should be made to enrich the curriculum of the community college in order to offer more courses that transfer, to develop strong articulation agreements between two- and four-year institutions for individual and block courses, and to enable community college students to co-enroll in two- and four-year institutions, therefore making the transfer process easier.
- *Academic advising.* Transfer students should have access to specially trained advisers. Moreover, institutions should create special transfer centers and appoint a transfer director or coordinator who continually addresses transfer issues.
- *Orientation.* Many of the strategies used to help other types of students' transition to the institution are needed for transfer students, such as summer transfer programs, pre-semester orientation programs, orientation courses, and peer mentoring programs.
- *Faculty involvement.* Faculty should be integrally involved in the transfer process as faculty mentors and should be adequately trained to understand transfer issues and provide support for those who transfer.
- *Assessment.* Institutions should embrace effective research and assessment including identifying accurate measures of successful transfer students, appropriate placement testing, studying the academic achievements of transfer students in relation to native students, as well as addressing the individual sub-populations of the overall transfer population.

Programs and Services

Cuseo (1998) suggests that orientation programs can offer support to incoming transfer students and can help them remove transfer barriers. A review of the literature suggests that the following steps need to be taken in the development of a program to ease the transfer transition: (a) assessing student needs, (b) determining program structure and components, (c) training, and (d) evaluating and using of results (Daniel, 1988; Goldsberry, McKenzie, & Miller, 2000). An assessment of the incoming transfer student population ensures an accurate picture of student characteristics and needs. Ultimately, the picture created by the assessment will give orientation professionals the structure on which to build a transfer program tailored to the needs of the incoming population. Once orientation professionals have a sense of who is coming to the campus and their specific needs, they can determine the program structure and components. Decisions that must be made about program structure include delivery method, timing of program (e.g., summer programs, pre-enrollment), location of program, (e.g., via the Internet, on campus), and length of program. This step also includes deciding who else in the institution needs to be involved with the planning and delivery of the program and identifying appropriate marketing strategies. Collaboration is vital and should include faculty, staff, and students from all areas of campus. Once the program structure has been defined, everyone involved in the process, from student orientation leaders to academic advisers, should receive training appropriate to the role he or she will play in the program. The training can include helping those involved understand the demographics and needs of transfer students, exploring appropriate language to use when addressing transfer students, and understanding the diversity of the transfer students. Finally, programs must be evaluated with an eye toward improving them in the future. Programs should be evaluated by the participants as well as by those who assist with their implementation. Chapter 14 in this monograph provides a more in-depth discussion of program evaluation and assessment.

A variety of programs and services are offered on American college campuses to assist transfer students with their transition to a new learning environment. Many institutions choose individual approaches to meet the needs of transfer students, including offering pre-enrollment programs, various types of orientation and mentor programs, specialized environments for transfer students such as living-learning environments and orientation courses, and other one-to-one outreach programs.

Some institutions have developed comprehensive methods to serve transfer students better, such as creating transfer centers and appointing staff and faculty to serve as transfer counselors. According to Harrison (1993), those institutions that are able to create these types of systems are better able to address a transfer's needs along a continuum instead of dealing with one issue at a time. For example, the issues facing a transfer student might range from "academic articulation, advising, and registration to the student's need to become familiar with the campus, the people, the support services, and the feelings of being a transfer" (Harrison, 1993, p. 134). Transfer centers can ease the transfer process for incoming students by centralizing many of the campus resources including, assisting with the credit transfer process, pre- and post-enrollment issues, identifying campus programs and services, and initial academic advising. In addition, many centers collaborate with campus-wide orientation programs to remind students continually about resources they may need throughout their college experience.

When asked why special programs and services were being offered for transfer students, respondents to a survey on the National Orientation Directors Association listserv (NODANet) offered a variety of reasons, such as to address transition issues, as a convenience for students and university offices, and to increase retention. In addition, many cited managing a large population as a reason for offering programs and services. Still others suggested that the institution was slow in realizing that not all of their incoming populations are served as fully as traditional first-year students and that the campus faculty and staff are working to make sure that all students feel comfortable on what can be a large and overwhelming campus. Another orientation professional suggested that the institution worked closely with former transfer students and state-wide community colleges to develop their program and that the resulting program was designed to address the needs of transfer students in a timely fashion and in a manner that would best help them make a successful transition. Other respondents suggested that programs and services were offered because transfer students were falling through the cracks on campus or because students returned to campus not remembering needed information that had been provided in an orientation session several months before enrollment.

"Transfer centers can ease the transfer process for incoming students by centralizing many of the campus resources including, assisting with the credit transfer process, pre- and post-enrollment issues, identifying campus programs and services, and initial academic advising."

Regardless of the reason programs are developed on campus, the authors believe that institutions need to respond more effectively to the needs of transfer students by offering specialized orientation programs; outreach programs; mentoring; opportunities to interact with peers, faculty, and staff; campus tours; access to services, and a general introduction to campus policies and procedures in a timely manner. Conversations we have had with colleagues across the country suggest that most institutions help students during the enrollment process and then assume the student will move into campus academic and social environments without additional assistance. Outreach to transfer students needs to occur from the time they express interest in the institution until they graduate in order to offer the maximum level of support for these students.

The following program descriptions are taken from two sources: (a) a survey conducted on the National Orientation Directors Association electronic listserv, NODANet and (b) the first edition of this monograph (Harrison, 1993). Common themes that emerge from the survey responses are offering transfer orientation programs before the student's enrollment on the new campus; involving small numbers of faculty and staff in the adjustment process of transfer students; reaching out to faculty, staff, and students at institutions from which large numbers of transfer students come; and acknowledging that the campus should offer transfer students more assistance with their transitions than is currently provided. In recognition of this last theme, many respondents noted that their campuses were in the process of developing new programs and services for the transfer population. These program and service descriptions offer very practical examples of strategies for assisting transfer students.

Orientation Programs for Transfers

Most institutions offer some type of program geared to helping transfer students and their families make the transition to the new college environment. Depending on the population size and campus resources, programs can vary from a few hours to several days. For example, Stephen F. Austin University, a mid-size institution (10,000 students) located in Nacogdoches, Texas, enrolls 1,000 transfer students annually. The University faculty and staff have offered a specialized transfer orientation program since 1975 that includes a review of support services; opportunities to take care of University business in such areas as housing, financial aid, and testing; introduction to campus resources; placement testing; academic advising; and course registration.

Virginia Tech, located in Blacksburg, Virginia, has an enrollment of 21,000 undergraduates and enrolls 700 transfer students annually. Virginia Tech offers Fast Track sessions for transfer students during the summer orientation sessions for first-year students. The sessions include an introduction to the University spirit and traditions; academic success messages; administrative greetings; college or departmental advising and registration; college business such as obtaining identification photos, paying bills, and parking; and the opportunity to come to campus one day during the summer to get ready for the new semester. The attendance rate is high; approximately 95% of transfer students attend the Fast Track sessions.

Located in West Lafayette, Indiana, Purdue University enrolls approximately 31,000 undergraduates and approximately 1,500 transfer students annually. Purdue University staff offer transfer students two specialized orientation programs, one at the beginning of the fall semester and one in the spring. The programs include components typical of most orientation programs; however, the staff has recently added more outreach to the regional campuses via online and personal contacts to reach the large populations transferring from these areas more effectively.

Washington State University, located in Pullman, Washington, has an enrollment of 16,431 undergraduates and enrolls 1,800 transfer students annually. The University offers transfer students the opportunity to attend specialized orientation programs designed to help them make a successful academic and social transition to campus. The programs are a day and a half in length and offer opportunities to ask questions and address concerns. The major draw to this program and the biggest benefit, according to the campus staff, is the opportunity to meet with an academic adviser and register for classes prior to all other new students. The program is held in May, which enables the students to see the campus while classes are in session. This program also offers a track for parents and family members.

Georgetown University, located in Washington, D.C., has an undergraduate population of 6,000 students and enrolls 275 transfer students each year. The University faculty and staff host a four-day program that includes many of the same functions as the program for new first-year students in terms of an academic convocation, advising, diversity education, and registration. The transfer program specifically introduces the transfer students to the Jesuit influence on campus through a reception where students can interact with members of the distinct and unique campus community.

The University of Iowa, located in Iowa City, Iowa, enrolls more than 20,000 undergraduates annually and this past year welcomed 1,900 transfer students. During the University orientation program, the school offers a campus resource fair staffed by various campus offices including computing, housing, student life, and family services, to name just a few. The campus staff found that transfer students did not attend this portion of the program, which was held later in the day, so they rearranged the program and moved the campus services to the check-in portion where all students could get their questions answered.

Clemson University, located in Clemson, South Carolina, enrolls approximately 13,000 undergraduates and 1,000 transfer students each year. Clemson offers a summer orientation program that includes a session where students meet with advisers and are able to learn about the college and their major expectations as well as the academic requirements.

Northern Illinois University in Chicago enrolls approximately 3,200 transfer students each year, with 73% of those students transferring from local community colleges. The campus staff hosts an orientation program specifically for transfer students to be advised and access the registration system. The University is also in the process of developing a transfer center with a coordinator to better assist incoming transfer students. The development of the center is in direct response to pressure from the community college system within Illinois to treat transfer students with special care.

Transfer Centers/Offices

A transfer office is a part of the structure at the Community College of Allegheny County (Pittsburgh, Pennsylvania) which, among other things, interprets articulation agreements to the students on campus, enabling them to transfer successfully to other institutions. The College begins this process as early as orientation (Harrison, 1993).

The University of Central Florida, located in Orlando, Florida, has a total undergraduate population of 31,000 and enrolls approximately 5,000 transfer students each year. The University has an office called Transfer Services, which works directly with community colleges to help transfer students make a smooth transition to campus. The office staff works directly with the orientation program in order to offer transfer students a general overview of transition issues they may face as well as to coordinate the advising for undecided students and any student who needs assistance. In addition, the office staff communicates with transfer students using e-mail, informing the students about important dates. The staff also communicates with advisers and community colleges by publishing a newsletter focusing on transfer issues and specific campus polices. The Transfer Services office has become well-known on campus for being student oriented.

Florida International University, located in Miami, Florida, has an undergraduate population of 26,000 students and enrolls approximately 4,000-5,000 transfer students annually. The University has an Office of College Relations and Transfer Services, which collaborates with other campus offices to offer programs and services that assist transfer students with their campus success. For example, the office hosts a survival tips program during orientation where the students learn about campus information, policies, procedures, and specific Florida International University practices.

SUNY-Cortland enrolls approximately 6,000 undergraduates and 1,000 transfer students each year. The campus enlists the assistance of a coordinator of transfer services who works with the transfer student residence hall living areas, provides guidance and information to the campus community about transfer students including issues and trends, collaborates with the regional community college faculty and staff to coordinate transfer activities and ensure assistance during the transfer process, and coordinates a transfer orientation.

Additional Types of Programs/Services

Circleville Bible College, located in Circleville, Ohio, enrolls approximately 200 traditional-aged and 45 transfer students annually. Retention at the institution is approximately 80%. To assist with transfer success and to retain students to graduation, the campus staff only recruits a limited number of students each year. Thus, all students have premium access to resources.

Located in Maryville, Missouri, Northwest Missouri State University has an undergraduate population between 5,000-5,500 students and enrolls approximately 375-400 transfer students each year. The University staff offer the Transfer Information Program (TIPs) as a way of assisting students with their transition to the University. This program immediately follows orientation and includes monthly newsletters and frequent e-mail updates. Also, when appropriate, the TIPs program has included speakers and workshops.

Kent State University enrolls approximately 16,000 undergraduates and 1,200 transfer students each year. The Admissions Office sponsors a Transfer/Regional Campus Student Day that provides incoming transfer students (both from regional campuses and other institutions) an opportunity to secure academic advising, tour the campus, meet with currently enrolled students, and learn about the campus policies, procedures, and expectations. In addition, Kent State University offers transfer students who achieve a 3.0 GPA or better the opportunity to join Tau Sigma, a transfer student honor organization. This group offers its members social programming service opportunities both on and off campus.

Using Technology to Reach Transfer Students

Technology may be an untapped resource for assisting transfer students. Much of the outreach to transfer students can be accomplished with the assistance of technology.

Miller and Viajar (2001) studied orientation professionals and their use of technology and found that orientation professionals believed that new students should have university-sponsored e-mail access and that class registration should occur online.

Beyond registration services, video conferencing is an option for providing orientation at a distance. Lask (1998) found the University of Colorado's orientation via video conferencing to be a cost-effective way to establish a positive relationship with incoming students and their families, but she believes it is more desirable to host them on the campus. The program was created using the staff in the academic technology department

> *"Ultimately, the capabilities of the Internet, college web sites, CDs, DVDs, and interactive online tools and resources offer transfer students access to information and processes that were once unavailable except on campus. In addition, the accessibility of online transfer articulation agreements, online registration, e-mail, and instant message capacity provides a level of service that is convenient and instantaneous."*

and included a method by which a two-way interaction could occur offering all of the participants involved the opportunity to see and hear each other (Lask, 1998). However, Lask (1998) found that offering advising and registration was a challenge through this process.

The expansion of these types of technological resources to include transfer students may be a viable option for institutions that historically transfer a significant number of students from a particular college or system of colleges. Ultimately, the capabilities of the Internet, college web sites, CDs, DVDs, and interactive online tools and resources offer transfer students access to information and processes that were once unavailable except on campus. In addition, the accessibility of online transfer articulation agreements, online registration, e-mail, and instant message capacity provides a level of service that is convenient and instantaneous. Although these initiatives are positive in some respects, a complete online orientation program may not be prudent. As students often transfer to a college with a different and unique culture, experiencing that culture in person is important for positive academic and social adjustment.

Articulation Agreements

Other types of services which offer support to transfer students are found in articulation agreements. Articulation agreements are cooperative relationships that can be legal, governed by state entities, or voluntary. Ultimately, they benefit the transfer student by easing the process for transferring course work between institutions (Lehning, 2000). Ignash and Townsend (2000) found that 79% of the states currently had articulation agreements; however, many of the agreements did not meet levels of good practice. Although many orientation professionals have little influence with the development of agreements, knowledge about such agreements will enable them to offer better service to incoming transfer students.

Much of the responsibility for facilitating transfer from two- to four-year institutions is placed on the community college or two-year institution, but Zamani (2001) argues that the responsibility of preparing for transfer success should be shared by both two- and four-year institutions. Moreover, both should partner to address the role of transferring, and many two- and four-year institutions have created unique collaborative efforts to assist transfer students (Zamani, 2001). These collaborations include creating and implementing transfer centers and admissions agreements; developing more effective outreach to transfer students including, information sessions and campus tours; and strengthening articulation agreements (Zamani, 2001). While many factors influence these collaborations, a mix of student affairs and academic approaches combined with appropriate pamphlets and brochures offered at the proper point in the transfer process seem to build the most effective programs (Harrison, 1993).

Cuseo (1998) has promoted the idea of collaboration between two-year and four-year institutions to develop articulation agreements that enhance the transferability of individual courses. Lehning (2000) hypothesizes that students who transferred between institutions with articulation agreements and transfer guides are more likely to persist in college but cautions that the articulation agreements should not replace advising for transfer students. Rather such agreements should offer the transfer student an understanding of expectations, requirements, and their role in the educational process (Lehning, 2000).

Summary

There are many pressing reasons to continue addressing the specific needs of transfer students both individually and as a population. Transfer students deserve a level of attention and service in parity with new first-year students and should be seen as assets rather than liabilities to the institution. The curricular, financial aid, policy and procedure, and service provision barriers that exist for transfer students must be overcome. Initiatives to maximize transfer have been instrumental to students' success in the transfer process. They include such initiatives as articulation agreements, admission and co-registration agreements, transfer advising, financial incentives, technological resources, orientation, transfer centers, support programs and resources, and evaluation.

Innovative programs at a variety of colleges and universities have addressed these issues. Orientation professionals need to learn from these innovative programs and implement them or workable prototypes at their own institutions. In particular, they need to identify ways in which technology can enhance the level of service provided to transfer students and ease their transition to a new environment.

The research and our informal review of institutional practice clearly suggests that many institutions develop basic articulation agreements and offer initial programs that assist with the transition. Unfortunately, few offer formal programs and services that extend beyond the first few weeks of the academic term. As the demand for education accountability continues to increase, orientation professionals and higher education administrators will be forced to develop effective vehicles for all students to be more successful in college, including transfer students. Gone will be the days when college and university faculty and staff can assume a new student will transfer successfully, as they will be held to a higher level of accountability to implement the programs and services that can provide opportunities for successful transitions.

References

Baxter Magolda, M., Terenzini, P. T., & Hutchings, P. (1999). Learning and teaching in the 21st century: Trends and implications for practice. In C. S. Johnson (Ed.), *Higher education trends for the next century: A research agenda for student success* (pp. 20-27). Washington, DC: American College Personnel Association.

California Community Colleges. (1994). *Transfer: Preparing for the year 2000.* Sacramento, CA: State Chancellor's Office.

Cohen, A. M., & Brawer, F. B. (1982*). The American community college.* San Francisco: Jossey-Bass.

Cohen, A. M., & Brawer, F. B. (1996). *The American community college.* (3rd ed.). San Francisco: Jossey-Bass

Cuseo, J. (1998). *The transfer transition: A summary of key issues, target areas, and tactics for reform.* (Report No. 141) (pp. 1-6). Washington, DC: ERIC Clearinghouse on Higher Education.

Daniel, B. V. (1988). Designing orientation programs for transfer students. In R. H. Mullendore (Ed.), *Orientation Planning Manual.* Bloomington, IN: National Orientation Directors Association.

Diaz, P. (1992). Effects of transfer on academic performance of community college students at four-year institutions. *Community College Journal of Research and Practice, 16,* 279-291.

ERIC Clearinghouse for Community Colleges. (n.d.). Frequently asked questions. Retrieved May 16, 2002 from the http://www.gseis.ucla.edu/ERIC/faq.html

Eggleston, L. E., & Laanan, F. S. (2001). Making the transition to the senior institution. In F. S. Laanan (Ed.), *Transfer students: Trends and issues* (New Directions for Community Colleges No. 114). San Francisco: Jossey-Bass.

Goldsberry, K. L., McKenzie, B. L., & Miller, D. (2000). Designing effective transition programs for transfer students. In M. J. Fabich (Ed.), *Orientation planning manual 2000.* Washington, DC: National Orientation Directors Association.

Harrison, C. H. (1993). Orienting transfer students (Monograph No. 13) (pp. 123-140). In M. L. Upcraft (Ed.), *Designing successful transitions: A guide for orienting new students.* Columbia, SC: University of South Carolina, The National Resource Center for The Freshman Year Experience.

Ignash, J. M., & Towsend, B. K. (2000). Evaluating state-level articulation agreements according to good practice. *Community College Review, 28*(3), 1.

Kim, K. A. (2001, July). Trends and issues in transfer. U.S. Department of Education: EDO-JC-01-06, pp. 1-4.

Kodama, C. M. (2002). Marginality of transfer commuter students. *NASPA Journal*, 39(3), 233-250.

Kozeracki, C. A. (2001). Transfer student adjustment. In F. S. Lannan (Ed.), *Transfer students: Trends and issues.* (New Directions for Community Colleges No. 114). San Francisco: Jossey-Bass.

Laanan, F. S. (2003, January). *Studying transfer students: Policies, research, and implications.* Presentation at the First Annual Institute for the Study of Transfer Students, Denton, Texas.

Laanan, F. S. (2001). Transfer student adjustment. In F. S. (Ed.), *Transfer students: Trends and issues.* (New Directions for Community Colleges No. 114). San Fransciso: Jossey-Bass.

Lask, T. (1998). Orientation from a distance: Connecting new students to campus by utilizing video conferencing. *Journal of College Orientation and Transition, 5*(2), 21-24.

Lehning, E. M. (2000). The influence of student development in articulation agreements. *Journal of College Orientation and Transition 7*(2), 33-40.

Miller, M., & Viajar, P. (2001). The integration of technology in new student orientation programs. *Journal of College and Transition, 9*(1), 33-38.

Parnell, D. (1986). *The neglected majority.* Washington, DC: Community College Press.

Pascarella, E. T., & Terenzini, P. T. (1991). *How college affects students.* San Francisco: Jossey-Bass.

Townsend, B. K. (2001). Redefining the community college transfer mission. *Community College Review, 29*(2), 15-29.

Vaughn, G. B. (2000). *The community college story.* (2nd ed.) Washington, DC: Community College Press.

Zamani, E. M. (2001). Institutional responses to barriers to the transfer process. In F. S. Laanan (Ed.), *Transfer students: Trends and issues.* (New Directions for Community College No. 114). San Francisco: Jossey-Bass.

Orienting Nontraditional Students to College: Creating Opportunities, Supporting Success

Cathie Hatch

Cathie Hatch

If there is one societal pattern that can be projected into the future, and with good reason, it is that higher education enrollment will steadily increase. . . . In good times and in bad times, in all regions of the country, among all types of Americans, education seems to be the answer to some goal. (Aslanian, 2001, p. xv)

Current and future statistics indicate that nontraditional learners will continue to be the largest emergent group of new college students (Aslanian, 2001; Caffarella, 2002). The complexities associated with shifting demographics, technological change, and sociocultural factors have encouraged this population to continue learning throughout their lives (Clark & Caffarella, 1999). At the same time, the 2001 National Survey of Student Engagement suggests that all institutions of higher learning across the country are being asked to extend their reach and expand functions to support a rapidly changing society. As student affairs personnel and especially as orientation professionals, we should envision these circumstances as opportunities (Tinto, 1998).

To capitalize on these opportunities, institutions ultimately need to revise missions, goals, and program and service delivery to ensure the persistence and success of nontraditional students. The purpose of this chapter is to develop a profile of nontraditional learners, including their motivations, interests, and needs related to gaining the most from college. Success for nontraditional learners in educational pursuits will depend on how campus programs, services, and environmental factors support their learning intentions. Therefore, this chapter also addresses a number of initiatives designed to help nontraditional students during the orientation process and throughout their entire college careers.

Increasing Numbers of Nontraditional Students

Nontraditional learning is no longer a luxury; instead, it is necessary to meet public needs for economic stability and social equity and to enhance quality of life (Aslanian, 2001). In addition, continuous changes in demographics, economics, and social trends have altered the characteristics of college-bound populations. Thus, institutions are seeing an influx of nontraditional students who seek higher education in response to a variety of personal and social issues (Brown, 2002; Gordon & Habley, 2000; Merriam & Caffarella, 1999). These students are also diverse in other significant ways—such as their age and life experience. For example, nontraditional students encompass a broad spectrum, including growing numbers of women, displaced homemakers, career changers, immigrants, single parents, second career retirees, and those seeking professional development (Aslanian, 2001; Caffarella, 2002; Merriam & Caffarella, 1999; Smith & Walter, 1995; Upcraft, Gardner, & Associates, 1989).

Between 1970 and 2000, the number of nontraditional students enrolling in college increased 170% (from 2.4 million to 6.5 million), while enrollment of

Chapter Nine

students aged 18 to 24 rose only 41% (from 6.2 million to 8.7 million) (Aslanian, 2001). By the year 2010, 7.1 million nontraditional students are projected to be seeking degrees. The National Center for Educational Statistics continues to forecast increases in part-time and full-time non-traditional student enrollment at two- and four-year institutions (qtd. in Aslanian, 2001). Under-graduate nontraditional students are growing older, following American popu-lation patterns. According to The College Board, 65% of college students are 25 years old or older, with a median age of 40 (qtd.

"By the year 2010, 7.1 million nontraditional students are projected to be seeking degrees."

in Aslanian, 2001). Further, Aslanian (2001) notes that 87% of nontraditional students are White and 66% are female. While 25% percent of today's undergraduates are members of historically under-represented racial and ethnic groups, 12% of the nontraditional student population are from under-represented groups.

Returning to College

For nontraditional students, the re-entry to college is a significant life cycle turning point (Aslanian, 2001; Brown, 2002; Cross, 1981; Knowles, 1980; Smith & Walter, 1995; Zemke & Zemke, 1995). It is a time when career and personal perspectives change, life priorities are reorganized, and cognitive interests motivate individuals to seek education (Merriam & Caffarella, 1999). The motivation for older students to seek higher education is often "a combi-nation of complex internal and external forces" (Caffarella, 2002, p. 24)—a factor that distin-guishes them from many of their traditional-aged counterparts. Most nontraditional students pursue education because of an event or experience that has triggered or will trigger a status change (Aslanian, 2001). For example, Schlossberg, Walters, & Goodman (1995) suggest that adult behavior is determined by transitions, not by age, and that more than one half of their transitions are career related and linked to mid-life development. Aslanian (2001) suggests that transitions are also related to family issues. Circumstances surrounding the return to higher education include, but are not limited to, becoming displaced in the workforce, experiencing family challenges, divorcing a spouse, needing additional training to maintain or improve career status, and experiencing health-related challenges (Caffarella, 2002). Nontraditional stu-dents are also motivated to make transitions by a continual need to belong, renew, and estab-lish social involvement; engaging in learning activities is one method they use to cope with life events and transitions (Caffarella, 2002; Cross, 1981; Wolf & Leahy, 1998). The wide variety of factors motivating nontraditional students means they will have high interest and strong de-termination to do well in college and will clearly articulate their goals upon initiating or re-suming education (Brown, 2002; Cross, 1981; Smith & Walter, 1995).

An Emerging Profile of the Nontraditional Learner

Nontraditional students enter college with past accomplishments, ongoing transitions, and an awareness of the need to adjust to change (Aslanian, 2001; Cross, 1997; Smith & Walter, 1995). Change in adulthood is determined more by social factors, race, and gender, than by individual maturation (Clark & Caffarella, 1999; Schlossberg et al., 1995). Nontraditional learners return to school because of unfinished agendas and find themselves positioned between future success and present survival. Ultimately, education may be the last opportunity to secure a better future.

Nontraditional learners are confronted with complex life challenges, and their time may be governed by ambiguous agendas. They commonly commute long distances, juggle family and ca-reers with limited resources, and know that success in education will depend on good management of multiple demands (Aslanian, 2001; Copeland, 1989; Siebert, Gilpin, & Karr, 2000; Smith & Walter, 1995). Nontraditional students want to meet educational goals directly and efficiently, and they do best with educational experiences that provide what they value. They consistently practice strong academic discipline, resourcefulness, and determination (Brown, 2002; Zemke & Zemke, 1995). Nontraditional students are pragmatic learners and study to improve their performance in other social and vocational roles (Dirkx, 1998). They prioritize having their talent and career interests assessed (Gordon & Habley, 2000; Sandler, 1998; Smith & Walter, 1995). These students also possess repertoires of thinking and learning strategies and wants to integrate new learning into their knowledge from previous experiences (Caffarella, 2002; Cross, 1981; Dirkx, 1998; Knowles, 1980; Nouwens, 1997). In addition, they are exemplary in goal setting and apply entrepreneurship to overcome barriers (Brown, 1999; Siebert et al., 2000; Zemke & Zemke, 1995). Nontraditional students seek continuity between their past experience, current education, and future plans. Where they were before college is a prologue to where they are going, and socio-economic status, lifestyle, and interests remain influential (Aslanian, 2001; Lefrancois; 1996, Wolf & Leahy, 1998).

Designing Learning Experiences to Meet the Changing Needs of Today's Student

The decision to return to college for nontraditional students is typically aligned with personal values, commitment to learning, and employment goals. Thus, these students are potentially the most promising learners in higher education. In their quest to achieve career aspirations, their focus remains constant over time—earning a degree. In addition, motivational and cognitive abilities tend to be linked positively with their age (Caffarella, 2002; Cross, 1981; Garrison, 1997; Knowles, 1980). Unfortunately, the structure of college curricula frequently is not designed to include the life and learning experiences of nontraditional students. Their past education featured books, blackboards, and memorization, whereas today's workplace requires computer literacy and application of new knowledge to changing systems.

Moreover, many colleges do not envision serving nontraditional students as within their missions. For this reason, higher education continues to be characterized by conditions that are inappropriate for these students, including excessive standardization, insufficient individualization, passive models of teaching and learning, failure to reward prior learning, rigid schedules, an emphasis on research, and support programs reflecting traditional student needs (Brown, 2002; Merriam & Caffarella, 1999; Nouwens, 1997; O'Brien & Merisotis, 1996). The consequence of shifting sociocultural conditions requires educational leadership to rethink roles of responsibility in addressing learning needs of older students and to recognize institutional accountability for how these imperatives are managed (Brown, 2002; Merriam & Caffarella, 1999; Noel & Levitz, 2001; Zemke & Zemke, 1995).

Providing education for nontraditional students requires creating academic and social climates that foster a convergence between what students bring to campus and what higher education can provide. The best college experience for nontraditional learners presents two lifelong benefits: the knowledge students gain and the relationships they cultivate. If knowledge is to be leveraged in support of learning over the lifespan, then learning cannot be left to chance. Institutions need to ensure the academic and personal development of diverse nontraditional learners (Brown, 2002; Cross, 1997; Merriam & Caffarella, 1999). Ultimately, nontraditional students need focused, sustained, and rewarding activities to enhance motivation for learning and educational persistence (Caffarella, 2002; Clark & Caffarella, 1999; Zemke & Zemke, 1995).

> *"The consequence of shifting sociocultural conditions requires educational leadership to rethink roles of responsibility in addressing learning needs of older students and to recognize institutional accountability for how these imperatives are managed."*

In today's world, colleges must model organizational resiliency, be proficient at change, and demonstrate emotional intelligence in their handling of adult students (Siebert, 2000). Increased nontraditional student enrollment highlights the need for a revised curriculum and for resources to support these students (Tinto, 1998). Nontraditional students desire teaching methods that accommodate their learning styles and initiatives that support their unique intellectual and social needs (Brown, 1999). Programs and services needed by nontraditional students include improved assessment, academic advising, career planning, and tutoring; enhanced faculty competence in teaching nontraditional students; programs accommodating work and family obligations; integration of work instruction with learning; more distance-learning methods; nontraditional student centers; affordable day-care; and priority parking (Brown, 1999; Copeland, 1989; Noel & Levitz, 2001; O'Brien & Merisotis, 1996).

Similarly, The College Board has identified 10 areas influential to nontraditional learner satisfaction:

1. Assessing their academic readiness skills for reentering school
2. Obtaining advanced placement in college courses
3. Documenting academic and non-academic achievements
4. Matching competencies and experiences to potential careers
5. Selecting educational providers meeting career goals
6. Balancing study, work, and family demands
7. Qualifying for traditional and alternative financing
8. Updating study skills for resuming learning
9. Assessing career interests, skills, and potential
10. Planning re-entry into higher education over a lifetime (Aslanian, 2001; Cross, 1997; Siebert et al., 2000).

In addition, the 2001 Adult Student Priorities Survey (Noel & Levitz) examines data from 6,807 nontraditional students attending 39 four-year public, four-year private, and two-year community, junior, and technical institutions. Their responses indicated five areas surrounding nontraditional student satisfaction with the college experience: (a) classes scheduled at times convenient to nontraditional students, (b) quality of class instruction, (c) value of course content within chosen major, (d) knowledgeable faculty, and (e) few conflicts with class registrations. Additional factors included, but were not limited to, a welcoming environment for nontraditional students, faculty concern about nontraditional students as individuals, safe and secure classroom locations, provision of career services focused on nontraditional student needs, consideration of nontraditional student circumstances in financial aid awards, academic advising accessible by telephone and e-mail, classes oriented toward nontraditional student needs, and a focus on improved technology skills.

The factors cited by The College Board and the Noel-Levitz survey, along with the recommendations of the Council for the Advancement of Standards (CAS) in Higher Education (1998), provide the framework needed to establish and maintain quality programs for the orientation and retention of nontraditional students. Orientation professionals can have a positive influence on the attitudes of campus leadership toward accommodating nontraditional students. One way to do this is by integrating faculty, academic advisers, administrators, and staff into all academic and social components of orientation programming (Gordon & Habley, 2000). Intentionally educating these groups on how to recognize nontraditional needs may also contribute to student success (Brown, 1999).

Meeting the Needs of Culturally Diverse Nontraditional Students

As with all new students, "orientation programs serve an important early socialization function" (Pascarella & Teranzinni, 1991, p. 650) for nontraditional learners. Nontraditional students seek orientation experiences that support their initiatives in pursuing education. They are entering new cognitive domains and want help in evaluating their resources, abilities, and knowledge (Gordon & Habley, 2000; Zemke & Zemke, 1995). Moreover, nontraditional students come to orientation seeking an ethic of college membership and desiring help normalizing transitions to college (Lefrancois, 1996; Siebert et al., 2000; Tinto, 1998). They hope to find guidance in translating past accomplishments into realistic goals for college (Brown, 1999; Noel & Levitz, 2001). Through orientation, nontraditional students anticipate establishing information networks with faculty, staff, and experienced students who can provide such guidance and help them become socially integrated into the college environment (Brown, 1999; O'Brien & Merisotis, 1996; Siebert et al., 2000; Tinto, 1998).

Learning occurs best in settings where participants are known by name, are respected as individuals, can interact with people from backgrounds different than their own, feel confident taking intellectual risks, and are given the opportunity to assume responsibility for their learning (Dirkx, 1998; Kuh, Lyons, Miller, & Trow, 1994). The needs of nontraditional students are no different from other students in this respect. Participation in orientation should help nontraditional students learn information influential to their intellectual and personal satisfaction and success in college. Nontraditional orientation needs to provide students with a sense of self in academic, social, and cultural contexts (Clark & Caffarella, 1999). Thus, programs should be clearly focused on helping nontraditional students establish comfort levels in new surroundings, providing accurate information, identifying academic and social expectations, and discussing policies (Aslanian, 2001; Brown, 2002; Noel & Levitz, 2001).

Because culturally and ethnically diverse nontraditional students will enter higher education during this decade (Aslanian, 2001; Clark & Caffarella, 1999), delivery of orientation programs should focus on strategies that successfully engage all cultural groups according to their learning norms (Sork, 1997). Thus, "academic and non-academic staff who work with nontraditional students need to understand different cultural learning styles, identify accommodating instructional and communication methods, and connect students to appropriate academic and social programs" (Chavez & Guido-DiBrito, 1999, pp. 44-45). Nontraditional orientation that features self-sharing and encourages a sense of respectful community among all participants can create a comfort level for students from special populations as they make the transition to college. As the number of ethnically and linguistically marginalized learners increases on college campuses, differences in cognitive styles, life experiences, and gender become more significant than age and maturity in developing inclusive learning environments (Clark & Caffarella, 1999; Tinto, 1998). Central themes of orientation should feature respect and recognition of student differences (Council for the Advancement of Standards, 1998).

The Joint Task Force on Student Learning (1998) suggests that colleges need to develop campus cultures that enable students from different cultural backgrounds to become aware of and experience each other's traditions. One way to ensure this is to involve currently enrolled nontraditional students in the planning and implementation of orientation programs. Nontraditional students from a variety of backgrounds can present keynote talks, facilitate small group discussions, lead campus tours, serve as peer academic advisers, help with family orientation, and write nontraditional student publications. Additionally, institutional demographics should determine whether new nontraditional students would benefit more from culturally integrated or separate culture group orientation. Chapter 7 addresses the transition needs of special populations and highlights strategies for responding to those needs in the orientation process.

Social and Learning Considerations for Nontraditional Orientation Programs

Upon arrival at orientation, nontraditional students want to identify and become associated with other students whose learning goals and social and cultural profiles mirror their own. Caffarella (2002) reminds us that "Adults are more receptive to the learning process in situations that are both physically and psychologically comfortable" (p. 25). Thus, questions of delivery and access, with consideration given to intellectual and physical factors and psychological points of view, become as important for orientation professionals as questions of what nontraditional students want and need in terms of information (Merriam & Caffarella, 1999). Programs where entering students interact with each other in environments that accommodate their diverse backgrounds, needs, and interests are recommended.

> *"Orientation should be an experience during which nontraditional students have learning experiences relevant to both cognitive development and behavioral change that will be helpful to their initiation and matriculation to college life."*

Nontraditional students will often question the merits of their participation in orientation. For example, they want to make connections with peers whose goals and energies are congruent with their own and are likely to value programs designed with this end in mind (Brown, 2002; Cross, 1981; Knowles, 1980; Merriam & Caffarella, 1999; O'Brien & Merisotis, 1996; Siebert et al., 2000; Tinto, 1998). Because many nontraditional students have experienced unsatisfactory outcomes in past learning experiences, they want immediate reassurance that their time and resource commitment to attend orientation and pursue education will be worthwhile. They will not necessarily find value in orientation programs and learning environments designed with traditional-aged students in mind.

While nontraditional students may have limited time to devote to orientation activities, the length of the program is less important than schedule order. Given that the first hour of any learning activity determines productivity of subsequent learning events (Knowles, 1980; Silberman & Casazza, 2000), the opening of the orientation program needs to communicate clearly a positive and inclusive climate for learning. Physical design of the orientation space is also important. Room arrangements featuring chairs in circles—rather than theatre-style—satisfy nontraditional student needs for learning cooperatively (Caffarella, 2002).

Effective orientation for nontraditional learners should help them identify an important truth: Time has been their friend. From previous life experiences, they can analyze and support diverse opinions, practice critical thinking skills, and identify reasoning skills helpful for intellectual challenges (Brookfield, 1999; Tinto, 1998; Zemke & Zemke, 1995). Their cognitive development has been shaped by life experiences including prior classroom learning, careers, community involvement, and family responsibilities (Aslanian, 2001; Brookfield, 1999; Cross, 1981; Merriam, & Caffarella, 1999). Additionally, these past experiences have given them competencies to work both independently and collaboratively (Caffarella, 2002; Gardner, 1996; Merriam & Caffarella, 1999; Nouwens, 1997; Tinto, 1998).

At the same time, nontraditional students possess an awareness of how they learn, an awareness of their reasoning assumptions, and evidence and justification that underscore their beliefs (Dirkx, 1998; Knowles, 1980; Merriam & Caffarella, 1999). They want a process-focused orientation, giving them the control over learning that leads to improved self-confidence. Orientation should be an experience during which nontraditional students have learning experiences relevant to both cognitive development and behavioral change that will be helpful to their initiation and matriculation to college life. Intellectual stimulation and social comfort must be present for learning engagement to occur (National Survey of Student Engagement, 2000).

The richest learning environments include clear, coherent educational purposes and outcomes with consideration for cultural backgrounds and participant aspirations (Brown, 2002). Orientation should include identification of expected academic demands; opportunities for social integration; an introduction to library resources; an introduction to campus technology, including e-mail and Internet tutorials; campus tours; and descriptions of counseling and health service programs (Brown, 1999; Noel & Levitz, 2001; O'Brien & Merisotis, 1996; Siebert et al., 2000). Nontraditional students respond best to orientation topics when information is presented in short sessions, allowing students to pace their own progress (Zemke & Zemke, 1995).

According to the literature, self-directed learning, experiential learning, and transfer of learning are three topics about which orientation staff, advisers, and faculty need a working knowledge in order to create an effective nontraditional orientation.

- ◆ *Self-directed learning* focuses on the process by which adults take control of their own learning, set goals, locate resources, and evaluate their progress. Knowles, (1980) and Caffarella (2002) identify skills such as working in teams, sharing resources, and forming peer networks as measurable, helpful outcomes for nontraditional students resulting from self-directed learning.
- ◆ Teaching techniques based in *experiential learning* are adults' preferred methodology be cause it allows them to incorporate their past experiences and knowledge while making use of preferred learning styles. Examples of experiential learning include case studies, role-playing, simulations, and self-assessments (Caffarella, 2002; Cross, 1981; Merriam & Caffarella, 1999).
- ◆ *Transfer of learning* is the affective application of learning to support changes contributing to student success (Caffarella, 2002; Dirkx, 1998). Reflective journal writing, storytelling, role playing, and metaphor analysis are transfer of learning methodologies that meet nontraditional student needs (Brown, 2002).

Nontraditional students appreciate multi-type communication methods, including interactive panel presentations; forum participation emphasizing sharing insights, opinions, experiences, and success strategies; discussions led by other nontraditional students; and lecture-driven information sessions (Chavez & Guido-DiBrito, 1999).

Orientation needs to focus on helping nontraditional students initiate transfer of learning behavior, which also occurs with self and career assessments, advising, career planning, and which has different meaning for each cultural group. Understanding the importance of communication with the academic adviser, developing faculty associations, acquiring academic help, building peer networks, initiating campus involvement, and learning campus geography require responsible and active behavior, thus satisfying transfer of learning imperatives.

Distance Learning

Web-based education provides new learning benchmarks for nontraditional students. The majority of nontraditional students (85%) favor a traditional, face-to-face learning environment. However, busy schedules and the convenient nature of distance learning make it a valuable option for many students, as evidenced by the increasing number of students enrolling in distance courses: "In 2000, 40% of distance learners took classes via the Internet, 35% by videotape, 30% by correspondence, 25% by computer disks and 15% by audiotapes" (Aslanian, 2001, p. 25). The flexibility of distance learning extends resources, expands the learning day, and opens the learning place (Gardner, 1996). In addition, individuals can determine their participation time and integrate learning into their lifestyles (Nouwens, 1997). Online coursework features student-centered education, self-directed learning, inclusive class participation, and small group work (Gardner, 1996; National Academic Advising Association, 2002a). Nontraditional students appreciate formal lectures with question time and opportunities for student and professor interaction through e-mail or chats.

If distance courses are available at the institution, orientation professionals should include information on this option during orientation. Nontraditional students need to know that degree programs can be completed in traditional campus classrooms, through this alternative course delivery method, or through a composite of both programs.

To support distance education students, the Academic Advising CAS Standards and the NACADA Task Force on Distance Education both indicate that institutions need to be responsible for implementing a required orientation course (i.e., DL 101 "What it takes to be a distance learner"). Both groups mandate that student services for distance learners be equal to on-campus programs and that distance learners receive academic advising for all courses and assessment of student progress over time.

Meeting Faculty: Communicating Academic Needs

"While it is impossible to remove all risk from the learning environment, nontraditional students want opportunities to communicate to faculty that they will learn more effectively in an environment where some mistakes are acceptable but a successful performance is finally expected ..."

The nature and quality of student and faculty relations are significantly important to student learning (Kuh et al., 1994). In addition, findings are consistent: the more faculty interact with students, the more likely they are to remain in college (Tinto, 1998). Faculty participation in orientation also potentially helps to communicate campus spirit and collegiality. Thus, as with all orientation programs, faculty involvement in nontraditional orientation is extremely valuable.

Nontraditional students want the opportunity to meet the faculty members who will be teaching them during the orientation process so they can discuss issues related to their learning. In short, they want to have the opportunity to talk about their academic concerns, to know what to expect from the learning environment, and to receive reassurance that their learning styles will be valued. Some of the issues of greatest importance in working with nontraditional students in the academic environment are outlined below.

Nontraditional students are time-conscious learners and want to understand academic expectations in measurable terms (Aslanian, 2001; Siebert et al., 2000; Smith & Walter, 1995). For example, they need to know how the material will be taught and how much work is expected of them. Because nontraditional students may be uncertain about their academic skills, they prefer learning environments where their fear of judgment is reduced (Cross, 1981; Merriam & Caffarella, 1999). They may work more slowly, be more cautious, ask more questions, and set higher standards for themselves than traditional-aged students. At the same time, they seek to minimize time pressures and prefer multiple choice formats in testing (Siebert et al., 2000). They want review sessions before exams so that the potential for failure is reduced and prefer exam content that moves from easy to difficult (Zemke & Zemke, 1995). While it is impossible to remove all risk from the learning environment, nontraditional students want opportunities to communicate to faculty that they will learn more effectively in an environment where some mistakes are acceptable but a successful performance is finally expected (Nouwens, 1997). In addition to preferring low-risk learning environments, nontraditional students often prefer hands-on, active experiences in the classroom. Because they are used to using concrete skills necessary in the professional world, they may find it difficult to adapt to the theory-driven, abstract style of many faculty members.

Nontraditional students also expect faculty to have an awareness of how different pedagogical styles influence their learning. Moreover, research suggests that nontraditional students' learning is enhanced when teaching strategies are matched with learning styles (Brown, 2002; Caffarella, 2002; Pascarella & Terenzini, 1991). Difficulties arise for many underrepresented populations and international nontraditional students when they attempt to negotiate learning environments that are based within a sociocultural set of values, behaviors, beliefs, and ways of doing things that are different from their own (Chavez & Guido-DiBrito, 1999). Faculty who teach nontraditional students need to focus on establishing inclusive learning environments where course content is "anchored" in more than one value system and where different life, development, and cultural backgrounds are considered (Chavez & Guido-DiBrito, 1999). These students also need to communicate with others from similar backgrounds who can support them in the learning environment. Failure to respond to the different cultural nuances of learning styles may result in disengagement for nontraditional students.

Nontraditional students anticipate that faculty will show interest in their learning agendas, identify helpful academic advocates, and help them inventory learning resources (Gordon & Habley, 2000). They expect that orientation programming will provide opportunities for them to inform faculty on how these factors will potentially influence what they gain from college. To help faculty be more receptive to the concerns and issues raised by nontraditional students, orientation professionals should consider requiring faculty development sessions as a prerequisite for those professors who are involved with nontraditional orientation programs and first-year seminars. Faculty need to be able to differentiate between traditional and nontraditional student expectations and interests, and faculty development programs can help them do this. Training should also help faculty develop skills to work with the multi-talented and diverse group of nontraditional students. Orientation professionals can help faculty develop this understanding, and they can also work to ensure that they create opportunities to discuss academic issues during orientation. Finally, orientation professionals should apply what is known about preferred learning styles of nontraditional students when they design both the content and delivery of orientation programs.

Initiatives Designed to Retain Nontraditional Students

In many ways nontraditional students are more similar to their traditional-aged counterparts than they are different. Many of the same types of programs and initiatives designed to help 18-year-old, first-year students make the transition to college and persist to graduation are valuable for nontraditional students. However, these efforts need to examine the kind and character of intellectual and personal experiences that shape nontraditional student life. For example, "degree utility (degree value to student), goal commitment, and career decision-making self-efficacy have all been found to have a statistically significant effect on the persistence decisions and behaviors of nontraditional students" (Brown, 2002, p. 3). Thus, programs for nontraditional students need to be designed with these issues in mind. Specific initiatives designed to aid in the retention of nontraditional students include being attuned to their unique cultural and community perspective; providing one-stop service centers for advising, registration, and fee payment; training faculty, advisers, and staff on culturally diverse nontraditional student development and learning; and providing internships, service-learning, and other experiential learning activities that satisfy higher order adult needs (Brown, 2002). This section addresses a range of educational initiatives designed to facilitate academic and social integration, with a special focus on their application with nontraditional students.

Family Orientation

Family orientation should focus on the impact of change and uncertainty on the nontraditional student's life (Brown, 2002). Because nontraditional students are involved with and committed to relationships and multiple roles that have primacy over educational goals (Chavez, & Guido-DiBrito, 1999), these relationships, including those with family, can influence their educational progress. The CAS standards mandate the provision of orientation for new students' primary support groups, underscoring nontraditional student expectations from family. Ultimately, nontraditional learners expect family orientation programs to explain to family members how they can support a nontraditional student's degree-earning efforts. Family orientation also needs to communicate that family systems will remain intact. These programs can help immeasurably both students and their families understand what changes to expect and develop the flexibility needed to support student educational intentions (Brown, 2002).

Events for family orientation might include campus tours; picnics or receptions; cultural group identity videos; family activities; and role play presentations portraying scenarios new student families can anticipate related to time management, impact of academic demands on student-family relationships, influence of family interest, and support with student success. The CAS standards also recommend providing family members with an orientation handbook (in a variety of languages, depending on the make-up of the campus community). Items might include welcomes from the college president and from a nontraditional student leader; academic calendars noting family events and particularly demanding times for students; faculty commentaries on working with nontraditional students; family member support services; answers to frequently asked questions for family groups; and lists of suggestions, advise, and lessons learned from experienced nontraditional students.

> *"Events for family orientation might include campus tours; picnics or receptions; cultural group identity videos; family activities; and role play presentations portraying scenarios new student families can anticipate related to time-management, impact of academic demands on student-family relationships, influence of family interest, and support with student success."*

Continuity with family orientation can be accomplished with year-long family orientation newsletters featuring nontraditional student success stories, articles reflecting family participation in events, invitations to spouses and children for campus events, campus-based pictures of family members with students, and listings of nontraditional student initiatives influencing campus life.

Because cultural expectations may compound the issues related to returning to school for nontraditional students, special attention should be paid to culture and ethnicity in enlisting family support for educational pursuits (Chavez & Guido-DiBrito, 1999). In particular, social events open to the family may help resolve one of their primary issues: "In what ways do I matter? How can I play a meaningful role here?" Involving currently enrolled students from a variety of cultural backgrounds in family orientation is also important.

Academic Advising

The academic advising process, specifically the relationships nontraditional students establish with advisers during orientation, can directly influence future intellectual growth and goal determination. The adviser and nontraditional student relationship is enhanced when advisers understand life changes that influence adult reentry to college (Gordon & Habley, 2000). The National Academic Advising Association's (NACADA) Core Values of Academic Advising (2002b) urges advisers to acknowledge the talents and skills nontraditional students need to manage study, work, and family. Thus, a knowledge of family system theory, adult development theory, and adult learning theory is important for academic advisors and career counselors so that students receive appropriate advocacy (Brown, 2002). Moreover, academic advisers need to be prepared to "address the characteristics and needs of a diverse population when establishing and implementing policies and procedures" (Council for the Advancement of Standards in Higher Education, 1996).

Because nontraditional learners need to be accommodated in terms of needs, knowledge, and readiness to learn (Smith & Walter, 1996), academic assessments become essential advising tools for helping students select courses that will showcase their competencies and provide support in needed areas (Brown, 1999; Clark & Caffarella, 1999). Further, these students expect advisers to evaluate current knowledge, work experience, and previous (potentially dated) coursework and to guide them into appropriate curriculum levels (Merriam & Caffarella, 1999). The Course Applicability System, an electronic system for evaluating transfer credits, can be an especially useful tool in advising nontraditional students (Gordon & Habley, 2000). As noted earlier, nontraditional students frequently return to college for career-related reasons. If they are hoping to enter a new career field, they may expect their advisor to understand the developmental and self-efficacy stages through which they will progress in choosing a career that is personally and professionally satisfying (Sandler, 1998). As they make decisions about career, nontraditional students may also need advisers to be supportive if they decide to change majors.

The setting of academic advising is also important. Because nontraditional students want to feel confident and prefer non-intimidating environments, advisers might consider holding meetings outside traditional office settings (Gordon & Habley, 2000). Nontraditional students may also find it difficult to meet with advisers during normal business hours. Therefore, e-mail, video, and telephone advising should be explored as options to accommodate nontraditional student schedules (Nouwens, 1997). No matter where or through what medium the meeting takes place, non-traditional students want to find academic advisers who are accessible and willing to commit time to listening (Brown, 1999; Gordon & Habley, 2000).

Academic requirements and implications of campus policies on learning demands are important information for nontraditional students (Brown, 1999; Siebert et al., 2000; Smith & Walter, 1995). The academic adviser can certainly help make students aware of these policies and understand their relevance, but nontraditional students might also benefit from a handbook written from the experienced student perspective. Helpful sections might include case studies of common challenges facing nontraditional students (e.g., failed day-care arrangements during finals week, work commitments causing missed classes, conflicts with the professor) with helpful management suggestions; merits of good academic adviser associations; methods for assessing syllabi assignments; a list of campus resources; classes to avoid taking concurrently due to the workload; nontraditional student quotes on lessons learned with managing school, family, and employment; and experiences helpful to future career placement. Brown (2002) suggests that the involvement of currently enrolled nontraditional students as peer advisers during orientation is often greeted with enthusiasm by older students. Such peer involvement might take the form of panel presentations, small group discussions, or one-on-one meetings.

First-Year Seminars

The efficacy of first-year seminars for improving academic performance and persistence has been well-established (see Chapter 12 of this monograph for a discussion of relevant research).

Such courses give students time to ensure not only the initiation but also the establishment and maintenance of academic and social engagement with college (Upcraft, Gardner, & Associates, 1989). In a study of institutions offering first-year seminars for nontraditional students, 52% of respondents indicated that participation in the seminar led to increased use of campus services, satisfaction with college and persistence to second semester and graduation (Julian, 2001). Most significantly, nontraditional student first-year seminars immeasurably support adult self-efficacy, helping students estimate their competency in interactions with others and in new environments (Lefrancois, 1996). Students define goals, assess efforts and abilities, identify learning styles, determine potential outcomes, and become engaged with college (Merriam & Caffarella, 1999). Nontraditional students realize the control that they have and the contribution they make to learning, based on self-perception of ability (Dirkx, 1998). They acquire needed help, interact more with faculty, and contribute to organizations. Seminars help adults understand that academic success depends on how they learn, as differentiated by how well they are taught (Smith & Walter, 1995).

Learning Communities

Curricular learning communities take many forms, but one type is a block of two to four classes for which a given group of students is co-registered (Tinto, 1996). Courses are scheduled at the same time each session, and student groups meet two to three times weekly for four to six hours. Students form study teams, with each member accountable for specific learning tasks. The scheduling and hands-on nature of learning activities in this type of learning community may be especially appealing to nontraditional students. One way to maximize the benefits of this structure is to include a first-year seminar within the block of required classes. Integrating first-year seminars as part of a learning community model has benefits for this student group. They are vulnerable to not becoming engaged and integrated with campus life as a direct consequence of lacking time needed to establish and maintain associations with faculty and peers (Merriam & Caffarella, 1999; Siebert et al., 2000), and the seminar is effective in helping students establish peer and faculty relationships. The inclusion of the first-year seminar may have a synergistic effect in that learning communities are highly successful in providing both academic and social integration (Merriam & Caffarella, 1999; Tinto, 1996).

Service-Learning and Internships

The Joint Task Force on Student Learning (1998) identifies service-learning and internships as strategies that promote interdisciplinary approaches to solving problems and balancing challenge and support, both of which enhance student learning. They also provide ample opportunities to synthesize and integrate material learned in the classroom and to test the value and worth of new ideas in real-world situations (Brown, 1999; Jacoby, 1996). Internships and service-learning invite and value diverse perspectives and critical thinking and foster opportunities for nontraditional students to develop learning partnerships with other students, faculty, and individuals external to the campus (Jacoby, 1996). As such, they provide the experiential learning opportunities nontraditional students prefer (Caffarella, 2002; Cross, 1981; Jacoby, 1996).

Integration of service-learning and internships with degree requirements has positive implications for nontraditional student career placement (Brown, 1999). Service-learning and internship programs can be designed to take place in community and work settings where nontraditional students are already engaged, where a wide spectrum of schedules and lifestyles can be accommodated (Jacoby, 1996), and where students can make use of prior knowledge and experience. Orientation can influence nontraditional student participation by working with faculty to include internships and service-learning as part of first-year seminar requirements and by integrating them into learning community curricula.

Student Support Groups

Nontraditional students enter college with a wealth of experience related to helping others (Brown, 1999; Jacoby & Associates, 1996). These skills, when applied to study and support group participation, can directly influence nontraditional learning and social satisfaction. Networking, mentoring, and support group participation commonly influence student satisfaction, success, and survival with peers whose backgrounds match their own (Siebert et al., 2000). Study groups provide leadership opportunities while enhancing learning and intellectual achievement (Smith & Walter, 1995). Mentoring groups also have merit for these students in transition (Brown 2002; Siebert et al., 2000). The voluntary sharing of problematic circumstances, topics needing resolution, and changing situations with peers who can give advice and support can boost determination. Consulting with others and hearing learned truths and wisdom helps decision making (Merriam & Caffarella, 1999; Smith & Walter, 1995; Tinto, 1998). Orientation professionals should identify how co-curricular participation provides opportunities for students to use their talents to the benefit of the institution and themselves.

Conclusion

Nontraditional student enrollment will continue to increase through the next decade, bringing a heightened awareness of the differences among socially, politically, and economically disenfranchised groups of students. The key to promoting nontraditional student retention and success is to help this audience feel a part of the institution. Orientation professionals need to work collaboratively with faculty and administration to create curricular and co-curricular programs that accommodate different learning styles and social expectations of changing nontraditional students. Moreover, they must encourage themselves and their colleagues to step outside the box where these students are concerned:

Not only must new degree programs and non-degree programs be developed, but academics, practitioners and policy makers working with nontraditional students need to recognize that retention efforts require vision and creativity to guide efforts that encourage the development and persistence of this student audience. (Brown, 2002, p. 2)

Such vision and creativity will ensure that nontraditional learners achieve successful integration between prior experience and new intellectual challenges.

References

Aslanian, C. B. (2001). *Adult students today.* New York: The College Board.

Brookfield, S. D. (1999). *Understanding and facilitating adult learning.* San Francisco: Jossey-Bass.

Brown, S. M. (1999). *Adult students speak out: A focus group research project.* Pittsburgh: University of Pittsburgh.

Brown, S. M. (2002). *Strategies that contribute to nontraditional adult student development and persistence.* Paper presented at Eastern Regional Adult Education Research Conference, University Park, PA.

Caffarela, R. S. (2002). *Planning programs for adult learners: A practical guide for educators, trainers, and staff developers.* San Francisco: Jossey-Bass.

Chavez, A. F., & Guido-DiBrito, F. (1999). Racial and ethnic identity and development. In C. Clark, & R. S. Caffarella (Eds.), *An update on adult development theory: New ways of thinking about the life course.* (New Directions for Adult and Continuing Education No. 84). San Francisco: Jossey-Bass.

Clark, M. C., & Caffarella, R. S. (Eds.). (1999). *An update on adult development theory: New ways of thinking about the life course.* (New Directions for Adult and Continuing Education No. 84). San Francisco: Jossey-Bass.

Copeland, B. A. (1989). Adult learners. In M. L. Upcraft, J. N. Gardner, & Associates (Eds.), *The freshman year experience* (pp. 305-315), San Francisco: Jossey Bass.

Council for the Advancement of Standards (CAS) in Higher Education. (1996). *CAS standards and guidelines for student services/development programs: Academic advising programs self assessment guide.* Washington, DC: Author.

Council for the Advancement of Standards (CAS) in Higher Education. (1998). *CAS standards and guidelines for student services/development programs: Student orientation programs self assessment guide.* Washington, DC: Author.

Cross, K. P. (1981). *Adults as learners: Increasing participation and facilitating learning.* San Francisco: Jossey Bass.

Cross, K. P. (1997, February). *Working on the puzzle of a college education.* A paper presented at the Annual Conference on The Freshman Year Experience, Columbia, SC.

Dirkx, J. M. (1998). Transformative learning theory in the practice of adult education: An overview. *Journal of Lifelong Learning, 7,* 1-14.

Garrison, D. R. (1997). Self-directed learning: Toward a comprehensive model. *Adult Education Quarterly, 48*(1), 18-33.

Gardner, P. (1996). Demographic and attitudinal trends: The increasing diversity of today's and tomorrow's learner. *Journal of Cooperative Education, 31*(2-3), 58-82.

Gordon, V. N., & Habley, W. R. (2000). *Academic advising: A comprehensive handbook.* San Francisco: Jossey Bass.

Jacoby, B., & Associates. (1996). *Service learning in higher education.* San Francisco: Jossey-Bass.

Joint Task Force on Student Learning. (1998). *Powerful partnerships: A shared responsibility for learning.* Washington, DC: American Association for Higher Education, American College Personnel Association, National Association of Student Personnel Administrators.

Julian, D. M. (2001). *Evaluation of first-year seminar/orientation programs and services offered for part/full-time reentering, transfer, and first-time adult/nontraditional undergraduate students attending AAU institutions of higher education.* Unpublished doctoral dissertation, University of Pittsburgh.

Knowles, M. (1980). *The adult learner: A neglected species.* Houston: Gulf Publishing.

Kuh, G., Lyons, J., Miller, T., & Trow, J. (1994). *Reasonable expectations: Renewing the educational compact between institutions and students.* National Association of Student Personnel Administrators. (Available from Thomas Miller, Vice President, Canisius College, 2001 Main Street, Buffalo, New York 14208)

Lefrancois, G. R. (1996). *The lifespan.* (5th ed.) Belmont, CA: Wadsworth.

Merriam, S. B., & Caffarella, R. S. (1999). *Learning in adulthood: A comprehensive guide.* San Francisco: Jossey-Bass.

National Academic Advising Association. (2002a). Task force on distance education. (Available from Kansas State University, 2323 Anderson Ave. Suite 225, Manhattan, KS 66502-2912.)

National Academic Advising Association. (2002b). Core values of academic advising. (Available from Kansas State University, 2323 Anderson Ave. Suite 225, Manhattan, KS 66502-2912.)

National Survey of Student Engagement. (2000). National benchmarks of effective educational practice. (Available from the Center for Postsecondary Research and Planning, Indiana University, Ashton Aley Hall Suite 102, 913 East Seventh Street Bloomington, Indiana 47405-7510).

Noel, L., & Levitz, R. (2001). Adult Student Priorities Survey. Iowa City, IA: American College Testing Program, National Center for Advancement of Educational Practices.

Nouwens, F. (1997). *Designing materials for adult learners.* PAGE: Melbourne

OBrien, C. T., & Merisotis, J. P. (1996). Life after forty: A new portrait of today's and tomorrow's postsecondary students. Boston, MA: Education Resources Institute. Washington, DC: Institute for Higher Education Policy. (ERIC Document Reproduction Service No. ED 401 813)

Pascarella, E. T., & Terenzini, P. T. (1991). *How college affects students.* San Francisco: Jossey Bass.

Sandler, M. E. (1998). Career decision-making self-efficacy and an integrated model of student persistence. San Diego, CA: Paper presented at the Annual Meeting of the American Educational Research Association. (ERIC Document Reproduction Service No. ED 419209)

Schlossberg, N. K., Walters, E. B., & Goodman, J. (1995). *Counseling adults in transition.* (2nd ed.). New York: Springer.

Silberman, S. L., & Casazza, M. E. (2000). *Learning and development: Making connections to enhance teaching.* San Francisco: Jossey-Bass.

Siebert, A. (2000). *Adult students need resilient, emotionally intelligent colleges.* Portland, OR: Practical Psychology Press.

Siebert, A., Gilpin, B., & Karr, M. (2000). *The adult student's guide to survival and success* (4th ed). Portland, OR: Practical Psychology Press.

Sork, T. J. (1997). Workshop planning. In J. A. Fleming (Ed.), *Newer perspectives on designing and implementing effective workshops.* (New Directions for Adult and Continuing Education No. 76). San Francisco: Jossey-Bass.

Smith, L. N., & Walter, T. L. (1995). *Adult learners guide to college success.* Belmont, CA: Wadsworth.

Tinto, V. (1996, February). *Student success and the construction of inclusive educational communities.* A paper presented at the Mid-Winter Conference of the Minnesota Technical College Student Services Association.

Tinto, V. (1998, March). *Learning communities: Building gateways to student success.* A paper presented at the annual meeting of the American College Personnel Association, St. Louis, MO.

Upcraft, M. L., Gardner, J. N., & Associates. (1989). *The freshman year experience.* San Francisco: Jossey-Bass.

Wolf, M. A., & , Leahy, M. A. (Eds.). (1998). *Adults in transition.* Washington, DC: American Association for Adult and Continuing Education.

Zemke, R., & Zemke, S. (1995). Adult learning: What do we know for sure? *Training, 32*(6), 31-34, 36, 38, 40.

The Connecting Point: Orientation at Community Colleges

Les Cook, Betty R. Cully, and Deneece Huftalin

America's college campuses are changing in response to both external and internal forces in widespread attempts to meet the challenges facing the higher education community. More students with differing degrees of preparation are enrolling in colleges and universities, and traditional models of higher education are no longer sufficient to respond to society's needs. Higher education is not immune from market forces, technological innovation, and an emerging globalization of access and resources. (Schroeder, 2000)

New student orientation has been a fixture on college campuses for many years; however, the existence of orientation-type programs appears to be less frequent on the two-year college campus. Two-year community colleges have had a significant impact on American higher education and continue to play a large role in providing access for students who might otherwise not be able to obtain postsecondary education. The evolution of the two-year community college and increased enrollments at these institutions have necessitated the introduction of comprehensive orientation and retention programs. Moreover, increases in attendance of women, people of color, students of differing socioeconomic backgrounds, and nontraditional students have clearly changed the framework of orientation programs for these and other institutions (Hazzard, 1993; Strumpf & Sharer, 1993). While little research has been completed detailing the value of new student orientation programs at two-year colleges, it can be assumed that, much like their counterparts in four-year schools, these programs are a valuable component of student goal attainment (Beatty-Guenter, 1992). Despite the positive evidence about orientation from other sectors and the presence of some form of orientation program on most two-year campuses, orientation professionals continue to struggle to raise the level of prominence of programs on these campuses (Cook, 1996).

This chapter provides a brief historical overview of the evolution of two-year colleges and explores current issues facing two-year institutions. The authors surveyed more than 100 two-year institutions across the nation about their orientation practices. Selected findings from this survey are highlighted. The chapter concludes with some recommendations for program components on the two-year campus.

A Brief History

From its beginnings, the two-year college has had two generic names applied to it: junior and community. For much of the first half of the 20th century, these schools were commonly known as junior colleges (Cohen & Brawer, 1989). In 1922, at the second annual meeting of the American Association of Junior Colleges, a junior college was defined as "an institution offering two years of instruction of strictly collegiate grade" (Bogue, 1950, p. xvii). Later, the term "community college" was developed to describe comprehensive, publicly supported state institutions. As college environments became more specialized, it became necessary to distinguish between environments that awarded degrees and those who strictly offered education courses, which could be applied at other institutions. For the purposes of this study we will use Cohen and Brawer's (1989) definition of the community college: "any institution accredited to award the Associate of Arts or the Associate in Science as its highest degree" (pp. 4-5).

Two-year colleges have had a dramatic impact on American higher education, most significantly by expanding access to it. The number of community and junior colleges increased from 70 in 1900 to almost 1,700 today (Burke, 2003; Thornton, 1972). A primary reason for the growth of community colleges and of increased enrollments in all institutions was the passage of the GI Bill, which increased the financial assistance available to students returning from World War II. Education was no longer just for sons and daughters of the elite; rather, it could now be obtained by a diverse cross-section of citizens. In addition to more students, institutions began to see more students from lower socioeconomic classes and disadvantaged cultures as well as those who were less prepared academically.

> *"Two-year colleges have had a dramatic impact on American higher education, most significantly by expanding access to it. The number of community and junior colleges increased from 70 in 1900 to almost 1,700 today."*

But increases in two-year college enrollments can be attributed to conditions other than general population growth and the GI Bill. Cohen and Brawer (1989) associate this growth with the increased participation of older students, increased physical accessibility, greater availability of financial aid, increased part-time attendance, the reclassification of institutions, the redefinition of students and curriculum, and increased attendance by low ability and culturally disadvantaged students. Students also choose to attend a community college for a variety of reasons: to complete the first two years of college and then transfer to a four-year institution for degree completion, to retrain, or to pursue personal interests (Cohen & Brawer, 1989; Fullerton & Hayes, 1993; Higbee, 1989; Thornton, 1972). With this expansion came the need for community colleges to begin examining the student affairs function and the importance of providing services designed to support the student.

Current Issues Facing Two-Year Institutions

In 2001, the authors contacted more than 100 orientation professionals at two-year institutions, asking them a series of questions concerning the institution and orientation practices (see chapter appendix for survey questions). The purpose of the survey was to assess the current state of orientation programs and services at two-year schools and to identify best practices. Best practices were determined based on self-reported positive evaluations of success or value to the campus. As orientation professionals at community colleges across the country assess individual campus orientation programs, they are faced with several issues that make their role challenging at best. Nearly half (47%) of those responding to the survey indicated that meeting the needs of an increasingly diverse population was for them the most difficult dynamic to address during their planning. Eighteen percent cited lack of institutional value and support for orientation programs demonstrated by an inadequate organizational structure and scarce human and financial resources as a particular challenge. And, like all other types of institutions, orientation professionals at two-year colleges report struggling with the role technology should play in helping students make the transition to college.

Unlike some of their four-year, residential counterparts, community colleges enroll a population of students who are difficult to respond to and far harder to classify because of their diversity. Given the comprehensive mission of most community colleges, a "typical" student profile for which the ideal orientation program can be created is rare. Students enter the college from a variety of paths: directly from high school, after a hiatus from formal education, from industry for retraining, from a four-year institution as a reverse transfer student, or through a desire to improve their economic status or career prospects. Within these subgroups, the personal skill level and savvy needed to navigate the intricacies of college life run the continuum from highly mature to underdeveloped and in need of great attention. Two-year institutions are challenged to create specialized orientations or at least particular tracks within a global orientation program to assist with these differing goals and competencies. Several authors argue for specialized orientation programs to create more meaningful experiences for student sub-populations. For example, Ramirez (1993) argues that

> student affairs professionals, more than any other group in the institution, must develop a team that reflects the varied nature of the population. Not only does this variety improve the probability that the information used for program and design management will be more accurate and relevant, but that information will also have more meaning and importance for the team. Student affairs professionals working with heterogeneous student populations must arrive at a commonly held philosophy or guiding principle of student development programming. Differences exist and must be recognized. (p. 437)

Given the diversity of student types and needs, community colleges should be responding with multiple offerings in their orientation programs. These programs could be defined by a demographic distinction among students, the major or degree type they are pursuing, or the method by which they are accessing the institution (e.g., at a distance or in person). A related challenge then becomes identifying, in advance, which students need which program and designing and marketing those programs in a supportive, cost effective manner.

Another challenge facing community college orientation professionals is the lack of perceived value orientation programs have at the community college level. Historically, orientation programs or new student weeks have been associated with residential, four-year colleges. For many faculty and staff at community colleges, especially those with their roots in the vocational-technical fields, orientations are seen not as a necessary part of their culture but rather as a nonessential bonus. This perception may contribute to a general lack of institutional support resulting in fewer dollars and human resources allocated to the program, limited expectations for faculty involvement and therefore few reward structures for those who are involved, and less than adequate marketing efforts to incoming students.

This lack of support is also demonstrated anecdotally by the number of professional staff who claim to have had orientation programming added to their list of job duties. Hired by the institution to provide another service, they are subsequently given the task of directing and planning a dynamic, inclusive orientation experience for students. In addition, orientation staff in the survey mentioned above (Cook, Cully, & Huftalin, 2001) expressed their frustration with the revolving staff assigned to orientations and to the limited, if any, budget dedicated to it annually. They felt the orientation program was tangential to the other programs or services on campus and not given the professional credibility and administrative support necessary for a meaningful program. Many administrators do not recognize that research and literature exists to share best orientation practices and that research over the years has pointed to a strong orientation program as a significant way to connect students to the campus and subsequently increase the likelihood of their persistence.

In *Four Critical Years*, Astin (1977) discusses the dilemma community colleges face in trying to capture commuting students and connect them with faculty and staff. He asserts that given the demographics of community college student bodies, institutions need to be much more intentional about connecting students to the environment because the structures that might provide those connections at a residential college may not exist at a two-year institution. In other words, community colleges should create environments that mimic the residential setting so that students spend more time on campus interacting with faculty and fellow students. Given the positive relationship between involvement and persistence, programs that encourage greater involvement from commuter students are likely to result in increased retention rates.

For many, one of the highlights of the community college system and structure is the open door philosophy and accessibility it provides to students who may not otherwise take advantage of an educational opportunity. Given this mission, any attempt to control the flow of enrollments by mandating an orientation may be met with resistance. It is difficult to balance the desire to allow students to step right into the institution, freely and without a lot of bureaucracy, with the desire to ensure that students are starting out with the knowledge and resources to support them in their educational pursuits.

The role that technology can and should play in orienting students to college complicates the debate. Gone are the days when a student had to physically come to campus to register for classes. Our once captive audiences, who came to be advised, select courses, and participate in orientation, can now take care of these enrollment services online or via the telephone. As distance and asynchronous learning are expanded and promoted, orientation professionals wonder whether they should be offering a cyber orientation to accommodate the needs of these students. Enter another paradox . . . high tech vs. high touch. Since one of the key goals of an orientation program is to build connections between students and other members of the college community, many are skeptical as to whether the cyber connection built by technology affords the same advantage as traditional face-to-face programs. Can we connect students with each other, create meaningful interactions between faculty and other students and share the same information about student success and the culture of the college through cyberspace? Is involvement through the web as strong a factor in persistence as other forms of involvement?

"Given the national move throughout higher education to fewer "brick" and more "click" environments, it seems justified that an effective, innovative method for providing key concepts and a sense of belonging via the web must be developed; at least as one alternative for the diverse student populations colleges will be courting in the years to come."

Given the national move throughout higher education to fewer "brick" and more "click" environments, it seems justified that an effective, innovative method for providing key concepts and a sense of belonging via the web must be developed—at least as one alternative for the diverse student populations colleges will be courting in the years to come. Orienting students to electronic learning, customized training programs, electronic integration of job listings, resumes, career information, and learning resources requires community colleges to adopt effective web-based tools (Morman, 2000).

Orientation professionals, then, in addition to their program development and implementation responsibilities, must become educators and champions for the role orientation plays in the retention and success of students. They must arm themselves with the research and literature which demonstrates the critical role orientation can play in the first year of college whether students are of traditional or nontraditional age, and they must use that information to build support and resources. In addition, they must increase their personal knowledge of adult learning theories, racial identity theories, and other research that broadens their understanding of diverse groups of students. These concepts, while widely discussed and often accepted at four-year colleges and universities, are slower to emerge and take hold at community colleges.

As the arena of higher education opens up to increasingly business-driven educational settings, community colleges need to position themselves to offer more than instruction, but in a responsive, progressive way. Resolving these issues will demand, in most cases, institutional conversations about the value of orientation to student learning and success, followed by sustainable financial and human support to create a diverse selection of orientation options for community college students. If we believe that students are more successful by belonging to a community of learners and by connecting to their environment, we need to accept that there may be different ways for them to make that connection. Research needs to examine the success and persistence of distance learners and the cyber components that replicate a successful orientation program for them.

Best Practices in Two-Year Colleges

When two-year college orientation personnel in all nine regions of the National Orientation Directors Association were contacted by the authors in a nationwide telephone survey (Cook et al., 2001) about best practices in orientation programs, many of them revealed similarities in what they identified as their most successful program components. Most orientation professionals at two-year colleges want a good fit with campus life for new students starting out and starting over, ending in successful completion of two-year college degrees. Providing a seamless transition from new students' past experiences to the culture of the college is both a goal and a challenge. The common threads for the best practices in the orientation tapestry of these urban and rural colleges are strong collaborations between student affairs personnel and faculty, the use of student orientation leaders, the design of unique orientation programs to match students' needs, and the incorporation of technology.

Collaboration with Academics

One of the best practices at many two-year colleges that highlights collaboration between academic and student affairs is offering extended orientation programs similar to the University 101 course at the University of South Carolina. These semester-long seminars of 20 to 25 students help first-year students adjust to the expectations of college, expose them to available resources for career searches, help them develop study and time management skills, and provide a supportive environment for academic growth (Upcraft, Gardner, & Associates, 1989). A more in-depth discussion of the first-year seminar as an effective extension of traditional orientation programs can be found in Chapter 12 of this monograph.

Using faculty in orientation is a great practice to help students make an immediate connection to the college. The most common involvement by faculty in orientation programs is through advisement and class scheduling. Some faculty members volunteer for social aspects of orientation, such as mingling with students during breaks or serving pizza. Others are involved in serving on committees, providing presentations, or teaching extended orientation courses.

Student Orientation Leaders

Although no formal research has been completed on the use of students in two-year orientation college programs, many four-year colleges and universities have used student orientation leaders for years with great success. The under-representation of orientation professionals and student teams from two-year colleges is usually quite apparent at National

Orientation Directors Association (NODA) conferences and regional workshops. More two-year colleges need to adopt the philosophy of using student orientation leaders.

Sponsoring an orientation team is extra work for the orientation professional but well worth the time involved. Students build rapport with other students quickly, and new students see orientation leaders as more credible, especially when discussing the college's expectations and the advisement process. Some orientation leaders volunteer, some are paid, and some are offered tuition waivers or scholarships for their involvement. Most teams are carefully selected, trained, and supervised by orientation professionals and are capable of performing nearly every task involved in an orientation program. The student leaders personally benefit by enhancing their communication, leadership, and team-building skills. The student orientation leaders also earn respect from faculty and staff for providing a much-needed service for the institution and from fellow students for helping them during their transition to college. The college benefits by having a more effective orientation program which serves as a key component in increased retention of new students.

It is evident that the best practices at each college are designed to promote institutional fit for new students through interaction with peers and faculty. In a recent study of 1,867 students at a private institution, entering multi-ethnic students (i.e., Black, American Indian, Asian or Pacific Islander, Hispanic) rated building relationships with faculty and discussing expectations with continuing students as important components of the orientation process. They rated these two factors more highly than their non-multi-ethnic counterparts (Nadler & Miller, 1999). Because two-year colleges are also experiencing a growth in international students, selecting multi-ethnic and international students as orientation leaders will provide more opportunities for diverse populations of entering students to succeed on campuses. The majority of the colleges surveyed (Cook et al., 2001) indicated the use of student orientation leaders as their ultimate best practice. Some examples of programs involving student orientation leaders follow.

Delgado Community College in New Orleans, Louisiana, enrollment 13,000, urban campus. OARS (Orientation, Advising, Registration Support Services) began in 1995 and has been well-received by new students and college staff. One asset to the OARS programs is the well-trained student orientation leaders (PALS) who manage to keep the program informative, but short, covering only essential information needed to make the transition to college.

Enterprise State Junior College in Enterprise, Alabama, enrollment 1,600, rural campus. The best practice at Enterprise State Junior College since 1988 has been using a select group of orientation student leaders, the First Impressions Team (FIT), to participate in get-acquainted activities, lead campus tours, offer presentations on clubs and organizations, participate in personality and cultural diversity activities, perform in skits relating to college-centered themes, teach policies and procedures using PowerPoint presentations, and assist with advisement and scheduling for new students. Returning, international, and military students are included in the orientation team to relate to and reflect the incoming student population better. The training for FIT includes a weekend retreat, a one-semester hour leadership course, and an overlap practice at an actual orientation with the previous year's leaders.

> *"In a recent study of 1,867 students at a private institution, entering multi-ethnic students rated building relationships with faculty and discussing expectations with continuing students as important components of the orientation process."*

A typical orientation session is delivered in two half-day sessions and serves 125 students who are divided into 10 to 15 smaller groups for which FIT is fully responsible. Placement testing is completed before orientation. Faculty and professional staff orientation advisers receive a list of their advisees with copies of their high school transcripts and results from ACT, SAT, Compass, or ASSET tests two days prior to pre-registration. This information helps the advisers know their advisees very well on paper before they actually meet them on the second day of orientation. Faculty, staff, and administrators are involved in various ways from serving pizza and leading student majors meetings to assisting students in pre-registration. All college staff and FIT staff wear orientation t-shirts at orientation sessions in order to be easily identifiable and to give students a warm welcome.

Georgia Perimeter–Lawrenceville Campus, enrollment 3,000, urban campus. Georgia Perimeter–Lawrenceville Campus is located near Atlanta, GA, and its best orientation practice is having a strong, well-trained group of peer orientation leaders. Training includes a retreat and a trip to the NODA Region 6 Southern Regional Orientation Workshop or Annual NODA conference. The college separates parents and students as much as possible, allowing students to make their own scheduling decisions. Breakout sessions with 12 to 20 participants are offered for parents or families, transfers, and traditional and nontraditional (more than 25 years of age) students with at least one orientation leader per group. The program allows time for meaningful icebreaker activities in smaller groups, but only after introducing the icebreaker concept in a larger group setting to establish a comfort level. Peer leaders perform skits and conduct professional follow-up discussions to introduce a variety of potential concerns or issues.

Meridan Community College in Meridian, Mississippi, enrollment 3,000, rural campus. Orientation is mandatory and directors are now in the process of making changes to involve more students at Meridian Community College. Orientation is tied to registration, and a team of student recruiters gives testimonials throughout the session. The program also offers fun and informative tours.

Unique Program Designs

Oakton Community College in Des Plains, Illinois, enrollment 10,000, suburban campus. At Oakton Community College, new students complete a three-step program: one for placement testing, one for advising, and one for orientation. Each workshop is limited to 15 students and is lead by a counselor, faculty advisor, or a staff member. The college also offers early orientation programs to seven feeder high schools where the placement tests are given and students are then bussed in for college advisement sessions.

Baltimore City Community College located in Baltimore, Maryland, enrollment 5,800, urban campus. Orientation is mandatory for full-time students at Baltimore City Community College (BCCC). BCCC considers its best practice to be providing one central location for academic counseling, advisement, and orientation. The faculty conduct the academic advising for registration at orientation, and New Student Orientation Program Student Ambassadors advise and provide student tours. Orientation professionals recently changed to a one-day orientation in response to customer concerns about being able to arrange a two-day leave from their places of employment.

Cowley County Community College in Arkansas City, Kansas, enrollment 3,800, rural campus. Cowley County Community College offers a month-long orientation program in a picnic-like environment held on Saturdays. Nontraditional students come in the morning, and traditional-aged students arrive in the afternoon. Students meet advisors who inform them of college policies. In addition, club officers attend to inform the students about involvement and co-curricular activities.

Florida Community College in Jacksonville, Florida, enrollment 20,800, urban campus. Orientation is mandatory for all new students at Florida Community College at Jacksonville (FCCJ). Students may choose to complete orientation in a large group setting, a small group setting, or

131

via video. Meeting the needs of its multi-ethnic students, FCCJ offers on one of its four campuses a special orientation for ESL students run by counselors and advisors trained to work with this special population. FCCJ is now in the process of designing a web orientation.

Manatee Community College in Bradenton, Florida, enrollment 7,800, suburban campus. As its best practice, Manatee Community College offers an extended semester orientation designed for at-risk students, but open to all. Also, an international student orientation is mandatory and offered once per month, designed to help ESL students succeed.

Salt Lake Community College in Salt Lake City, Utah, enrollment 21,500, urban campus. Enrolling in the First Step orientation program at Salt Lake Community College allows new students the earliest registration opportunities with assistance from academic advisors. Also, the First Step program focuses on alleviating student fears, getting students connected to the campus, and exploring campus resources.

Spokane Community College in Spokane, Washington, 6,200, urban campus. Spokane Community College has formed an orientation committee to strengthen its program. Some of its best practices are involvement of staff and faculty in breakout orientation seminars, student tours of the campus, and the use of student government members in orientation activities. Giving college credit for orientation and linking orientation to advisement is the most significant incentive for full participation by new students.

Technology

Ideally, incorporating online technology into orientations may free administrative time and lower clerical costs, allowing more time during on-site orientations for new student concerns, such as cultural awareness, career searches, substance abuse, date rape, enhancement of learning techniques, and self-concept development. The reality is that most new student populations will still need the actuality of the "high touch" traditional orientation, but the incorporation of Internet options should be helpful in attracting and facilitating the transition to the two-year college environment for commuters and distance education learners.

As increasing numbers of new students arrive on campus with Internet experience in surfing, shopping, chatting, e-mailing, and researching online, two-year college orientation professionals are beginning to see the importance of first meeting them in cyberspace. Two-year college web sites range from providing general information such as dates for orientation, contact information, cost, and e-mail addresses to sites where students can actually complete orientation, register, link to other helpful sites, and even pay fees. For example, the College of DuPage in Glen Ellyn, Illinois, has a web site where students can download applications and register for orientation sessions (http://www.cod.edu/Service1/CTA/NewStud/orientation.htm).

Brevard Community College, Cocoa, Florida, enrollment 20,000, urban campus. As a convenient alternative to its on-campus orientation, Brevard Community College offers a one-hour online orientation that must be completed before registration (https://web2010.brevard.cc.fl.us/orientation/).

Broward Community College, North Campus in Coconut Creek, Florida, enrollment 35,000, urban campus. Broward Community College, North Campus has created a Cyber-Orientation that may be accessed 24 hours a day via the Internet. Cyber-Orientation acts as a substitute for or supplement to the on-site orientation program and provides information on programs of study; scheduling courses; procedures for registering online or by phone; classroom culture; behavioral expectations; academic standards; strategies for balancing school, work, and family; and support services. The site also contains a college catalog. Students also receive personal assistance in reviewing test scores and determining proper course placement. When students select their choice of degree, the site informs them of requirements and other pertinent information.

At the end of the program, students complete a 20-question quiz that ensures they have learned the appropriate information. New students, distance learners, and returning students can all benefit from this program initiative (http://www.broward.edu/cyber/index.jsp).

Richland College, enrollment 2,000, urban campus. Richland College has a required orientation for all students who have failed a portion of the Texas Academic Skills Program (TASP) test and has restructured their entire orientation program using an upbeat 20-minute orientation CD-ROM. The CD-ROM allows students to orient themselves at their convenience, reviewing the college's policies and procedures and providing web links for intramural sports, campus activities, and clubs. Recent changes provide drop-in advising in a year-round office staffed by full-time advisors 10 hours per day. An advising manual is an online tool that helps students build both two-year and four-year programs (Lords, 2000).

Recommendations

Most successful orientation programs use the Council for the Advancement of Standards (CAS) in Higher Education's (1986) Guidelines for New Student Orientation to develop and assess their orientation programs. Although the CAS standards list many goals as part of the mission of orientation programs, two-year college programs need to modify those goals to reach the diverse populations of traditional and non-traditional students on their campuses. Two-year institutions are designed to serve not only students planning to transfer to four-year institutions, but also the workforce needs of their local communities. The wide variety of curriculum offerings is often confusing to incoming students. The authors suggest that, to enhance orientation programs, two-year colleges

- ♦ Provide college-wide involvement by administrators, faculty, staff, and students.
- ♦ Encourage new students to participate in orientation by providing some type of early registration.
- ♦ Involve students in the delivery and design of orientation programs.
- ♦ Have faculty or counselors lead majors meetings explaining curriculum, preferably in small groups.
- ♦ Offer learning styles inventories to new students, which help them identify their preferred method of processing and receiving information and inform them of other methods that may help them succeed in the college classroom.
- ♦ Offer personality, career, or study skills inventories, which personalize orientation for new students, helping them to select or affirm a major or career choice.
- ♦ Meet new students where they are using web or computer technology.

Summary

Orientation is the starting point for most students and is essential in making a successful transition to college. Campuses today are increasingly complex and present challenges for all entities involved. Literature on orientation programs suggests that these initiatives provide some of the most dynamic, rapidly changing components of the college student's educational experience. However, the traditional models of orientation are not always successful at two-year institutions, and innovative models must be developed and used to help students make a successful transition to this environment. However, more research should be conducted that describes program content and assesses their effectiveness, so that orientation professionals may better assist students in their educational pursuits.

Without further study that clearly demonstrates the impact of orientation on retention and student success at the community college, it is unlikely these programs will reach the desired level of support. This chapter has not attempted to prescribe a single model for orientation in two-year and community colleges. Ultimately, each institution will have to make the decision about how to invest scarce resources to enhance the retention of students. Studies at four-year institutions clearly demonstrate the impact of orientation. In short, the most practical way to ensure the successful retention of students lies in programs that manage, from the outset, the first interaction the student has with the institution. The authors suggest that the same impact experienced at four-year institutions can be experienced at two-year and community colleges if the resources are available and used appropriately.

References

Astin, A. W. (1977). *Four critical years.* San Francisco: Jossey-Bass.

Beatty-Guenter, P. (1992). *Sorting, supporting, connecting, and transforming: Student retention strategies at community colleges.* A report prepared for the school of education. University of California, Berkley.

Bogue, J. (1950). *The community college.* New York: McGraw Hill.

Burke, J. M. (Ed.). (2003). *2003 higher education directory.* Falls Church, VA: Higher Education Publications.

Cohen, A. M., & Brawer, F. (1989). *The American community college.* San Francisco: Jossey-Bass.

Cook, L. P. (1996). A description of orientation programs at two-year colleges in the United States (Doctoral dissertation, Brigham Young University, 1995).

Cook, L., Cully B., & Huftalin, D. (2001). *Orientation and its effects on two-year colleges – phone survey.* (Available from the authors. Enterprise State Junior College, P.O. Box 1300, Enterprise, AL 36331).

Council for the Advancement of Standards (CAS) in Higher Education. (1986). *CAS standards and guidelines for student development services/development programs: Student orientation programs self-assessment guide.* Washington, DC: Author.

Fullerton, F. E., & Hayes, I. (1993, November). *Orientation at the community college: Sometimes one size does not fit all.* Paper presented at the meeting of the Missouri Community College Association, Springfield, MO.

Hazzard, T. (1993). *Programs, issues and concerns regarding nontraditional students with a focus on a model orientation session.* Florida State University: Continuing Education Paper.

Higbee, J. (1989). *Orientation courses: Meeting the needs of different student populations.* Paper presented at the National Conference on Student Retention. Chicago, IL.

Lords, E. (2000, September 22). Revolution in academic advising in a Texas community college. *Chronicle of Higher Education,* p. A48

Morman, D. A. (2000). New web tools click with community colleges. *Community College Journal, 71* (2), 34-37.

Nadler, D. P., & Miller, M. T. (1993). Designing transitional programs to meet the needs of multi-ethnic first-year students. *Journal of College Orientation and Transition, 6,* 20-26.

Ramirez, B. (1993). Adapting to new student needs and characteristics. In M. J. Barr &Associates (Eds.), *The handbook of student affairs administration.* San Francisco: Jossey-Bass.

Schroeder, C. C. (2000). *Collaboration and partnerships.* Paper presented at the meeting of the American College Personnel Association, Washington D.C.

Strumpf, G., & Sharer, G. (1998). *National Orientation Directors Association data bank.* College Park, MD: National Orientation Directors Association.

Thornton, J. (1972). *The community junior college.* New York: John Wiley & Sons.

Upcraft, M.L., Gardner, J. N., & Associates. (1989) *The freshman year experience: Helping students survive and succeed in college.* San Francisco: Jossey-Bass.

Appendix

Orientation and Its Effect at Two-Year Colleges

Phone Survey

Demographic Information

Institution:

Enrollment:

Private/Public:

Name of respondent & title:

Date:

---

1. How is your program designed? Who was involved in the decision and program design?

2. Are your programs mandatory or optional? If optional, how do you get the students to attend? What percentage of students participate in orientation?

3. How is your program funded? Are the students assessed a fee? How much? Have you had any success with corporate sponsors? If yes, please describe.

4. Do you conduct orientation for special populations? If so, which populations and who facilitates these programs?

5. Are you using technology in orientation?

6. How long have you had an orientation program on your campus? What do you feel are the best practices?

7. Is orientation tied to assessment? Advising? Registration?

8. Are faculty involved? How?

9. How do you use students/peers in your program?

10. How does your institution evaluate your orientation program (student outcomes, satisfaction)?

11. Are you aware of other models of successful orientation programs?

12. What are some current issues (challenges/roadblocks) facing your institution?

13. Any unique trends or ideas you see emerging?

Additional comments or feedback:

The Role of Family Influence on Student Success

Diane M. Austin*

Chapter Eleven

When we look at new students, we realize we know very little about them in terms of the complexities of their individual psyches and in terms of their interpersonal support systems. Students arrive on campus with many significant relationships in place—relationships with parents, spouses or partners, friends, neighbors, and colleagues. These relationships are as important to the academic success of new students as are their familiarity with the layout of the campus, curriculum requirements, and support services. Long before and long after new social and collegial attachments form, students rely on these previously established relationships for feedback, reassurance, and guidance.

This chapter focuses on the ways in which orientation professionals can work with the important people in students' lives, helping them to understand how their attitudes and behaviors may influence students' satisfaction and success. Special attention is paid to the parents (or step-parents and guardians) of traditional-aged students. Because the number of nontraditional students on campuses is increasing, this chapter also addresses some of the issues relevant to spouses, partners, and children of college students.

Rationale for Expanding the Audience for Orientation

Why not just orient the student, since it is the student who is joining the college community? Most traditional-aged students would probably ask the same question. Throughout the pre-collegiate educational experience, family members may have been highly involved and were probably kept directly informed about their student's progress by school officials. The entry into college is seen by most 17- or 18-year-olds as an end to parental involvement in their academic (and personal) lives in all ways but financial. Parents may expect to be kept at arm's length, both by their student and by the college administration, but often prefer greater involvement in their student's educational experience.

There are a number of reasons why it makes educational sense for the college to provide clearly defined opportunities for parents to stay involved in their student's academic experience. The underlying aim in student development theory and practice is to provide an educational environment that acknowledges the multidimensional aspects of human development and strives to enhance the growth process. Students may tell us that they are coming to college to "get a degree so I can get a job." But as educators, we know that they will be tackling much more than just their course requirements. In a similar way, students may indicate that they cannot wait to get to college in order to be independent, but as Cohen (1985) notes, they are still very much a part of their family systems. Cohen suggests "if we can view students as dual citizens of both the college community and the family-of-origin, we can begin to deal more comfortably with them and their parents" (p. 7).

---

* Diane Austin updates her chapter "Orientation Activities for the Families of New Students" from the first edition.

Parents and students are often unclear about what they want their relationship to be with each other at this point—and that uncertainty can characterize what they *say* they want in their relationship with the institution. It may happen that on a given day a student will tell a college administrator not to involve her parents at all and call home the next day asking her parents to hold the college accountable for the issue at hand. Parents will call the campus demanding that the institution address their student's problems while at the same time insisting that we not reveal that they have called us, lest their student get upset. Developing programmatic interventions for parents, such as orientation activities, provides a mechanism for staff to educate parents about the separation process and the ways in which they can appropriately be a part of their student's new experience.

> "A healthy student-parent relationship is positively linked to overall college adjustment, including academic achievement and affective health, and these issues are all clearly demonstrated factors in student retention."

Because "letting go [of the parent-child relationship] is a long-term process"(Mullendore & Hatch, 2000, p. 10) that often begins on the college's doorstep, institutions should play a role in helping students and their families begin this process. Research data accumulated in recent years make a compelling case for devising orientation programs for parents of traditional-aged students, and for the spouses and partners of nontraditional students—programs that are predicated on keeping family members *attached* in a renegotiated relationship.

Many researchers have explored the role of parents in the transition to college. In reporting the results of a study on traditional-aged student perceptions of parental attachment, Kenny (1990) reminds us that "parents can be an important source of support for their college-age children" (p. 45). Langhinrichsen-Rohling, Larsen, and Jacobs (1997) discuss "… the importance of the family in the transition of children to college life" (p. 59). An article by Hickman, Bartholomae, and McKenry (2000), reports on the relationship between first-year student adjustment and parents' level of education, finding that first-generation college students are at greater risk of finding the transition difficult. Wintre and Sugar (2000), looked at the impact of students' personality and their parental relationships on the students' transition into postsecondary education, and concluded, "…the role of parents cannot be dismissed" (p. 212).

However, students' desires for independence and their perception that college means separation from parents may make maintaining the relationship difficult at times. Kenny (1987) notes that

> College student affairs staff members can be critically important in communicating revised views regarding the value of parental ties to students, parents, and other college staff. Students need reassurance that it is all right to value their parental relationships and to turn to parents as a source of support and that these are not unnatural signs of immaturity or dependence. (p. 441)

The theme in these and other studies (Henton, Lamke, Murphy, & Haynes, 1980; Kenny & Donaldson, 1992; Lapsley, Rice, & FitzGerald, 1990) is the important ongoing connection that needs to exist between adolescent and parent. A healthy student-parent relationship is positively linked to overall college adjustment, including academic achievement and affective health, and these issues are all clearly demonstrated factors in student retention.

One example of how the student-parent partnership can positively affect academic achievement comes from the University of Maryland, College Park. After designing and distributing a resource directory to the parents of incoming first-year students, staff members at the University studied the effects on academic success when parents agreed to be "referral agents" for their own students. They found that students whose parents did so were more likely to be in good academic standing than those students whose parents did not serve in this capacity (Boyd, Hunt, Hunt, Magoon, & Van Brunt, 1997).

The significant sources of support and connection for nontraditional students may include relationships with parents but are more likely to involve those with spouses or partners and may also include the students' children. Results of a study focused on wellness issues for this population show that being able to balance personal needs with the demands of others enhances feelings of wellness, while "'feeling overwhelmed or conflicted about fulfilling all my role responsibilities'" (Hybertson, Hulme, Smith, & Holton, 1992, pp. 52-53) was detrimental to wellness. The respondents in the study clearly identified environmental influences as key to their successful functioning and overwhelmingly endorsed items that related to support systems and interpersonal relationships including those with family members, friends, and neighbors. The authors concluded that "helping commuter students, especially non-traditional-age commuters, develop responsive and reliable support systems" (Hybertson et al., 1992, p. 53) was of particular importance. The implications for orientation professionals are clear. Programs designed for nontraditional students and their families must focus on strategies for maintaining relationships and renegotiating roles and responsibilities within those relationships.

Separation from the Family of Origin

Understanding the separation process is central to understanding what is going on with traditional-aged students as they move from late adolescence to early adulthood. Separation in this context refers not to physical distance but rather to a sense of autonomy in the young adult and "a reciprocal lessening of the emotional and psychological ties between parents and children" (Lopez, 1986, p. 509). The separation process is a mutual one for the adolescent and the parent, with both parties experiencing developmental changes. Separation that has successfully been achieved brings with it an ability on the part of the young adult to function independently while still maintaining an important emotional tie to his or her parents. For the parents, evidence of successful separation is their ability to develop an adult-to-adult relationship with their young adult and feel comfortable with the change in the role of "parent." Separation does *not* mean a lack of connection; in fact, where there is no interdependence between young adult and parent, healthy developmental separation has not happened.

Bloom (1980) describes five stages in adolescent-parental separation. In the first stage, both the adolescent and the parent are caught between wanting to stay in the relationship as it has been (i.e., parent and child) and wanting to move on to the next stage (i.e., adult-to-adult.) No one word better characterizes this stage (and, in many ways, the entire separation process) than "ambivalence." Adolescents and parents alike find themselves vacillating in their expressed and unexpressed feelings and actions.

The second stage occurs when the adolescent comes to terms cognitively with the idea of separation. During this stage he or she may argue with parents about almost everything in order to establish a unique sense of self. In the third stage, after the cognitive integration of separation has taken place, affective processing is addressed. Both adolescent and parent deal with nostalgia for the past, feelings of guilt and anger, and the challenge of negotiating individuation without sacrificing a loving attachment.

During the fourth stage, adolescents adopt those qualities of their parents that have perceived value to them; it is at this point that the adolescent has come to understand that being "like" one's parent does not mean being an "extension" of one's parent. Similarly, during this stage parents learn how to translate the best parts of the parenting role into the next stage of their life, while enjoying the knowledge that they have been successful parents. The final stage is marked by the ability of the young adult to develop emotionally intimate relationships outside the family and to make commitments. Both the parent and the young adult can enjoy their shared relationship, knowing that they are able to function separately while retaining a special connection.

Most student development professionals are well-versed in the developmental tasks facing traditional-aged students (e.g., wrestling with identity, exploring and navigating interpersonal relationships, developing a sense of purpose and direction). As orientation professionals, we may be less familiar with the developmental tasks facing the parents of students. However, for anyone designing programs for this population, this knowledge is crucial. Many parent orientation programs over the years have been built on the foundation of educating parents about the changes inherent in the passage from late adolescence to early adulthood but have ignored the parents' own issues (except in terms of the adolescent). Knowing that the separation process is a mutual one, we do only half the job if we view the process solely through the adolescent lens.

Research conducted by Austin and Sousa (1987) sought to obtain more information about the separation transition from the parents' perspective. They found

- No major differences existed between the response patterns of parents of commuters and parents of residents.
- Very little difference was found in the response patterns of parents of daughters and those of sons.
- Parents in general tended to endorse items that demonstrated their wish to retain control in, or over, their student's life after he entered college.
- Parents were more concerned about their students' potential for success in college if they perceived their students' academic or social abilities as average or below average.
- Parents who had not been to college demonstrated a greater sense of loss and desire for control.
- Parents who were sending their first child to college responded in similar ways to those parents who have not been to college.

This type of information provides a basis for developing programs that meet the specific needs of parents while concurrently attending to the transitional needs of students. An aspect that has not been extensively researched is what differences (if any) are manifested in the college student-parent transition process with regard to the variables of ethnicity and race. This is an area where more work must be done, as cultural factors undoubtedly play a role in the separation process. In the absence of data, orientation professionals should rely on what they have learned through survey work and program evaluations to fine-tune their programs and meet identified cultural needs.

Understanding the need for workable boundaries is also essential to professionals. Lopez (1986) speaks of the importance of boundaries in the family system and indicates that "'clear' boundaries facilitate contact between the various subsystems while permitting distinct, generationally appropriate functioning" (p. 508). For the purposes of this chapter, boundaries may be defined as observable behaviors and tangible mechanisms that provide for healthy connections without forestalling the process of individuation. When orientation staff members understand that keeping family connected to their students is important *and* that there are better and worse ways for those connections to happen, they can play a critical role in teaching family members how to stay attached appropriately.

Determining Program Goals

Institutional program goals may be quite different from the goals that parents, families, or significant others bring to us. Family members choose to attend orientation programs designed for them for reasons both expressed and unexpressed. Consistent with those issues, program participants will often tell us that they are in attendance because they want to show support for their students, are interested in learning what the college is all about, need to be (re)assured that their student's choice of the college is a good one, wish to stay actively involved in their student's life, and are looking for specific information regarding such issues as financial aid, housing, safety, and security.

Program participants are less likely to share with us that they are also attending programs because they are concerned about how attendance at the college may change their student's life *and* their life, want to try to determine what the college values, wish to retain some level of control in their student's life, and are hoping to hear that the institution cares about *them* as well as their student. The goals that participants tend to state are often more cognitively based; those they tend not to state are more often affectively based. As a result, orientation professionals have frequently devised programs that provide a lot of factual information but that never speak directly to the emotional component.

The goals for orientation professionals when working with family members come from what we know of family dynamics. These goals are first, to help establish and maintain appropriate boundaries and to provide the means for the participant to continue to be a "good partner" or "good parent" while observing the necessary boundaries, and second, to address directly the myriad ambivalent feelings being experienced by everyone—students, parents, and partners—and which are undoubtedly coloring the relationships as the time comes closer for the academic year to begin. In the case of the adolescent-parental relationship, dealing with the emotional dimension can set the stage for helping the participants gain insight into the separation process.

Family members want to know how to be the best husband, wife, father, mother, or partner to their students. Family members also know *much* more about their students than any of us at the college may ever know. It is critical that orientation staff acknowledge that the *family members* are the experts about their own students. Hatch (2000) states it this way: "Parents benefit most from orientation if their importance as mentors to students is clearly recognized" (p. 41). Preferably, that mentor role should be noted and acknowledged by the college in appropriate ways.

> "Similarly, family members should know that while it is appropriate to contact the college when they are anxious about the well-being of their students, in most cases, representatives of the institution will be legally prohibited from discussing the student's academic, disciplinary, or medical status without his or her permission."

However, we also need to share our expertise about adolescent and adult development and family dynamics in general and allow them to make applications in their own way. For example, in addressing the issue of appropriate boundaries, two types of interactions need to be kept in mind: those between the students and the family members and those between the family members and the college. Family members need to be given examples of ways to be helpful and supportive without compromising boundaries. For example, if parents are knowledgeable about the college, they can serve as referral agents for their students to the campus community. However, in providing a lot of tangible information to parents and families, it should be made clear that the aim is not to have them do for their students what the students are capable of doing for themselves. Similarly, family members should know that while it is appropriate to contact the college when they are anxious about the well-being of their students, in most cases, representatives of the institution will be legally prohibited from discussing the student's academic, disciplinary, or medical status without his or her permission.

Orientation programs can help family members explore strategies for enhancing the changing relationship with their students, but these programs also need to provide opportunities for the family members' feelings to be acknowledged and affirmed. Kenny (1987) suggests that parents need to know that it is all right to respond to their sons' or daughters' request for involvement but that they "need to recognize, however, that lending their support may mean supporting the development of interests, ideas, and values different than their own . . ." (p. 441). Orientation staff should speak to the fact that the family members in attendance may also be redirecting their interests and that part of their task in the renegotiated relationship is to help their students understand that they are not the only ones in the family who are changing. Orientation programs for family members have historically tried to make the participants aware of the demands that exist in the life of a college student so that the family can adjust *its* level of expectation for the student. At the same time, family members need to be reassured that it is appropriate for them to continue to rely on their students (within reasonable parameters). Family members and students alike can be reminded that as a member of a family there are expectations and tasks that must be fulfilled and that membership in an academic community does not absolve anyone of all other relationship responsibilities.

This theme (of the student's continued membership in the family-of-origin) might be one to integrate into various aspects of a comprehensive first-year experience program. In many ongoing orientation courses, topics such as relationship building and communication skills have frequently been included but focused specifically within the university community. It would not be difficult to expand the focus of these discussions to include the evolving relationships with one's family members. If the topic of "community" is one that is included in a syllabus, that would be an opportunity to discuss the roles and responsibilities attendant to being a member of a family unit. Finally, prior to holiday breaks or vacations, topics related to family re-integration could be introduced and strategies devised for navigating these times.

Developing and Implementing a Program

Translating all of this into an orientation program is both a challenge and an opportunity. Hundreds of colleges and universities throughout the United States have chosen to devote resources to the orientation of family members. In the most recent edition of the *National Orientation Directors Association Data Bank, 2000* (Strumpf & Wawrzynski, 2000), 89% of the 278 member institutions surveyed indicated that they have some type of orientation for parents. A small number of institutions (30) stated that they offered no parent orientation program; of these, one third were junior or community colleges. Only 3% of the institutions indicated that they had experienced a decline in parent participation in the previous one or two years, and 49% of the institutions noted that attendance had increased in that same time period. Of the institutions offering parent orientations, 62% of their incoming students had one or more family members in attendance at a parent orientation program.[1]

> *"In the most recent edition of the* National Orientation Directors Association Data Bank, 2000, *89% of the 278 member institutions surveyed indicated that they have some type of orientation for parents."*

Orientation Program Models

The definition of "orientation activities" varies from one institution to another, but for purposes of this chapter we define the term broadly, so that we can consider all contacts with family members from the point of a student's first inquiry with the college through the first year of enrollment.

Earliest interactions. During the pre-acceptance and pre-deposit periods of contact, students and their families form their opinions about institutions and try to determine if what they see and what they hear mesh with their image of "the right college." Students and family members are looking for signs that bespeak a good fit. Regardless of the tangible concerns, the often unvoiced questions center on issues of psychic safety. For the student this means, "Will I be liked here?", "Will I find people like me here?", and "Will I succeed or fail here?". For the family the questions are "Will these people value the uniqueness of my student?", "Will my student get the attention he deserves here?", and "Will my student survive here?". Given the emotional dimension attached to the decision to attend a college, it makes sense that the perceived approval and support of the family is valuable to the student.

In all the various contacts during this time period (e.g., mailings; web site content; on- and off-campus interviews; open house activities; on-campus tours; regional receptions held by staff, alumni, and families of current students), it should be remembered that *both* the students and their families are important. It should also be remembered that these earliest interactions set the tone for how families learn about their future relationship with the college. Staff members need to be clear about boundary issues and to model behavior that reinforces appropriate boundaries. Questions that students need to answer should not be directed at other family members. Likewise, family members who accompany their students to a pre-acceptance program should be acknowledged directly and permitted to voice questions.

Formal orientation programs. At the point where students indicate a clear commitment to attend the college, the institution's relationship with them takes on a new tone. The process of bringing the students into the college community as its newest members begins in earnest, and rare is the week in the few months prior to enrollment that a mailing, visit, or phone call from a college office or representative does not occur. When all of these interactions are coupled with participation in the college's formal student orientation program, it is quite likely that the transition process from the previous educational or work experience to the college environment is made smoother. The relationship between the institution and the new students has become less uni-dimensional and has begun to develop an intangible, emotional aspect. A sense of shared purpose and of affiliation has started to emerge. The new students begin to learn the language (i.e., both "academic-speak" and the specific college's own jargon) spoken by the college community members, and they pick up on the mores and nuances of the community.

Extending an invitation to an orientation program designed expressly for family members sends a clear message to them that they have not been forgotten. To be inclusive, promotional materials need to be sensitive to the different cultural backgrounds of families and students. The program content and manner of delivery communicate volumes about the way the college regards the family members of its students and about the type of ongoing relationship that can be anticipated throughout the students' experience at the college.

In developing a family orientation program, the two major considerations are structure and content. Regarding structure, questions that need to be answered include the following:

♦ Will the program run in conjunction with the students' programs, as a separate entity, or will they intersect at some points?
♦ Will the program be offered during the summer, just before the start of classes or after classes start?
♦ Will the program run on weekdays, evenings, or weekends?
♦ How long will the program be—a half day or one, two, or three full days?
♦ Will the program be facilitated by professional staff, student staff, faculty, family members of current students, or a combination thereof?
♦ Will participants be charged a fee, and if so, how much will it be?
♦ How will the program be evaluated?

The answers to these questions need to reflect the culture, parameters, and demographics of the given college as well as complement the delivery model of the students' orientation programs.

The *NODA Data Bank* (Strumpf & Wawryznski, 2000) indicates that of the institutions surveyed, approximately 69% of the family orientation programs run partially in conjunction with the students' program. The modeling implicit in this format is solid: The family members will share in some of the students' college life, but not all of it. This would also imply that programs for family members are generally, but not exclusively, held at the same time as students' programs. A college running a multi-session summer orientation program may provide the opportunity for parents to attend *any* of the sessions, not just the one in which their student participates. The same college may also provide the chance for parents who were unable to attend in the summer to join a catch-up program that might be offered on the day that students move to campus.

The content of an orientation program for family members should be designed to expand on the themes determined for the students' program. In addition to the overarching goals already outlined in this chapter, appropriate themes for a parents' program might include the following:

♦ The kinds of "predictable crises" that parents can anticipate as their students move through late adolescence in a college setting
♦ The decreasing degree of control that parents can expect to exert over their students' lives
♦ The challenges inherent in renegotiating the parenting role
♦ The ways in which parents can refocus their energies as their own lives undergo change

Themes specific to a partners' or children's program include

♦ The rhythm of the academic year and times of particular stress
♦ Time management
♦ The possible need for redefining acceptable levels of participation in each other's lives
♦ Structured ways in which family members can discuss the changes and their reactions to them
♦ The need for renegotiating the role responsibilities in the partnership and the home

Family program components that deal directly with college information and that might be included in any family orientation program include

♦ Tours of the campus
♦ Sessions about academic programs, policies, and procedures
♦ Presentations about student life concerns (e.g., the residential/commuter experience, safety and security issues, community rules and regulations, opportunities for co- and extra-curricular involvement)
♦ Sessions on the financial aspects relative to enrollment
♦ Meetings with significant campus representatives (e.g., faculty members, academic and Student development administrators, the provost, the president)
♦ Information about the institution's expanded first-year experience and its importance to the institution
♦ Information about the extended campus community and the surrounding geographic area

Program time focused on the more subtle, affective areas can take many forms. The welcoming address is a wonderful occasion to get to the emotional themes immediately and set a tone for the entire program. Skits, role plays, and videos have been developed by colleges that raise issues that might be encountered by the student during the academic experience. Family members are quick to respond to presenters who are knowledgeable *and* demonstrate a genuine interest in their experience at the institution; program participants often extrapolate about the care that will be accorded to their students by the manner in which they are treated.

Written Materials/Electronic Communications

As a component of many family orientation programs, and sometimes as a part of an ongoing orientation effort, institutions frequently publish handbooks, produce newsletters, and establish focused web sites or links. Materials written especially for family members serve as structured devices through which the institution is able to communicate directly with the families and educate them at the same time.

Handbooks designed for family members should provide a condensed version of the students' handbook, capturing the central philosophic and conceptual foundations for the college's operations. An assessment should be done to determine whether materials need to be made available in multiple languages. Key items for inclusion in a family handbook are an academic calendar, names and phone numbers of staff to whom family members can turn, a final exam schedule, and a glossary of academic terms and college-specific jargon. Policies pertaining to critical areas of student life (e.g., alcohol and other drugs) are also worthy of inclusion, especially if the institution has adopted a procedure of parental notification in the case of a policy violation. A newsletter for family members can carry similar information and also provides a mechanism for distributing articles that are developmental in nature. The articles can be timed to correspond to seasonal events (e.g., the reintegration of the resident student into the family when he or she comes home for a holiday) and to more intangible "events" (e.g., mid-semester slump, spending one's birthday away from home for the first time). Articles that feature the accomplishments of students can emphasize successful individuation by presenting evidence of students who have changed from dependent, immature adolescents to more autonomous, mature adults.

> *"The traditional parents' day or weekend is a mainstay on many campuses with a schedule that features welcoming receptions, home athletic activities, and campus tours."*

All of the information noted above can also be effectively woven into an online format through the institution's web site. For example, on the orientation page of Western Illinois University's web site, one can click on "Family Members" and find links to "Top 10 Tips for Parents," "Frequently Asked Questions," and information on the WIU's Parents and Family Association and a variety of student-related topics. From the "Alumni, Friends and Visitors" section on the University of Iowa's web site, one can reach an area designed for parents. This portion of the site includes an "Insider's Guide for UI Parents" with multiple links (e.g., academic calendar, information on the surrounding community, academic advising, financial aid), many of which contain content written specifically for parents. The page also includes information on Family Weekend, the Parents Fund for Student Support, the emergency phone system, and a link to "Parents' Time," UI's online parents' newsletter. An archive of prior issues is also available. One caution relating to accessibility stands out regarding the use of electronic means for communication with family members. Because not all family members have access to a computer and the Internet, making information available in multiple formats is recommended.

Since the publication of the first edition of this monograph, there has been a proliferation of publications directed at the parents of college students. Many colleges and universities have adopted a publication that they distribute to family members as a means of providing more extensive information about the transition process; other institutions make publications available in the bookstore for purchase. In 2000, the National Resource Center for The First-Year Experience and Students in Transition, in collaboration with the National Orientation Directors Association, published *Helping Your First-Year College Student Succeed: A Guide for Parents* (Mullendore & Hatch). This publication highlights 10 aspects of the first-year collegiate experience, including "Developing an Attitude for Success," "Building a Support Network," "Developing New Habits for a New Learning Experience," and "Identifying and Overcoming Problems." The focus is on educating parents about the issues students will face in making the transition to college and offering strategies that parents can use to help students navigate these issues.

Ongoing orientation activities. In much the same way that institutions provide programmatic support for their students *throughout* their first year, family programs can be planned that occur beyond the opening of the academic year. The traditional parents' day or weekend is a mainstay on many campuses with a schedule that features welcoming receptions, home athletic activities, and campus tours. It is becoming more common for colleges to stage events that are planned to go beyond that agenda. Often renamed as "Family Day" or "Family Weekend," these programs are aimed at *all* the significant others in the students' lives.

Complementing the activities usually built into these events (i.e., athletic competitions; program-focused meetings; opportunities to meet with faculty, staff, and administrators; receptions; meals; and student performances and exhibits) colleges are offering sessions with developmental themes that continue to respond to the task of separation for the adolescents and their parents, to the task of role renegotiation for the non-traditional students and their partners, and to the changes happening in the lives of all involved. Examples of topics for parents that could be addressed might include the following:

♦ Career change issues (presented by career development staff)
♦ Creative use of leisure time (presented by student activities staff)
♦ Dealing with aging parents (presented by social work faculty or counseling staff)
♦ Preparing for the financial changes that accompany retirement (presented by business faculty)

Summary

We who are in the business of working with students must not lose sight of the influence of the family system. Although our primary relationships will always be with students, we diminish our potential to enhance their development if we discount the relationships that can be initiated with their families. Students and family members alike should be assured that remaining integral parts in each other's lives is appropriate. Helping students establish and maintain reasonable boundaries with their families is a task that we should approach purposefully and with consistency across the institution.

Notes

[1]The *Data Bank* instrument did not ask about orientation programs for spouses/partners.

References

Austin, D. M., & Sousa, G. M. (1987). *Helping parents to understand the process of adolescent-parental separation.* (Unpublished manuscript.)

Bloom, M. V. (1980). *Adolescent-parental separation.* New York: Gardner Press, Inc.

Boyd, V. S., Hunt, P. F., Hunt, S. M., Magoon, T. M., & Van Brunt, J. E. (1997). Parents as referral agents for their first-year college students: A retention intervention. *Journal of College Student Development, 38,* 191-192.

Cohen, R. D. (1985). From in loco parentis to auxilio parentum. In R. D. Cohen (Ed.), *Working with the parents of college students.* (New Directions for Student Services No. 32) (pp. 3-14). San Francisco: Jossey-Bass.

Hatch, C. (2000). Parent and family orientation—programs supporting student success. In M. J. Fabich (Ed.), *Orientation Planning Manual.* Pullman, WA: National Orientation Directors Association.

Henton, J., Lamke, L., Murphy, C., & Haynes, L. (1980). Crisis reactions of college freshmen as a function of family support systems. *The Personnel and Guidance Journal, 58,* 509-511.

Hickman, G. P., Bartholomae, S., & McKenry, P. C. (2000). Influence of parenting styles on the adjustment and academic achievement of traditional college freshmen. *Journal of College Student Development, 41,* 41-51.

Hybertson, D., Hulme, E., Smith, W., & Holton, M.A. (1992). Wellness in non traditional-age students. *Journal of College Student Development, 33,* 50-55.

Kenny, M. E. (1987). Family ties and leaving home for college: Recent findings and implications. *Journal of College Student Personnel, 28,* 438-442.

Kenny, M. E. (1990). College seniors' perceptions of parental attachments: The value and stability of family ties. *Journal of College Student Development, 31,* 39-46.

Kenny, M. E., & Donaldson, G.A. (1992). The relationship of parental attachment and psychological separation to the adjustment of first-year women. *Journal of College Student Development, 33,* 431-438.

Langhinrichsen-Rohling, J., Larsen, A. E., & Jacobs, J. E. (1997). Retrospective reports of the family of origin environment and the transition to college. *Journal of College Student Development, 38,* 49-61.

Lapsley, D. K., Rice, K. G., & FitzGerald, D. P. (1990). Adolescent attachment, identity, and adjustment to college: Implications for the continuity of adaptation hypothesis. *Journal of College Student Development, 68,* 561-565.

Lopez, F. G. (1986). Family structure and depression: Implications for the counseling of depressed college students. *Journal of Counseling and Development, 64,* 508-511.

Mullendore, R. H., & Hatch, C. (2000). *Helping your first-year college student succeed: A guide for parents.* Columbia, SC: University of South Carolina, National Resource Center for The First-Year Experience and Students in Transition.

Strumpf, G., & Wawrzynski, M.R. (Eds.). (2000). *National Orientation Directors Association data bank.* University of Maryland: National Orientation Directors Association.

Wintre, M. G., & Sugar, L. A. (2000). Relationships with parents, personality, and the university transition. *Journal of College Student Development, 41,* 202-213.

The First-Year Seminar: Continuing Support for New Student Transitions

Mary Stuart Hunter, Tracy L. Skipper, and Carrie W. Linder*

Although the first-year seminar is not new to higher education, its evolution since the middle of the 20th century has brought national, and even international, attention to its ability to ease the college transition for incoming students and to influence positively student retention, academic performance, and a variety of other student success measures. As a course concerned with the needs and development of new students, the first-year seminar has much in common with traditional orientation. While the methods of delivery are different, both orientation and first-year seminars reflect an institution's commitment to helping its first-year students adjust to their new environment and prepare for the challenges of the collegiate culture. On some campuses, one person may lead both orientation and the first-year seminar. If not, it is important that the directors of these initiatives work together to ensure consistency of messages, reinforce important content presented to students, and smooth the transition for new students as much as possible.

The first-year seminar is flexible and, therefore, allows an institution to create and maintain a course that speaks to its unique mission and to the particular needs of its incoming students. While first-year seminars vary significantly from one institution to another, the vast majority can be classified as one of the following types: extended orientation seminars, academic seminars with common content across all sections, academic seminars on various topics across sections, professional or discipline-linked seminars, or basic study skills seminars (National Resource Center for The First-Year Experience and Students in Transition, 2000). Occasionally, a first-year seminar combines elements from two or more of the above mentioned seminar types and cannot be easily placed into any one of these categories.

The extended orientation seminar, sometimes referred to as a student success course, continues to be the most frequently reported type of first-year seminar (National Resource Center, 2000) and is the seminar type most reflective of traditional activities, but the authors of this chapter have chosen to discuss first-year seminars in general rather than isolate the extended orientation type. At their core, all first-year seminars, regardless of content and structure, are student success courses. Some may focus on academic skills, critical thinking, problem solving, or introduction to the major, while others may emphasize time management, adjustment to social pressures, or career development. Each seminar, however, strives to enhance student growth and development in one way or another. This, coupled with the knowledge that academic seminars are on the rise and that seminars in general are incorporating more skills development into their curricula, led us to broaden the focus of our discussion in the second edition of this monograph.

---

*The authors would like to acknowledge the important contribution of Betsy O. Barefoot and John N. Gardner who developed a chapter on this topic for the first edition of this monograph. We have used the framework they established in shaping the content of this chapter.

Our intention in this chapter is to show that the first-year seminar is a logical and proven method of extending orientation. We will discuss the history and development of the first-year seminar, its relationship to traditional orientation programs, its foundation in student development theory, and its current status in the United States. We will then discuss positive outcomes associated with first-year seminar participation and offer a number of guidelines and considerations for starting and maintaining a first-year seminar.

Antecedents of the Contemporary First-Year Seminar

College seminars for new students have their origins in the earliest American college, Harvard College, which was founded to "train the schoolmasters, the divines, the rulers, the cultured ornaments of society—the men who would spell the difference between civilization and barbarism" (Rudolph, 1962/1990, p. 6). Over the years, as increasing numbers of students attended college, higher education became more inclusive and accessible to larger numbers of people. At the same time, the close bond between students and teachers in the college environment evolved, by necessity, to a much less personal and individualized teaching and learning relationship. By the late 1800s, institutions began seeing a need for a more intentional effort to help students succeed as college students. Johns Hopkins University formed a system of faculty advisers in 1877, and a board of first-year advisers was in existence at Harvard University in 1889 (Gordon, 1989). These examples of early institutional efforts to address the needs of new students outside the realm of classroom academic engagement were antecedents to the current first-year seminar.

Prior to World War II, faculty had primary responsibility for virtually all facets of student life from orientation, or whatever passed as orientation, to graduation. Since that time, faculty roles have become increasingly specialized within disciplines, and faculty rewards have been linked almost exclusively to discipline-based research, scholarship, and teaching. Gradually, and all too willingly, many faculty have relinquished any involvement in or responsibility for out-of-class activities. During this same period, the student affairs profession began its own process of professionalization and specialization, assuming more and more responsibility for student life outside the classroom. As the interests and activities of faculty and staff became more specialized, institutions became increasingly fragmented by discipline or program and by scholarly interest so that by the middle of the 20th century, there was little that brought together educators across departmental or division lines—a trend that continues on many campuses today.

"Current estimates on the prevalence of seminars for first-year students indicate that approximately 74% of the institutions in the United States have such a course."

Concurrent with this specialization and fragmentation during the first half of the 20th century, orientation courses spread throughout America. At the turn of the century, such courses existed at the University of Michigan, Boston College, and Oberlin College (Gordon 1989), and records indicate that Reed College created the first for-credit orientation course in 1922 (Fitts & Swift, 1928). In 1948, 43% of institutions responding to a survey of first-year orientation techniques indicated the existence of a required orientation course (Gordon, 1989). By 1988 when the National Center for The Study of The Freshman Year Experience conducted the first National Survey on Freshman Seminar Programs, 68.5% of institutions responding reported offering a seminar for first-year students (Fidler & Fidler, 1991). Current estimates on the prevalence of seminars for first-year students indicate that approximately 74% of the institutions in the United States have such a course (National Resource Center, 2000; Policy Center on the First Year of College, 2000).

Although higher educators despair over the various schisms that divide the campus and create a fragmented, incoherent educational experience for many students, creation of meaningful partnerships between student affairs professionals and faculty is a difficult and uncommon occurrence in American higher education. The first-year seminar is one means of bringing together these two sides of the academic "house" to share perspectives, expertise, and creative ideas on behalf of a common goal—the success of first-year students. Several publications in the last two decades of the 20th century provide evidence and support for the development and institutionalization of first-year seminars. Special attention was given to the first college year in the 1984 Report for the Study Group on the Conditions of Excellence in American Higher Education, *Involvement in Learning: Realizing the Potential of American Higher Education*. This notion of improving the higher education enterprise by directing considerable institutional resources to the first year, a practice called front-loading, provided the impetus many institutions needed to focus more intentionally on the first-year experience. The 1987 release of Chickering and Gamsen's "Seven Principles of Good Practice in Undergraduate Education" underscored practices central to many first-year seminars, thus providing support for the existence of such courses. The principles outlined by Chickering and Gamsen include contact between faculty and students, cooperation among students, active learning, time on task, prompt feedback, high expectations, and a respect for diverse talents and ways of learning.

Orientation and First-Year Seminars

As this brief history indicates, the first-year seminar evolved from an early recognition that college students needed assistance making the transition to a higher education environment. Orientation programs can claim similar historical roots as seen in Chapter 3. Yet traditional orientation and first-year seminars are neither a single intervention nor mutually exclusive. Each has its important place in an institution's strategy to aid in the student's transition to higher education. Although these structures share many goals, the settings and the focus differ. Ideally, an institution will ensure that the orientation and the first-year seminar work together to create transition experiences for students that encourage student success. Many elements of a successful transition can only be addressed in the orientation setting. Such elements include students' taking placement tests, beginning to develop a relationship with an academic adviser, and choosing appropriate courses for the first term. Other elements such as developing new friendships and learning about campus resources and facilities can be started in orientation and continued during a term-long new student seminar. And still other elements—such as involving students in the process of career development, developing and helping them apply academic success skills, and instilling in them the importance of campus involvement—are best addressed over time in a seminar setting. Thus, both programs make unique contributions to the transition experience and to student success.

Upcraft and Gardner (1989) have defined success for first-year students as making progress toward fulfilling the following educational and personal goals: developing academic and intellectual competence, establishing and maintaining interpersonal relationships, developing personal identity, deciding on a career and lifestyle, maintaining personal health and wellness, and developing an integrated philosophy of life. Together, orientation and the first-year seminar are more likely to succeed in helping students achieve these goals. The specific contributions first-year seminars bring to this synergistic relationship are discussed below.

Joining Theory and Practice in First-Year Seminars

Not all first-year seminars are created after careful consideration of student development research and theory. In fact, many of today's first-year seminars have evolved from courses initiated before any substantial student development research was conducted (Barefoot & Gardner, 1993). But while these seminars may have been shaped without the benefit of student growth and development theory, surely course content at the time of inception was a reflection of perceived student needs—a guiding principle of today's student development theories. Even with the information available today, it is unlikely that all seminars are designed with theory in mind. But like those seminars created in the early 20th century, today's seminars are grounded, whether intentionally or merely intuitively, in philosophies supported by student development theory.

Theories such as those proposed by Sanford (1966), Chickering (1969), Astin (1984), Tinto (1987), and Chickering and Reisser (1993) are examples of the ideas intentionally and unintentionally shaping first-year seminars. These theories suggest that students develop intellectually, socially, and emotionally and that their development is contingent on support from others and their level of involvement and integration within the campus community. The first-year seminar, with its small class size and attention to individual student needs, is a likely and appropriate setting for aiding students in their development and encouraging on-going campus involvement.

Chickering (1969), and later Chickering and Reisser (1993), suggest that there are seven emotional, social, and intellectual vectors along which students develop. Upcraft and Gardner's (1989) definition of first-year student success (noted above) is rooted in this theory. Specifically, these vectors suggest that students develop along a continuum in the following areas: intellectual, physical, and interpersonal competence; recognition, acceptance, and control of emotions; interdependence and self-direction; acceptance and appreciation of differences in others; conception and acceptance of self; sense of purpose and commitment to personal interests and relationships; and integrity and a personal value system. First-year seminars often address these areas by initiating discussions and constructing course assignments on topics related to essential academic skills, health and wellness, relationships, communication skills, stress management, goal setting, time management, diversity, career exploration, and values clarification.

By asking students to think about, discuss, and reflect on these topics, the first-year seminar promotes Astin's (1984) theory that students learn best when they invest physical and psychological energy in various activities, tasks, or objects. He suggests that student learning and development are directly proportional to the quality and quantity of that investment or involvement. Involvement can be specific and short-term, such as participation in a campus event, meeting with a professor, or studying for a test, or it can be broader and ongoing, such as fitting in with the campus environment and adjusting to college-level work. The first-year seminar is capable of promoting and encouraging both specific and broad levels of investment and is often a catalyst for increased involvement past the first year of college.

> *"The first-year seminar is capable of promoting and encouraging both specific and broad levels of investment and is often a catalyst for increased involvement past the first year of college."*

Tinto (1987), in his model of student institutional departure, discusses the importance of intellectual and social development and how it relates to student involvement. He explains that student persistence requires separation from past forms of association, transition to a new environment, and incorporation into the social and intellectual communities of the institution. Tinto suggests that students, if they are to continue to graduation, must be involved, either socially or intellectually, in at least one college community. For him, such involvement is the lynch pin: "It is the daily interaction of the [student] with other members of the college in both the formal and informal academic and social domains of the college . . . that in large measure determines decisions as to staying or leaving" (1987, p. 127). The structure of the first-year seminar is conducive to the development of a community that is both intellectual and social in nature. First-year seminars often emphasize not only the necessity of college-level academic and critical thinking skills, but also the importance of self-concept, personal responsibility, and effective communication skills. In addition to these explicit intellectual and social goals, implicit goals of the course often include increasing the level of student/faculty interaction and developing student support groups and friendships among peers.

Closely related to Tinto's theories on student persistence is Sanford's (1966) theory of challenge and support. Sanford suggests that levels of challenge and support must be balanced for student development to occur and that the level of challenge students can handle depends on the level of support they are given. While many individuals on campus can offer advice and provide guidance (e.g., academic advisors, faculty mentors, student affairs professionals, counselors), membership in a supportive and inclusive community—whether social, intellectual, or a combination of both—provides students with a support network that is beyond compare. By requiring students to deal with issues openly and honestly, and by emphasizing the importance of open-mindedness and trust in community, the first-year seminar can play a key role in helping students achieve a balance between levels of challenge and support.

Clearly, student development research and theory provides educators with valuable information for intentionally creating a first-year experience that leads to greater student success. Through its small, supportive communities of first-year students and its ultimate goals of encouraging involvement and supporting academic and social integration, the first-year seminar offers institutions a suitable structure for joining theory and practice. In this chapter, we have selected for discussion those theories we find most applicable to the development of the first-year seminar. Chapter 2 of this monograph contains a more wide-ranging discussion of student development research relevant to orientation professionals.

Current First-Year Seminars in American Higher Education

In 2000, the National Resource Center for The First-Year Experience and Students in Transition at the University of South Carolina conducted its fifth triennial National Survey of First-Year Seminar Programming. The survey, sent to regionally accredited colleges and universities in the United States, provides a wealth of information about the current status and structure of first-year seminars in America. As mentioned earlier in this chapter, survey data indicate that nearly three-fourths (73.9%) of U.S. higher education institutions offer some type of seminar for first-year students; nearly half of those institutions require the course for all their incoming students (National Resource Center, 2000). The percentage of institutions offering a first-year seminar was verified that same year by a stratified random sample survey conducted electronically by the Policy Center on the First Year of College at Brevard College in which 73% of the institutions reported first-year seminars (Policy Center, 2000).

Traditionally, first-year seminars have addressed a number of topics related to the development of academic and life skills and the attainment of knowledge about the institution and higher education in general (Barefoot & Fidler, 1992). Respondents to the National Resource Center's 2000 survey were asked to list "the most important topics that comprise the content of the first-year seminar." The most frequently reported course topic was academic or study skills, followed, sequentially, by time management, personal development/self-concept, career exploration, campus resources, transition to college, diversity, academic advising/planning, personal wellness, and critical thinking (National Resource Center, 2000). Many of these echo topics recommended by Cuseo (1991). Using empirical evidence of positive student outcomes as a criterion, he identified the following seven topics as "top-priority" for the first-year seminar: (a) the meaning and value of a liberal arts education, (b) self-concept and self-esteem, (c) selection of a college major and a future career, (d) goal setting and motivation, (e) learning skills and strategies, (f) time and stress management, and (g) interpersonal relationships.

The survey also found that the majority of first-year seminars are offered for academic credit toward graduation, though the amount and type of credit vary from campus to campus. Usually, the seminar carries between one and three credits, but nearly 12% of U.S. institutions responding to the survey reported offering more than three semester or quarter hours to students completing the course. Generally, the seminar credit is applied as a general education, core requirement, or elective credit. About 80% of first-year seminars are offered for a letter grade (National Resource Center, 2000).

Moreover, first-year seminars are generally limited to no more than 20 students and are taught by faculty, student affairs professionals, campus administrators, and by undergraduate or graduate students on some campuses. Nearly one-third of institutions responding to the survey indicated first-year seminar instruction was a collaborative effort, with sections being taught by more than one instructor. Instructors are frequently provided opportunities for training and development before teaching the course, and nearly half of all institutions consider training a prerequisite for teaching the seminar (National Resource Center, 2000).

"Involvement in the first-year seminar program has been connected to increased innovation in teaching, improved attitude toward first-year students, and greater knowledge of resources available at the institution."

Survey data revealed no one prevailing administrative home for first-year seminars on U.S. campuses: They are housed in various offices, departments, and academic colleges. The largest number of institutions reported an academic college or division as the overarching structure, but this accounted for less than one-fourth of responding institutions. Seminars are also likely to be found in academic affairs offices, student affairs offices, and a variety of other offices and departments whose missions support the development and success of first-year students (National Resource Center, 2000).

While a heterogeneous grouping of students is ideal for first-year seminars (since this allows for richer in-class discussions and a greater variety of learning experiences), select student groups on some campuses may benefit from being in class with students with whom they have something in common. In these cases, first-year seminar content is often adapted to meet the unique needs of the specific group of students. Survey results indicate that special sections of the first-year seminar are most likely to be offered for students within a specific major, academically underprepared students, honors students, students in a learning community, and nontraditional students.

Outcomes of First-Year Seminars

The first-year seminar has probably been subject to more forms of systematic evaluation than any other course in American higher education (Barefoot, 2001; Cuseo, 1991). The most frequently reported outcomes associated with the seminar involve retention and academic performance. The National Resource Center has compiled two volumes (*Exploring the Evidence:*

Reporting Outcomes of First-Year Seminars) of institutional reports on the outcomes of first-year seminars that profile nearly 80 seminars (Barefoot, 1993; Barefoot, Warnock, Dickinson, Richardson, & Roberts, 1998). Fifty-eight of these reports examined the impact of the first-year seminar on retention; 46 examined its impact on academic performance, typically measured by GPA. Barefoot (2001) cautions that the quality of research designs varies widely among the institutions profiled, but clear trends regarding the two most frequently assessed variables emerge. Even when differences were not significant, the majority of the institutions examining persistence found that participants in first-year seminars were more likely to be retained than nonparticipants, a trend confirmed by a decade of research (e.g., Davis, 1992; Fidler, 1991; Fidler & Moore, 1996; Starke, Harth, & Sirianni, 2001; Strumpf & Hunt, 1993). First to second year retention rates have been a major focal point of first-year seminar assessment, but less frequently the seminar has been linked to improved graduation rates. Eight of the institutions profiled in *Exploring the Evidence* examined graduation rates, and Shanley and Witten (1990) have found a positive correlation between successful completion of a first-year seminar and persistence to graduation.

The first-year seminar is also tied to improvement in academic performance. Again, many of the institutional profiles in *Exploring the Evidence* cite higher GPAs among students who enroll in a seminar versus those who do not, and similar findings are reported by other researchers (Davis, 1992; Maisto & Tammi, 1991; Odell, 1996). Some of these institutions (see Irvine Valley College in Barefoot, 1993 and Floyd College and Massachusetts College of Liberal Arts in Barefoot et al., 1998) examined academic performance in the seminar as a predictor of academic success and persistence in college (for a more in-depth discussion of the Massachusetts College of Liberal Arts, see Hyers and Joselin, 1998).[1] Fifteen institutions profiled in *Exploring the Evidence* examined a related indicator of academic performance: hours earned. Most of these institutions found that students who enrolled in the seminar successfully completed more credit hours than students who did not take the seminar. Using a slightly different measure of academic performance, Missouri Western State College and the United States Air Force Academy found that seminar participants were also less likely to be placed on academic probation than non-participants (Barefoot, et al., 1998).[2]

The institutions included in *Exploring the Evidence* also examined a variety of other student outcomes associated with the first-year seminar course. These included

♦ Increased student satisfaction with the institution as a result of taking the seminar course
♦ Increased involvement on campus, use of campus resources, and self-reported feelings of academic and social integration on the campus among seminar participants
♦ Self-reported feelings of increased academic competence and lower stress levels
♦ Greater emphasis on academics and higher levels of engagement in learning among seminar participants versus non-participants (Barefoot, 1993; Barefoot et al., 1998)

Evidence also suggests that first-year seminars expedite academic and social integration, a finding borne out by other research on such seminars. For example, students enrolled in first-year seminars make better academic and social adjustments to college (Schwitzer, 1991; Rice, 1992), have more knowledge about institutional resources (Chapman & Reed, 1987; Fidler, 1991), and report more interactions with faculty and greater satisfaction with the quality of those interactions (Chapman & Reed, 1987; Maisto & Tammi, 1991).

While the impact of the first-year seminar on students has been most widely studied and reported, assessment of related aspects has also revealed positive results. For example, institutional reports note positive outcomes for the institution itself and for faculty teaching the seminar. Both

Baptist Bible College and Central Connecticut State University note that the resources allocated for the first-year seminar are a sound investment, given the potential return created by increased retention and graduation rates (Barefoot, et al., 1998).[3] Because they frequently cross departmental boundaries and sometimes feature interdisciplinary teaching teams, seminars may also result in productive partnerships and collegial relationships. For example, Champlain College reports that its seminar has improved the working relationships between members of its academic affairs and student affairs divisions (Barefoot, et al., 1998).[4]

The importance of the seminar as a faculty development tool is also the subject of a growing body of research. Involvement in the first-year seminar program has been connected to increased innovation in teaching, improved attitude toward first-year students, and greater knowledge of resources available at the institution. A survey of first-year seminar faculty at the University of Colorado suggests that involvement in the seminar program affects faculty in a number of ways (Wanca-Thibault, Shepherd, & Staley, 2002)[5]. Faculty members indicated that they were better able to make informal connections with others outside of their departments; they cited the personal and professional benefits of this informal networking as one of the most important advantages of teaching in the program. They expressed a greater feeling of integration into the campus and a better understanding of how various departments functioned in relation to one another. First-year seminar faculty at the University of Colorado are selected for their teaching abilities, but respondents indicated that the experience had helped them expand their classroom skills. In particular, they felt better able to relate to their students on a personal and professional level.

Perhaps, though, the most important impact of the first-year seminar on faculty participants is the extent to which student-centered teaching techniques common to the seminar transfer to discipline-based courses. Central Missouri State University reported that 79% of 81 first-year seminar instructors surveyed tried, at least once, new or innovative techniques learned in the first-year seminar in their discipline-based courses (Barefoot, 1993).[6] About half of the instructors surveyed continued to use some of those techniques in their regular courses. The University of Wyoming and Montana State University-Bozeman report similar findings, suggesting that faculty used more student-centered approaches to instruction in their regular courses after teaching a first-year seminar (Barefoot, 1993; Barefoot et al., 1998).[7] One of the reasons that the first-year seminar has such an effect on instruction is that faculty often have the opportunity (and are frequently required) to participate in training workshops in preparation to teach the course. The College of William and Mary examined the impact of such training on first-year seminar instructors, finding that those who participated in the training used a "larger, more varied group of strategies" than instructors who did not participate in training (Barefoot, et al., 1998).[8]

Fidler, Neururer-Rotholz, and Richardson (1999) also investigated whether the impact of such training went beyond the first-year seminar course to transfer to other courses taught by the instructor. Faculty reported using a greater variety of teaching techniques (47.2%), lecturing less and facilitating discussions more often (32.1%), being more interested in students' academic needs (28.3%), and modifying the content of syllabi in discipline-based courses (20.8%). Faculty also reported having met more colleagues outside of their discipline (56.7%), being more confident about their teaching abilities (33.3%), and feeling more committed to instructional excellence (33.3%). Fewer than 10% of faculty surveyed indicated that they had made no changes as a result of their experience in a first-year seminar program.

Principles for Establishing and Maintaining First-Year Seminars

By their very nature, first-year seminars, if they are to be effective and enjoy strong campuswide support, require the input and interest of both faculty and student affairs professionals (Gardner, 1986). And when student affairs professionals and faculty work together, they learn from each other and value the contributions that each make to the campus community. Faculty, who are generally unfamiliar with the body of literature and research on student characteristics

> *"Regardless of who teaches the first-year seminar, though, the initial planning for and maintenance of such a course should be accomplished by a campuswide coalition representing faculty, student affairs professionals, and students."*

and development, have the opportunity to learn and apply that new information in the first-year classroom. Student affairs professionals, conversely, can gain a clearer understanding of the academic goals of the institution and a better understanding of the classroom experience of students, enabling them to design programs that better support institutional goals and student growth and development.

As noted earlier, first-year seminars are taught on American campuses by faculty, student affairs professionals, campus administrators, and a host of other interested individuals including alumni, trustees, graduate students, and upper-level undergraduates. Many excellent first-year seminars use a team of instructors to teach the course. Regardless of who teaches the first-year seminar, though, the initial planning for and maintenance of such a course should be accomplished by a campuswide coalition representing faculty, student affairs professionals, and students. In particular, the director of the first-year seminar should work closely with the director of traditional orientation programs to ensure that the course and the orientation program work together in mutually beneficial ways, each supporting the goals of the other.

Elsewhere, Gardner (1989), Smitheram (1989), and Von Frank (1985) have discussed strategies for initiating a first-year seminar program. A few of their principles are included here, as are some strategies for maintaining a first-year seminar program.

Principles for Initiating a First-Year Seminar Program

- ◆ Find a credible proponent who will advocate the first-year seminar concept. When he or she argues for such a course, other campus leaders will rally around, listen, and follow. For student affairs professionals initiating a course, this means identifying key faculty members and academic administrators who can help shape course goals and who can help sell the course to other faculty members. Nationally recognized advocates for first-year students note that the support of the president or chief academic officer is often crucial to the successful implementation of first-year initiatives (Anttonen & Chaskes, 2002)—the first-year seminar is no exception.

- ◆ To ensure the broadest range of support for the course, create an initial planning "task force" with representation from all key sectors of the institution. For example, faculty, academic administrators, academic support professionals, student affairs professionals, and students might compose such a task force. Determine what other initiatives are being undertaken on the campus on behalf of first-year students, and be sure to include the directors of these programs on the planning team. In particular, the first-year seminar is a natural outgrowth of traditional orientation activities. Therefore, first-year seminar directors and orientation professionals should work closely together to assure that there is a logical flow from one set of activities to another.

- ◆ Identify and articulate the institutional issues or student needs that the first-year seminar is designed to improve, such as the need for more writing, better study skills, or preventive health education. Moreover, these issues should be explicitly connected to core institutional values or the institutional mission.

- On a related note, consider offering seminar sections for all types of new students including transfer students and others with specific needs (e.g., nontraditional students, undecided students, honors students). As with orientation programs, special student populations may present unique academic, cultural, and social needs to an institution that more general sections of the seminar cannot easily address.

- Widely circulate the work of the initial planning group, and any subsequent reviews. Invite feedback and criticism from your opponents. If people do not know what is being proposed or how the course is operating, rumors may proliferate. Maintaining an open and inviting stance will help defuse possible opposition. Once the proposal has been finalized, use the appropriate channels, especially faculty governance mechanisms, to have the course sanctioned or to institute changes. Educate faculty senate members in advance so that they are thoroughly informed about the proposal before it is considered on the floor of the senate.

- Propose to offer the seminar experimentally for one or two years. Agree to evaluate and then to continue offering the course only if it succeeds in achieving its objectives. Such an eminently fair and reasonable proposal will make rejection less likely and is an important strategy to meet the concerns of detractors. Particularly during this early stage, offering pilot sections of the seminar is a wise move. Start with a few sections to ensure greater quality control, evaluate those sections, disseminate the results, make whatever course modifications are indicated by the results of the evaluations, and then expand.

- As a part of the initial stages of course development, create an assessment plan linked to those issues the seminar is designed to address. To avoid unnecessary data collection or duplication of efforts, conduct a data audit (Ewell, 2001). For example, find out what information is collected and maintained on first-year students by the admissions office, financial aid, the registrar, institutional research, and the orientation program. Such information might provide important baseline data on first-year students or allow cohorts to be matched so that the impact of first-year seminars can be more easily measured.

- Develop a plan for recruiting qualified and enthusiastic instructors for the first-year seminar. Specifically, recruit instructors who are most likely to teach in ways that assure that the objectives of the seminar will be met, and provide *mandatory* preparation experiences for these instructors. Such preparation experiences might include, among other things, an introduction to student development and learning theories, a discussion of student-centered pedagogies, an introduction to campus resources, and a discussion of strategies for classroom management (Hunter & Skipper, 1999). Instructor training programs involving faculty members, staff, and administrators are also an excellent vehicle for bridging the divides among disciplines, departments, and programs. Providing ongoing opportunities for instructors to share teaching strategies, lesson plans, and assignments and encouraging team-teaching are other strategies for minimizing fragmentation.

- In addition to qualified faculty and staff instructors, involve upper-level students as co-teachers or mentors. Like faculty, some experience should be required to prepare students for their co-teaching/advising roles, and the students should be compensated in some way for their time and effort (e.g., money, academic credit, free residence hall accommodations). A more in-depth discussion of using peer leaders in the first-year seminar classroom, including discussions of recruitment and selection, training and program management, is available in Hamid (2001).

♦ Before launching a first-year seminar program, ask and answer some basic questions:

- How large will the classes be? Small class sizes (15 to 20 students) ensure substantive interaction among the students and between the instructor and each student.
- How much academic credit will be assigned, and how will that credit be applied? How will the course be graded? Will students receive a letter grade, or will they take the course on a pass/fail basis? If students and other campus constituencies are to take the first-year seminar seriously, students should receive a letter grade and academic credit should apply toward graduation. Ideally, such courses should comprise 45 to 48 contact hours per semester (three semester hours). Courses with fewer contact hours limit the quantity and quality of information that can be covered.
- What will the primary focus of the course be? Ideally, the first-year seminar will integrate the academic and social aspects of college orientation through substantive academic work such as reading, writing, library work, examinations, and public presentations. Moreover, it will introduce students to higher education and the relationship of its various curricular components (i.e., liberal arts, the major, professional curricula).
- If students are not required to take the course, how will they be recruited? The course, its purposes, and positive outcomes associated with participation should be actively marketed to first-year academic advisors, parents, and students.

Strategies for Maintaining a First-Year Seminar Program

♦ Periodically call on a standing committee, representing a wide range of institutional departments and functions, to help review seminar goals and to identify new goals. Similar to the initial planning group, this structure will help maintain ongoing awareness of and enthusiasm for the seminar across the institution.

♦ Once the seminar has become established, work with an advisory committee to implement the assessment plan for the course. Members of such an advisory committee should include key stakeholders, institutional researchers, and faculty from areas such as educational research, statistics, psychology, or sociology. Such assessment efforts should move beyond measures of retention and academic performance, to include an examination of student learning outcomes.

♦ Consider integrating the first-year seminar into other curricular structures that have proven successful in increasing student learning and engagement, such as learning communities or service-learning. Link the first-year seminar with one or more other first-year courses and develop connections between or among course content for the linked courses. Incorporate service into the seminar, connecting it to course content and goals and building in significant time for reflection on that service experience.

A carefully designed first-year seminar can intentionally and successfully link in-class and out-of-class experiences into a coherent whole for the benefit of first-year students. Such a classroom experience can dramatically increase the likelihood that entering students will experience both academic and social integration—key elements of a successful transition to college life (Tinto, 1987).

Summary

Orientation programs and first-year seminars are different yet complementary interventions, each with some common and some unique abilities to facilitate successful transition experiences for college students. First-year seminars provide a setting and structure for "front-loading" significant resources in the critical first year and for implementing "good practice" in undergraduate education.

These seminars have existed for more than a century, but their dramatic growth since the mid-20th century has brought wide attention to their potential as a tool for easing the transition to college, for improving student retention, for enhancing academic performance, and for having a positive impact on other success measures. Current survey research reports indicate that approximately 74% of institutions in the United States have a first-year seminar, but these seminars vary in type and reflect specific student and institutional needs. Regardless of the type of seminar, most are designed to enhance student growth and development in an academic setting and to incorporate success skills into the curriculum.

The first-year seminar is also arguably the most systematically assessed course in the American collegiate curriculum. Assessment strategies and foci vary from campus to campus but typically address such student-centered factors as retention/persistence, academic performance, student satisfaction, student involvement on campus, and academic and social integration. Additionally, other assessment efforts focus on positive outcomes for the institution and for the participating faculty.

Specific strategies for initiating first-year seminars have proven successful on campuses of all types. These strategies include but are not limited to identifying credible proponents to advocate for the concept; involving a broad-based planning committee with representation from key sectors of the campus community; addressing institutional issues and student needs in the content development of the seminar; ensuring that the development process is an open and widely communicated process; starting small with a pilot program; including an assessment component in the program from the beginning; involving quality and enthusiastic instructors and upper-level students in course delivery; and providing instructor development opportunities for the instructional staff. Maintaining existing seminar programs also demands attention and should include the involvement of an advisory committee, ongoing assessment and distribution of the assessment results, and a continual effort to institutionalize the seminar fully by ensuring that it is central to the first-year curriculum.

The first-year seminar is a dynamic and constantly evolving course that has been in existence for more than a century. As institutions evolve and student needs and characteristics change, so must the first-year seminar. If fully embraced for its educational potential, the first-year seminar can allow institutions to ensure proactively that first-year students will adjust to their new learning environment and make successful transitions to higher education.

Notes

[1] Irvine Valley College is a two-year institution in Irvine, California, with an enrollment of 11,200 students. Floyd College, in Rome, Georgia, is also a two-year institution and has an enrollment of 2,085. Massachusetts College of Liberal Arts is a four-year institution in North Adams, Massachusetts, with an enrollment of 1,590.

[2] Missouri Western State College in St. Joseph's, Missouri is a four-year institution with an enrollment of 5,118. The United States Air Force Academy, a four-year service academy located in Colorado, has an enrollment of 4,334.

³ Baptist Bible College is a four-year institution in Springfield, Missouri, with an enrollment of 796. Located in New Britain, Connecticut State University is a four-year institution enrolling 12,252.

⁴ Champlain College is four-year institution located in Burlington, Vermont, with an enrollment of 2,521.

⁵ The University of Colorado at Colorado Springs is a four-year campus enrolling 6,617 students.

⁶ Located in Warrensburg, Central Missouri State University is a four-year institution with an enrollment of 11,282 students.

⁷ The University of Wyoming in Laramie is a four-year institution enrolling 11,743. Montana State University-Bozeman is a four-year campus with an enrollment of 11,761 students.

⁸ The College of William and Mary, located in Williamsburg, Virginia, is a four-year institution with an enrollment of 7,530.

References

Anttonen, R. G., & Chaskes, J. (2002). Advocating for first-year students: A study of the micropolitics of leadership and organizational change. *Journal of The First-Year Experience & Students in Transition, 14*(1), 81-98.

Astin, A. W. (1984). Student involvement: A developmental theory for higher education. *Journal of College Student Personnel, 25*(4), 297-308.

Barefoot, B. O. (Ed.). (1993). *Exploring the evidence: Reporting outcomes of freshman seminars* (Monograph No. 11). Columbia, SC: University of South Carolina, National Resource Center for The Freshman Year Experience.

Barefoot, B. O. (2001). First-year experience jeopardy. In R. L. Swing (Ed.), *Proving and improving: Strategies for assessing the first year of college* (Monograph No. 33) (pp. 95-98). Columbia, SC: University of South Carolina, National Resource Center for The First-Year Experience & Students in Transition.

Barefoot, B., & Fidler, P. (1992). *1991 national survey of freshman seminar programming: Helping first-year college students climb the academic ladder.* (Monograph No. 10). Columbia, SC: University of South Carolina, National Resource Center for The Freshman Year Experience.

Barefoot, B. O., & Gardner, J. N. (1993). The freshman orientation seminar: Extending the benefits of traditional orientation. In M. L. Upcraft, R. H. Mullendore, B. O. Barefoot, & D. S. Fidler (Eds.), *Designing successful transitions: A guide for orienting students to college* (Monograph No. 13) (pp. 141-153). Columbia, SC: National Resource Center for The Freshman Year Experience.

Barefoot, B. O., Warnock, C. L., Dickinson, M. P., Richardson, S. E., & Roberts, M. R. (Eds.). (1998). *Exploring the evidence: Reporting outcomes of first-year seminars, Vol. II* (Monograph No. 25). Columbia, SC: University of South Carolina, National Resource Center for The First-Year Experience and Students in Transition.

Chapman, L. C., & Reed, P. J. (1987). Evaluation of the effectiveness of a freshman orientation course. *Journal of College Student Personnel, 28*, 178-179.

Chickering, A. W. (1969). *Education and identity.* San Francisco: Jossey-Bass.

Chickering, A. W., & Gamson, Z. (1987). Seven principles for good practice in undergraduate education. *AAHE Bulletin.* Retrieved June 7, 2002 from http://www.aahe.org/bulletin/sevenprinciples1987.htm

Chickering, A. W., & Reisser, L. (1993). *Education and identity* (2nd ed.). San Francisco: Jossey-Bass.

Cuseo, J. (1991). *The freshman orientation seminar: A research-based rationale for its value, delivery, and content* (Monograph No. 4). Columbia, SC: University of South Carolina, National Resource Center for The Freshman Year Experience.

Davis, B. O., Jr. (1992). Freshman seminar: A broad spectrum of effectiveness. *Journal of The Freshman Year Experience, 4*(1), 79-94.

Ewell, P. (2001). Observations on assessing the first-year experience. In R. L. Swing (Ed.), *Proving and improving: Strategies for assessing the first college year* (Monograph No. 33) (pp. 3-5). Columbia, SC: University of South Carolina, National Resource Center for The First-Year Experience and Students in Transition.

Fidler, P. (1991). Relationship of freshman orientation seminars to sophomore return rates. *Journal of The Freshman Year Experience, 3*(1), 7-38.

Fidler, P. P., & Fidler, D. S. (1991). *First national survey on freshman seminar programs: Findings, conclusions, and recommendations* (Monograph No. 6). Columbia, SC: University of South Carolina, National Resource Center for The Freshman Year Experience.

Fidler, P. P., & Moore, P. S. (1996). A comparison of effects of campus residence and freshman seminar attendance on freshman dropout rates. *Journal of The Freshman Year Experience and Students in Transition, 8*(2), 7-16.

Fidler, P. P., Neururer-Rotholz, J., & Richardson, S. (1999). Teaching the freshman seminar: Its effectiveness in promoting faculty development. *Journal of The First-Year Experience and Students in Transition, 11*(2), 59-74.

Fitts, C. T., & Swift, F. H. (1928). The construction of orientation courses for college freshmen. *University of California Publications in Education, 1897-1929, 2*(3), 145-250.

Gardner, J. N. (1986). Student affairs and academic affairs: Bridging the gap. *Carolina View II,* 46-49.

Gardner, J. N. (1989). How to start a freshman seminar program. In M. L. Upcraft & J. N. Gardner (Eds.), *The freshman year experience: Helping students survive and succeed in college* (pp. 330-346). San Francisco: Jossey-Bass.

Gordon, V. P. (1989). Origins and purposes of the freshman seminar. In M. L. Upcraft & J. N. Gardner (Eds.), *The freshman year experience: Helping students survive and succeed in college* (pp. 183-197). San Francisco: Jossey-Bass.

Hamid, S. L. (Ed.). (2001). *Peer leadership: A primer on program essentials* (Monograph No. 32). Columbia, SC: University of South Carolina, National Resource Center for The First-Year Experience and Students in Transition.

Hunter, M. S., & Skipper, T. L. (Eds). (1999). *Solid foundations: Building success for first-year seminars through instructor training and development* (Monograph No. 29). Columbia, SC: University of South Carolina, National Resource Center for The First-Year Experience and Students in Transition.

Hyers, A. D., & Joselin, M. N. (1998). The first-year seminar as a predictor of academic achievement and persistence. *Journal of The First-Year Experience and Students in Transition, 10*(1), 7-30.

Maisto, A. A., & Tammi, M. W. (1991). The effect of a content-based freshman seminar on academic and social integration. *Journal of The Freshman Year Experience, 3*(2), 29-47.

National Resource Center for The-First Year Experience and Students in Transition. (2000). [National survey of first-year seminar programming]. Unpublished data.

Odell, P. M. (1996). Avenues to success in college: A noncredit eight-week freshman seminar. *Journal of The Freshman Year Experience and Students in Transition, 8*(2), 79-92.

Policy Center on the First Year of College. (2000). [National survey of first-year curricular practices]. Unpublished data.

Rice, R. (1992). Reaction of participants to either pre-college orientation or freshman seminar courses. *Journal of The Freshman Year Experience, 4*(2), 85-100.

Rudolph, F. (1990). *The American college and university: A history.* Athens, GA: University of Georgia Press. (Original work published in 1962)

Sanford, N. (1966). *Self and society*. New York: Atherton.

Schwitzer, A. M. (1991). Adjustment outcomes of a freshman seminar: A utilization-focused approach. *Journal of College Student Development, 36*(2), 484-489.

Shanley, M., & Witten, C. (1990). University 101 freshman seminar course: A longitudinal study of persistence, retention, and graduation rates. *NASPA Journal, 27*, 344-352.

Smitheram, V. (1989). The politics of persuasion and the freshman year experience course. *Journal of The Freshman Year Experience, 1*(1), 79-95.

Starke, M. C., Harth, M., & Sirianni, F. (2001). Retention, bonding, and academic achievement: Success of a first-year seminar. *Journal of The First-Year Experience and Students in Transition, 13*(2), 7-35.

Study Group on the Conditions of Excellence in American Higher Education. (1984). *Involvement in learning: Realizing the potential of American higher education*. Washington, DC: National Institute of Education.

Strumpf, G., & Hunt, P. (1993). The effects of an orientation course on the retention and academic standing of entering freshman, controlling for the volunteer effect. *Journal of The Freshman Year Experience, 5*(1), 7-14.

Tinto, V. (1987). *Leaving college: Rethinking the causes and cures of student attrition*. Chicago: University of Chicago Press.

Upcraft, M. L., & Gardner, J. N. (1989). *The freshman year experience*. San Francisco: Jossey-Bass.

Von Frank, J. (1985). Setting up a special program for freshmen: Mastering the politics. *College Teaching, 33*(1), 21-26.

Wanca-Thibault, M., Shepherd, M., & Staley, C. (2002). Personal, professional, and political effects of teaching freshman seminar: A faculty census. *Journal of The First-Year Experience and Students in Transition, 14*(1), 23-40.

10 Years Later: The Web Phenomenon and New Student Orientation *

Gary L. Kramer

During the last decade, web technology has not only come of age but has almost single handedly revolutionized the college campus. The vital and interactive roles technology and new student orientation play in higher education have not changed much during the past 10 years. However, as a consequence of the significant advances and ubiquitous, if not pervasive, use of web technology, orientation professionals' dependence on this tool is becoming more apparent. Exposure to technology heightens student expectations and increases demands for its use and access to it.

This chapter explores web technology and the college campus. In particular, it examines the impact, strengths, challenges, and opportunities for enhancing new-student orientation's information, programs, and services through new technologies. Further, this chapter presents several institutional examples of web technology used as a tool for orienting prospective and incoming students. Finally, the chapter concludes with a discussion of the human-technology nexus, particularly as it applies to new-student orientation and its leaders.

The Web and New-Student Orientation

Web technology, historically speaking, is a result of the brilliant, sometimes awkward, but nevertheless evolutionary computing chain that began in 3000 B.C. with the Babylonian sand abacus—lines drawn in the sand with small pebbles representing amounts placed between them. A later iteration was the hand-held bead-and-wire abacus, which originated in Egypt about 500 B.C. In 1612, Napier invented logarithms. The punch-card readers that emerged in the 1890s led to the founding of IBM, and the first all-electronic computer was produced in the 1940s. Now we enjoy the sophistication and universal availability of modern computers and access to the world through the Internet.

The current link in this evolutionary chain—web technology—uses communication lines to connect the world in ways not thought possible just a few years ago. It has transformed the way people interact with each other, do business, provide services, and process information. This new technology empowers students by putting information at their disposal 24 hours a day, seven days a week. And just as important, student services providers have greater freedom to move to the forefront of helping students through meaningful personal contacts. Given the strengths of web technology, there has perhaps never been a better time for student services leaders in their quest to provide exceptional student support.

Examples in the next section demonstrate that web technology today significantly increases the timely availability of, accuracy of, and access to *information*—the lifeblood of individuals, institutions, and industry. Ten years ago access to campus orientation information was at best uneven across the higher education spectrum. While providing the timely delivery of information, web technology

---

* Some of the materials in this chapter are adapted from Kramer, G. (2002). *EDUCAUSE Center for Applied Research (ECAR) Research Bulletin*, 2002 (15).

has also connected the campus and its services in important ways for students, especially prospective and newly admitted students. In some respects, these advances have broken down the organizational barriers among student academic services and across the campus generally. Put another way, web technology has flattened organizations, putting them on a horizontal rather than a vertical plane. In the past, most campus departments have defined themselves by the latter model, thus indirectly disconnecting students from the services they need most. George Fisher, former CEO of Motorola, explains this phenomenon: "Organizations are not built to serve customers—they are built to preserve internal order. To customers, the internal structure may not only mean very little, it may serve as a barrier. Organizational charts are vertical and serving the customer is horizontal" (qtd. in Burnett, 2000). In the context of student academic services in general and new student orientation specifically, what Fisher described might look something like Figure 1.

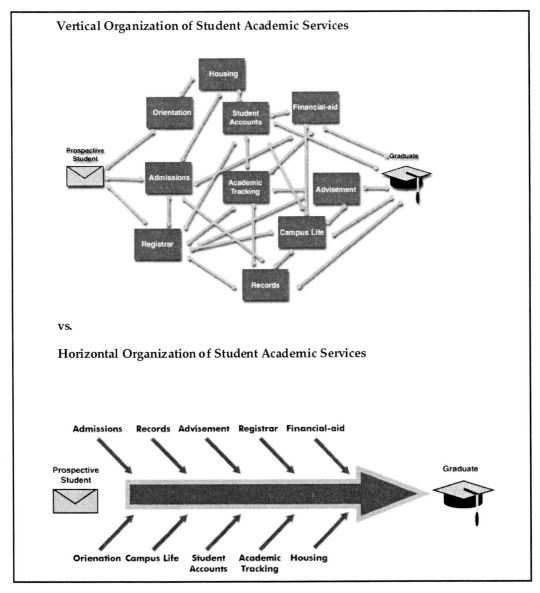

Figure 1. Vertical organization of services often creates a confusing web of pathways that students are asked to navigate.

The campus structure is not the only thing that has changed; the technology it seeks to blend into the institution has also evolved. Our constituents—students—have also changed, especially in their expectations for immediate information and service. Certainly technology has had a dramatic influence on the way all of us, including our students, do things. Perhaps because of the influence of web technology there have also been extraordinary changes in students' expectations for quality services. Levine and Cureton (1998) perceptively observe "students are bringing to higher education exactly the same consumer expectations they have for every other commercial enterprise they deal with. Their [and our] focus is on convenience, quality, service, and cost" (p. 5). Jacobsen (2000) notes that such expectations present challenges for higher education, as they do for all other business:

> We are living the revolution of the digital economy: a revolution that is transforming business, education, and society. This rapid transformation is so complete and significant that a new class of business has resulted: e-business. Today's e-business solutions break the molds of organizational identity and process ownership. E-business shifts power from service provider to customer. These forces challenge the institutional status quo while providing new opportunities to revamp business practices and improve customer service. (p. 7)

Odd as it may seem today, a decade ago use of the Internet in higher education was a discussion item (albeit an interesting one) in limited circles on campus and at selected national higher education conferences. Now campuses everywhere are busily engaged in wiring classrooms to accommodate the Internet as a means to improve the teaching-learning process. They are also encouraging students to bring laptops to the classroom to integrate technology into student-learning initiatives. Most notably in the student academic services arena, campuses are using web technology as the medium to admit, register, and advise students; provide financial aid; track academic requirements; and help students graduate. We are forever changed by the Web in how we conduct our business in higher education, teach one another, learn, and, most importantly, work with students.

Web Applications and the First Year

Using information technology to provide students timely and convenient access to important personal academic information takes the pressure off advisors and orientation leaders, who would otherwise routinely have to provide mundane and routine data for students. In the web technology environment, students can access the data themselves and then seek advice from professional staff and faculty members as needed. This section demonstrates this interrelationship between people and technology in providing services to the new student. There are many superior web-based initiatives on today's campuses; unfortunately, only a few can be presented here. Those presented, however, highlight the following transitions and information needs of prospective and first-year students: (a) selection and preparation for entry into higher education, (b) orientation to the campus, (c) first-year academic planning and registration, (d) transfer academic planning and registration, and (e) the individualization of information.

College Selection and Entry—The UC Gateway Program

Beginning in the mid-1990s, the regents of the University of California (UC) studied ways to improve the data available on precollegiate programs, which led to the building of a single, multi-campus, web-based database called UC Gateways. This database provides the platform for middle school and high school students to track their progress toward eligibility for college admission online. According to Thompson, Heisel, and Crass (2002), "Students build a multidimensional portfolio incorporating their academic work, extracurricular activities, and career and college interests into a single web-based system." (p. 240). The academic portfolio incorporates courses taken (or courses that students plan to take) and grades earned at the middle or high school level, as well as the official list of all courses that satisfy UC's admissions requirements for each high school. The activities portfolio includes information about a student's participation in UC-sponsored program activities, school-based activities, community service, and work experience. The social capital portfolio allows the students to take a series of online surveys that help them understand their personalities, interests, and learning styles (Thompson, et al., 2002). Figure 2 provides a sample page for the UC Gateways site.

Campus Orientation–The CD Interactive and Online Orientation

As an enhancement to an online orientation program, Brigham Young University (BYU) created a Virtual New Student Orientation CD that combines video, sound, special effects, and Internet links to campus services. It comes with a program brochure that provides an overview of the upcoming on-campus orientation program. From a virtual tour of the library, bookstore, and other campus facilities to a classroom experience to an integrated video preview of the cultural, athletic, and social happenings on campus, new students get a taste of what life is like at BYU before they arrive. The purpose of this virtual orientation experience is to get newly admitted students excited about their upcoming enrollment at BYU and about attending the on-campus new-student orientation program.

Figure 3 is the menu or introductory page for the interactive CD, which provides orientation options for students to explore. From this page, students can connect to six separate areas to explore academic and social life at BYU:

1. *Educational Journey.* Describes academic, spiritual, and cultural life at BYU
2. *Cool Links.* Links to BYU's web site, including pages for new students, orientation, prospective students, and a calendar of events
3. *Getting Around.* Offers a virtual tour of campus, an interactive campus map, and a link to BYU's web cam
4. *Campus Life.* Highlights student life at BYU, including information on getting involved, living on campus, and obtaining tickets for sports and other special events
5. *Academic Planning.* Connects students to the first-year registration and planning system
6. *Frequent Questions.* Provides answers to frequently asked questions broken down by categories: new student orientation, employment, tuition and fees, campus computing, and transfer students

A Web-Based First-Year Advising and Registration System

Years ago, BYU made the organizational decision to connect new student orientation with first-year advising and registration. As a result of this decision, a web-based first-year advising and registration system was created. The guiding principle behind this system was to encourage and support academic advising and registration for entering first-year students through online materials. This system helps first-year students look at the big picture of their academic career—understanding what the course requirements are, how they can be met, and when courses should be taken.

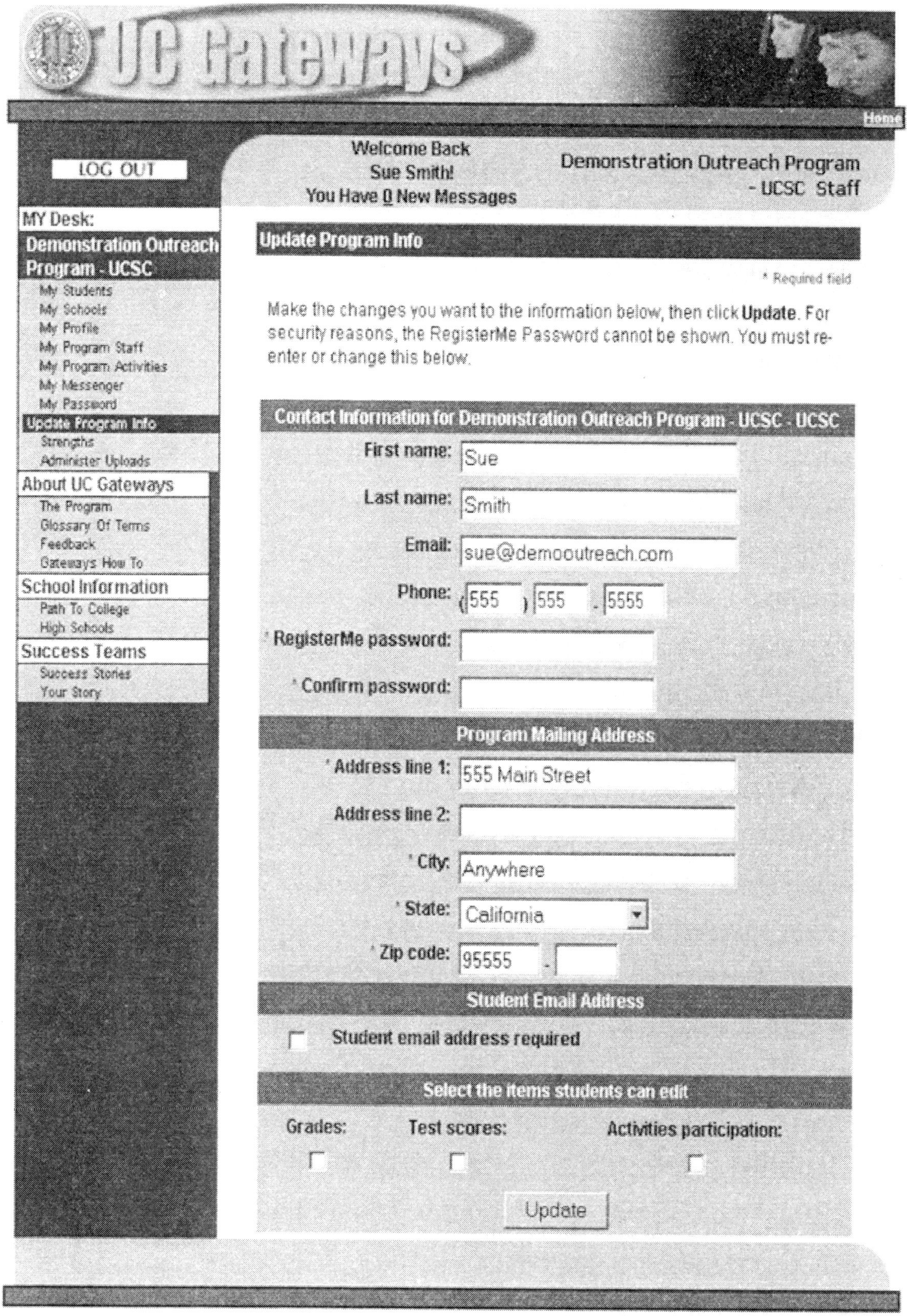

Figure 2. This sample page from the UC Gateways Program allows users to update their program information.

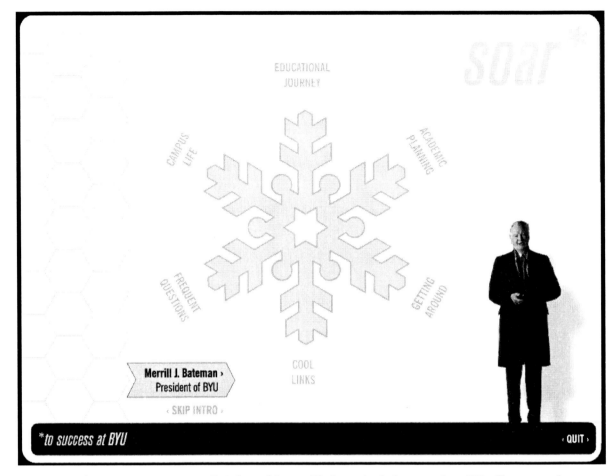

Figure 3. The gateway page on Brigham Young University's interactive CD allows students to explore all areas of college life.

With a "Freshman Resources for Planning and Registration" packet to guide them, newly admitted students begin the orientation process by logging onto BYU's student information system. Once they have logged on, first-year students immediately find an array of academic advising resources available to them, which, incidentally, are coordinated with the interactive CD described above.

The opening page of the system includes the student's biographical summary, which lists the major selected, advisement information, and the assigned registration time (see Figure 4). Links to other features include a menu of key advising sources; a five-step planning worksheet to complete the advising process and, thus, registration; an option to change majors; and a textbook reservation form (Kramer, Peterson, Webb, & Esplin, 2002).

Transfer Student Planning–Automated Transfer Evaluation

Web technology makes it possible for new and prospective transfer students to acquire course equivalency information in a timely manner and in a user-friendly environment. For new transfer students, delays in transfer course evaluations are often the result of a process that involves several offices, including admissions, registration, records, and the academic department. The delay often leaves students without vital academic information for weeks into their first semester or term. Sometimes students are left uniformed about course equivalencies

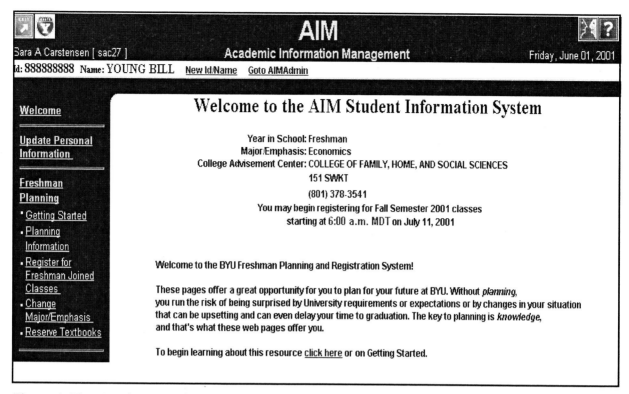

Figure 4. The Academic Information Management System at Brigham Young University allows students to do academic planning online.

until they apply for graduation, which leads to poor academic planning, courses unnecessarily taken, and even program change. Today, what used to take days or weeks (sometimes months), depending on institutional policies and procedures, requires only a matter of seconds. Enhanced by web technology, an automated transfer-evaluation system streamlines the communication of course equivalencies by routing transfer courses to a database of all past and current evaluations. Automated transfer evaluation is a welcome relief to new transfer students, allowing them to get on with the planning process and making it possible for orientation leaders to address the new transfer student's expectations, needs, and other orientation interests.

One of the premier transfer systems in higher education is Ball State University's Automated Course Transfer System (ACTS). The ACTS interactive web site permits students to enter transcript data from their current institution and receive two reports in a matter of seconds. The first report details courses accepted and the Ball State course equivalents. The second report, the degree audit, applies the transferable courses to the student's intended major and lists the courses students can take at their current school until the transfer is finalized (King, McCauley, & Shafer, 2002; McCauley, 2000).

Individualizing Information–Personalized Service Portals

The University of Buffalo is among a host of institutions that have effectively implemented web portals, the ultimate tier of personalizing the Web. The creation of "MyUB" as a personalized web portal has decreased the distance among students, faculty, and student services, and, most importantly, increased a sense of community. MyUB (see Figure 5) makes it easy for students to find the information they need by providing an easy-to-navigate, personalized,

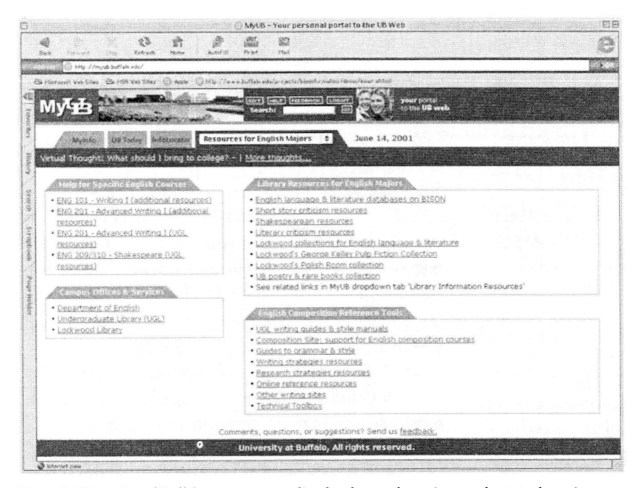

Figure 5. University of Buffalo uses a personalized web portal to orient students to the university and guide them to graduation.

and customizable portal. The portal coaches students from orientation through graduation and builds awareness of the many virtual and physical campus services. It also works as a proactive university communication tool (Wright, Gorman, & Bernstein, 2002).

The Human-Technology Nexus

Amid all of this wonderful technology, you might ask, what about the human interface, let alone the human-to-technology connection? Does human interaction matter anymore given such sophisticated technology? If so, how, where, and when should it occur? One might also ask: Given the advances in technology, could we not use technology to make the connections among the academic community, its resources and programs, and its students more seamless?

As evidenced by the past, technology will only get better, more powerful, and more viable as an enabler or tool to accomplish a variety of tasks or purposes. The challenge for orientation professionals is to get better at managing technology as an enabler, to bridge and match technology advances with equally effective student support services (see Figure 6). Thus technology becomes effective only as it is integrated into, supports, and humanizes the service environment for providers and students. As technology transforms the way we do things, so too must the providers transform themselves. Service providers' focus should be on high touch as much if not more than high tech and high effect.

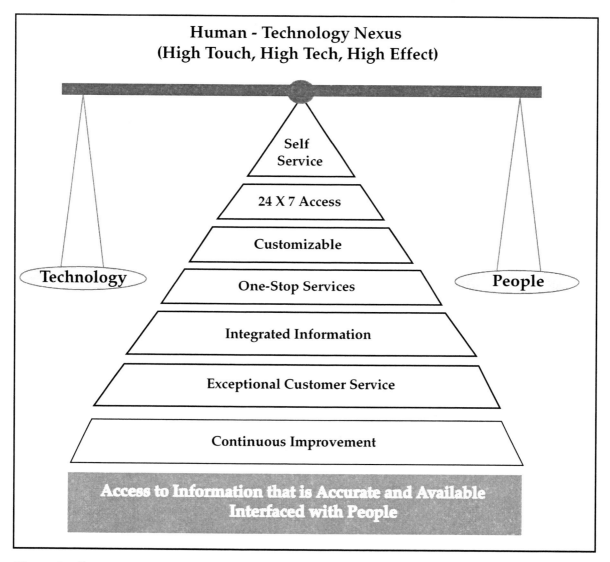

Figure 6. Effective use of technology requires a balance of high-touch personalized approaches with the efficiency of high-tech systems.

Dolence and Norris (1995) understood this dilemma as new information infrastructures were beginning to be developed in the 1990s, as the following comment makes clear:

> Higher education has invested in information technology infrastructure and in restructuring our organizations, redefining roles and responsibilities of employees, and re-engineering our systems and processes. While we have changed a great deal, American higher education has not transformed. The reasons are clear. We have not formulated a compelling vision for the learning required to succeed in the Information Age. Absent this vision, we have not reshaped structures, roles, functions, and services to address those changing needs. (p. 3)

The challenges, opportunities, connections, and possibilities we address with technology largely remain with the providers of services to solve and dictate. But how do we achieve this transformation to a human-technology nexus?

1. *Continue the conversation on the campus.* Namely, create and foster an ongoing dialogue among faculty, service providers, and administrators about using technology in effective, humanized ways. Regardless of the information technology advances on the campus, it is up to service providers to ensure that the human face of the institution is preserved. Thus the tension between information technology (high tech) and institutional goals to offer personalized services (high touch) cannot be resolved with the same thinking and practices that created them. Institutions must ask: Will the new technology add value for students or the institution? How will the appropriate human touch be integrated into the new technology? Finding an answer to these questions and others are perhaps best achieved through campus collaboration and networking.

2. *Determine essential and personalized academic information needs with key users and developers on the campus.* Anticipate needs of students, especially those needs that cannot be answered through technological advances. Most important, determine what technology can do to assist and enhance the role of the service provider in supporting student needs.

3. *Carefully and comprehensively define the roles of orientation professionals and their connection to information technology services.* Ask questions like: "What are the responsibilities of students, orientation leaders, the institution, and technology?" and "How do these roles relate to each other and, more broadly, to defined orientation outcomes for students?". Information technology can complement the institution's goal of encouraging students to be self-reliant, while at the same time freeing service providers to help students make informed, responsible decisions, and set realistic goals. (Kramer, 1996)

Summary

As leaders in orientation and related student academic services, we must embrace the technology revolution, while safeguarding our primary role as enablers of student success. As Kanter (2001) observes, our evolution as a digital society will "require a deeper emphasis on human skills that build meaningful community out of mere connections" (p. 12). And building community and integrating new students into that community are an integral part of the mission of orientation programs.

References

Burnett, D. (2000). [Slide Presentation]. Best Practices Forum, University of Delaware.

Dolence, M. G., & Norris, D. M. (1995). *Transforming higher education: A vision for learning in the 21st century.* Ann Arbor, MI: Society for College and University Planning.

Jacobsen, C. (2000). E-business: Change, challenge, and opportunity. In G. L. Kramer, & M. W. Childs (Eds.), *The "e" factor in delivering advising and student services* (NACADA Monograph Series No. 7). Manhattan, KS: National Academic Advising Association.

Kanter, R. M. (2001) *Evolve!: Succeeding in the digital culture of tomorrow.* Watertown, MA: Harvard Business School Publishing

King, D. D., Jr., McCauley, M. E., & Shafer, P. M. (2002). Web-stop shopping. In D. J. Burnett, & D. G. Oblinger (Eds.), *Innovation in student services: Planning models and blending high touch/ high effect.* Ann Arbor, MI: Society for College and University Planning.

Kramer, G. L. (1996). The human-technology nexus. In G. L. Kramer, & M. W. Childs (Eds.), *Transforming academic advising through the use of information technology* (NACADA Monograph Series No. 4). Manhattan, KS: National Academic Advising Association.

Kramer, G. L., Peterson, E. D., Webb, C., & Esplin, P. (2002). A web-based freshman advising and registration system. In D. J. Burnett and D. G. Oblinger (Eds.), *Innovation in student services: Planning models and blending high touch/high effect.* Ann Arbor, MI: Society for College and University Planning.

Levine, A., & Cureton, J. S. (1998). What we know about today's college student. *About Campus, 3*(1), 4-9.

McCauley, M. (2000). Transfer evaluation. In G. L. Kramer, & M. W. Childs (Eds.), *The "e" factor in delivering advising and student services* (NACADA Monograph Series No. 7). Manhattan, KS: National Academic Advising Association.

Thompson, J. M., Heisel, M., & Crass, L. (2002). Empowering students through portfolio management. In D. J. Burnett, & D. G. Oblinger (Eds.), *Innovation in student services: Planning models and blending high touch/high effect.* Ann Arbor, MI: Society for College and University Planning.

Wright, R. W., Gorman, J., & Bernstein, R. (2002). MyUB: A personalized service portal. In D. J. Burnett, & D. G. Oblinger (Eds.), *Innovation in student services: Planning models and blending high touch/high effect.* Ann Arbor, MI: Society for College and University Planning.

Evaluating and Assessing Orientation Programs

Richard H. Mullendore, Gary Biller, and Ralph Busby*

Chapter Fourteen

Understanding and applying national standards is paramount within any higher education program. Such standards help educators set and evaluate the goals associated with specific programs. More important, program directors must anticipate how unique institutional characteristics will influence the successful adoption of national standards and make necessary adjustments. They must also work to raise awareness of such standards within the campus community and to involve a variety of constituents in meeting those standards and in evaluating programs in relation to them. The local value of one program over another is often a very pragmatic decision involving the allocation of resources. A program, without evaluation, is left to stand on the perceived merits or deficiencies held by a local audience, and in an era of declining resources this is a very precipitous position. This chapter discusses the use of standards as an evaluation and assessment tool and examines the importance of evaluating and assessing orientation programs.

Using Standards for Self-Assessment

Throughout this monograph, chapter authors advocate the use of the Council for the Advancement of Standards in Higher Education (CAS) standards as a model for designing and implementing orientation programs. As Mullendore (1992) suggests, using the standards is a potent way to involve the entire institution in the orientation program and to legitimize its work. Moreover, "[p]utting the standards into place can . . . assist in program planning, staff development, self-study for re-accreditation, budget request justification, educat[ion] of the campus community, and political maneuverability" (Mullendore, 1992, p. 43). CAS also provides student affairs professionals with tools for assessing their work in a variety of service areas. *The CAS Self-Assessment Guides* (CAS, 2002) provide 13 specific rating scales for program self-assessment.

Implementation of CAS standards requires a functional area review (assessment) that should be conducted by a group including students, faculty, staff, and the person(s) responsible for the program. This broad base of involvement allows the implementation process to be an educational effort for other campus constituencies and increases the objectivity and credibility of the assessment.

The self-assessment guides are designed for completion by a variety of individuals, but preliminary training of those involved in the self-study is essential to a successful review process. Once all members of the self-study group have completed an individual review, differences can be identified and discussed until consensus is reached. Use of this process can be tedious due to the depth of the assessment and the reliance on collecting and documenting supporting evidence. Discrepancies between accepted national standards and the local program may require the development of an action plan aimed at correcting identified program deficiencies

---

* Ralph Busby joins Richard H. Mullendore and Gary Biller in updating "Orientation Standards, Evaluation, and Assessment" from the first edition.

and maintaining program strengths. However, institutions should also identify areas where departure from national standards is appropriate because of student characteristics, institutional type, and other contextual issues. Even when national standards are found to be in conflict with the local context, final reports developed by the self-study group "should include areas of excellence, required actions, program enhancement actions, and program action plans" (Bryan & Mullendore, 1991, p. 34).

Program Evaluation

Program review or self-assessment is a necessary first step for evaluation. The report of the self-study group establishes where the program is currently and outlines a course of action for taking the program toward a desired outcome or goal. Programs should be evaluated regularly to determine if the strategies and remedies outlined in the self-study report are moving them toward desirable outcomes. CAS (1997) recommends the use of a range of qualitative and quantitative measures "to ensure objectivity and comprehensiveness" (p. 136). Moreover, program participants and "other significant constituencies" must be the subjects of any comprehensive evaluation process (CAS, 1997, p. 136). Once the results of these evaluations have been analyzed, they should be used to inform decisions about program revisions and improvement and staff recognition (CAS, 1997).

When evaluating a program, orientation professionals need to know (a) if the services, programs, and activities offered during orientation meet identified or perceived student needs and (b) if the students who participate in orientation are satisfied with these services, programs, and activities, and what the students consider to be the strengths and weaknesses of the institution's orientation program. Orientation professionals should also determine if the needs of parents and families are being addressed appropriately. Some researchers highlight the difficulty in evaluating student satisfaction with orientation, suggesting that students often do not know what to expect from these programs. For example, Nadler and Miller (1997) note, "[Since orientation is] often presented as a vast series of somewhat interrelated events, students may not know what they expect from the experience, and may decide for themselves the value of the program only after they are well into various sessions" (p.12). Rather than negating the importance of evaluating student satisfaction or perceptions of usefulness, such comments underscore the importance of delaying or repeating program evaluation.

Which Aspects of the Program Should Be Evaluated?

Orientation professionals should understand that everything and everyone connected with the orientation program needs to be evaluated. Orientation, probably more than any other single program, involves virtually every department within the institution.

Facilities. From the moment new students and their families arrive on campus for orientation, they form lasting impressions that often influence decisions about staying at the institution. Whether or not they are asked specific questions about campus facilities, orientation participants make judgments about the institution based on those facilities. Knowing the perceptions of campus newcomers can provide valuable information about changes needed to the physical plant. Thus, questions about campus facilities and the grounds should be added to the evaluation. For example, the adequacy of the residence hall rooms and food service should be addressed for those programs requiring

"Whether or not they are asked specific questions about campus facilities, orientation participants make judgments about the institution based on those facilities."

an overnight stay; after all, many students will be living and eating on campus for the next nine months. In some cases, problems noted with housing or food service during one session can be addressed before future sessions in the same cycle.

Program components. Each component and activity of the orientation program should be evaluated "to determine participants' satisfaction with the program and to highlight concerns not being addressed" (Robinson, Burns, & Gaw, 1996, p. 65). This should include the quality of interaction with the academic adviser and whether or not the schedule of classes received was satisfactory. The timing of the program (early summer, mid-summer, or fall) and program length should be evaluated as well.

Staff. The warmth, friendliness, and helpfulness of staff and faculty are judged in the many interactions they have with new students. While evaluations of the orientation leaders (Tremblay & Nolan, 2001) and other orientation staff are essential, perceptions of staff in key offices (e.g., the registrar, financial aid, academic advising) should also be gathered. Specifically, the degree to which faculty, administrative, professional, clerical, and student staff are friendly, helpful, and knowledgeable should be evaluated.

Perceptions of faculty and staff outside orientation that are less positive may indicate areas where more training for faculty and staff about the goals and purposes of orientation are needed. Further, such evaluations point to campus constituencies with whom orientation professionals should build stronger partnerships.

Perceptions of orientation leaders may shed light on changes that need to be made in the selection and training process. Thus, participant evaluations of the orientation program can supplement the evaluations of recruitment, selection, and training conducted by orientation professionals. Finally, orientation leaders must be evaluated by the orientation professional, who should, in turn, be evaluated by orientation leaders.

Who Should Evaluate the Orientation Program?

First, and most important, the participants in orientation (i.e., students, parents, families) must be given the opportunity, and be strongly encouraged, to evaluate the program, facilities, and the staff. In addition to program participants, those who are involved in the program delivery should be provided an opportunity to evaluate orientation. Professional and clerical staff from each university division involved with orientation (e.g., admissions, financial aid, food service, housing, registrar) should evaluate the program either formally or informally.

How Should the Program Be Evaluated?

In evaluating programs, both quantitative and qualitative data can be gathered about student satisfaction with the programs, activities, staff interaction, and services offered. Because each provides us with different kinds of information and because some types of information simply cannot be quantified, Fidler and Henscheid (2001) recommend collecting both types. They suggest that quantitative data provides the best picture of understanding the outcomes associated with a program or intervention but suggest collecting qualitative data if learning "how the participant . . . understands or makes meaning of an event, activity, program, or period of time" is important (p. 17). For example, if orientation professionals want to evaluate the academic advising component of orientation, they can ask students to rate along a Likert scale how well the courses selected met their academic goals, how friendly or accessible the advisor was, or how useful the information provided was. Such ratings would represent a quantitative measure of the advising component's effectiveness (or more accurately, of students' perceptions of its effectiveness). Students might also be asked to describe what happened during their meetings with advisers. The qualitative data gathered from these free responses might supplement or explain how students rated the effectiveness of their advising appointments. These responses would also provide a picture of the kinds of things that were happening (or just as important, not happening) during the advising component—information that closed-ended survey responses might not provide.

Evaluation responses can be collected through closed (e.g., yes/no, Likert rating scale) or open-ended questions on surveys, individual interviews, or focus groups. The development of the evaluation process will differ considerably from one institution to the next, depending on the number of participants, the type of information desired, budget constraints, and the personnel available to collect and analyze data. A brief description of some evaluation techniques follows.

Surveys. Nadler (1992) suggests that survey instruments used to evaluate orientation programs should serve two functions. The first is to provide immediate feedback, so that problems identified at one session can be addressed before the next one. The evaluation instrument should also "provide a comprehensive feedback summary to everyone involved in the program planning and delivery. This feedback not only promotes continuous program development but can also enhance staff morale and cooperation" (Nadler, 1992, p. 39). In developing an evaluation instrument, questions should relate to the goals of the program or the participants. Because the program components for a parent or transfer orientation may vary significantly from those of the first-year program, each type of program needs a separate evaluation instrument. Space may be provided for open-ended comments on these forms. Some institutions prefer to ask directed questions that require written responses regarding specific program components and activities.

> "Orientation professionals may consider conducting focus groups among first-year seminar participants, asking them to reflect back on which elements of the program proved most helpful over the course of the first semester."

Evaluation forms vary considerably, but computer-scored Likert scale responses are used by many campuses. Software is available to develop evaluations that can be scanned and the results stored digitally, allowing for the manipulation of data and publication of the results in easy-to-understand formats. Another option is to develop a web-based evaluation, "which provides several new ways to acquire information from students" (Hansen, 1997, p. 34). Those who use the computer-scored forms enjoy immediate feedback and the ability to adjust problem areas between orientation sessions. Another benefit of electronic forms is the elimination of printing, postage, and data-entry costs (Hansen, 1997). Whether the survey is a paper-and-pencil questionnaire or online, program planners should pilot the instrument to ensure that questions are clear and generate the types of responses anticipated.

Interviews and focus groups. If you choose to use the interview, focus group, or another interactive method, interviewers must be trained to ensure consistency in the collection and recording of information from program participants. The benefit of the interview method is that it provides the opportunity for non-standard feedback, and the trained interviewer is keenly aware of the opportunity to record this data. Some institutions conduct phone interviews during the first semester to determine how the student is adjusting to college, what concerns he or she may have, and in retrospect, whether the orientation experience was helpful.

Like interviews, focus groups provide opportunities for rich data collection. Moreover, the interaction of focus group members frequently prompts participants to report information or impressions that they might not have considered in responding to a survey or an individual interview. Orientation professionals may consider conducting focus groups among first-year seminar participants, asking them to reflect back on which elements of the program proved most helpful over the course of the first semester.

Both interviews and focus groups can be used to follow up on questions on survey instruments, especially if orientation professionals are interested in uncovering why participants responded as they did. A disadvantage of both of these methods is that that they can be time and labor intensive.

Informal feedback. While the interview is one method of gathering qualitative data, the orientation professional should never overlook the obvious. Do participants appear to be engaged? Which sessions have the highest attendance rates? Which the lowest? What are the most commonly asked questions? Simple observation and nonverbal communication are important sources of qualitative data. The orientation professional should also be attentive to informal feedback from staff, students, parents, and families during the program.

When Should the Program Be Evaluated?

Evaluation occurs not only in a variety of ways but also during different time frames. Some institutions place evaluation forms in participants' folders at orientation. Participants are encouraged to complete and leave the forms at the program's conclusion; others are asked to mail them back to the institution. To encourage participants to respond, some institutions provide incentives such as bookstore gift certificates. Other institutions, as noted above, may seek feedback from participants some time after the orientation process.

Evaluating orientation immediately upon completion of the program is very useful for getting information that may help staff make adjustments for future sessions and acknowledge a job well done. Care should be exercised in interpreting the results, however, since the long-term impact of the program cannot yet be determined. To determine orientation effectiveness more comprehensively, research and evaluation efforts during and after the first semester and later have merit.

The timing of the evaluation may be influenced by program intentions. With each goal, a specific timetable for measurement needs to be established. Most goals can be measured immediately following orientation, while others require evaluations at longer intervals. An example of an evaluation that should take place after a longer interval might be examining the impact of orientation on retention and persistence. Studies might measure attrition from the first to second year or compare time to graduation against a national standard.

Many institutions evaluate program components on an annual basis, finding that an annual review prior to the planning of the next year's efforts is essential to program revision and improvement. However, the individual components of orientation may be evaluated at times throughout the year, without being tied to the annual review process specifically. For example, the evaluation of human resources may be an ongoing process with a formative evaluation conducted at the conclusion of the work period. For some staff members this evaluation may become part of an annual review of their work, but usually student staff members are evaluated continuously and formally upon completion of their specific responsibilities (Tremblay & Nolan, 2001). Facility evaluation, usually conducted on an annual basis, should be established as a part of the planning cycle when staff are considering the size of the audience and the type of program(s) offered. Fiscal resource evaluation is often tied into the institutional budgeting process. If fiscal resources are allocated on an annual basis, the cycle for evaluation of fiscal resources should be timed to coincide with the institutional budget planning cycle so that orientation professionals are able to justify current budget levels and request increases when needed.

Orientation staff should consider doing participant follow-up evaluation either at the middle or end of the first semester. At both of these times, new students should have had an opportunity to attend classes, take tests, make friends, join organizations, use campus services, and participate in campus activities. They should be able to remember orientation and relate that experience to their current level of comfort with and knowledge about the institution. Program evaluations at these times can and should be qualitative in nature, including personal interviews or focus groups.

How Should the Results of Evaluation Be Disseminated?

Whether participants evaluate orientation upon completion of the program or through a focus group during the first semester, it is critical that the results be compiled in a concise format for annual reports, future planning, and for dissemination within and perhaps beyond the institution. Evaluation reports are not effective if they do not receive wide review, especially by those stakeholders who have the power to influence the future course of a program.

Reporting low ratings for units involved with orientation, but over which the orientation program has no control, must be handled with diplomacy and tact in order to avoid alienating staff unnecessarily, and these results should be communicated privately.

Copies of evaluation reports, including quantitative data and participant comments, should be made available to all professional and support staff who are significantly involved in implementing the program. Because orientation involves so many constituencies within the institution, there may be a large number of people in this category. Those involved in the program are quite likely to read the material provided. Student staff should have ac-

> *"Evaluation reports are not effective if they do not receive wide review, especially by those stakeholders who have the power to influence the future course of a program."*

cess to reports and be encouraged to review them. All orientation advisory committee members (if applicable) should be given copies, and the report should be discussed in-depth with this group. Deans, vice-presidents, and presidents should also receive these reports. Follow-up meetings scheduled with upper-level administrators provide a forum to discuss the program, its success, and its needs. One way to gain the essential support of deans, vice-presidents, and presidents is to use the sharing of evaluative data as a springboard for discussion. It may also be appropriate for the members of the student affairs division (or other applicable group) or the governing board of the university to receive copies of the report.

Assessment

Thus far, this chapter has focused on evaluation of orientation programs, or the examination of participants' perceptions of the effectiveness or usefulness of the orientation program. Assessment differs in that it is more focused on outcomes. In other words, assessment asks in what ways has the orientation program affected or influenced participants or the institution. As with the design of evaluation, the CAS standards can be a useful guide for determining how well program goals were met by measuring some change in participants' attitudes or behaviors as a result of experiencing the program.

The self-assessment process discussed at the beginning of this chapter is also a useful point of departure for assessment. Reviewing the goals of the orientation program and of the division in which it is housed and examining how these goals fit within larger institutional goals are important first steps in the assessment process. The 11 goals for orientation programs outlined by CAS (1997) are useful benchmarks, but they may need some modification in order to be consistent with the mission and goals of a specific institution. For example, one of the CAS goals is to help students understand the mission of the institution. Each institution will need to articulate its own criteria for success in achieving this goal.

Student development models also provide a useful framework for program assessment. In an article on standards and outcomes assessment, Winston and Moore (1991) advocate using Lewin's (1951) model of person-environment interaction. Terenzini (1989) has identified the basic components of a student development model, focusing on knowledge, skills, attitudes and values, and behavior. Students come to a campus with a variety of development issues, and orientation professionals should examine the impact of programs on development within the parameters of the accepted model on their campuses. Assessment efforts must contain some baseline achievement such as those identified by Terenzini (1989), as well as demographic data on program participants and program specific information. This information will help orientation staff develop criteria for program assessment efforts.

As with evaluation, there is no one approach to assessment that all institutions should adopt. The characteristics of the student body, the mission of the institution, and the goals of the program are the bases for an assessment of the orientation effort. In order for a comprehensive

> "In a national study conducted by the American College Testing Program and the National Center for Higher Education Management Systems, orientation was ranked as the third most effective retention activity."

assessment to be made, a wide range of constituencies should be a part of the assessment effort. This means that admissions, the registrar, academic advising, housing, and other concerned areas need to be involved in planning and conducting the assessment. Recommendations from this group should be forwarded to the appropriate decision-making body on the campus. Feedback and discussion concerning the nature of the program should take place during formal assessment and should focus on developing or shaping a program that meets the needs of students, their families, and the institution.

By establishing a team to formulate the assessment, staff can educate team members on positive outcomes associated with orientation programs, and through this process, broaden the base of campus support for orientation programs. Blimling and Whitt (1999) note the important role orientation plays in "retention, graduation, and student learning" (p. 181) but argue that student affairs professionals must be prepared to provide evidence of these outcomes. Assessment efforts should provide the evidence needed. Programs that can demonstrate a positive impact on student development and that are consistent with the goals of the department and mission of the institution will be viewed as valuable.

One very visible way to demonstrate the importance of orientation is to determine its relationship to academic performance (grades), student retention, and persistence to graduation (Busby, Jeffcoat, & Gammel, 2001). In a national study conducted by the American College Testing Program and the National Center for Higher Education Management Systems, orientation was ranked as the third most effective retention activity (Beal & Noel, 1980). In another study, the combination of comprehensive orientation and advising activities appeared to have a positive effect on student retention to graduation (Forrest, 1982). These findings underscore Hossler and Bean's (1990) conclusion that programs designed to facilitate the student's transition from high school or from another institution are key factors in student success and essential components of enrollment management programs.

More recently, studies of student persistence cite Tinto's (1987, 1993) model of social and academic integration. Pascarella, Terenzini, and Wolfle (1986) tested "the influence of . . . a pre-college orientation program designed both to increase the student's knowledge of the institution and its traditions, and to facilitate his or her integration into the institution's social and academic systems" (p. 156) on persistence/withdrawal behavior. This longitudinal study found that attendance at orientation had a significant direct effect on the variables "social integration" and "institutional commitment." Interestingly, these two variables "had the largest direct effects on freshman year persistence of all variables in the model" (Pascarella et al., 1986, p. 169). As a result, the impact of the orientation experience was primarily indirect but substantial. Replication of these types of study on your campus may be a powerful assessment activity.

Suggested Timeline for Formal Assessment

A functional area review is recommended if CAS standards are not part of an institution's mission statement. This review would allow staff to assess compliance with established national standards as well as review the value of the orientation effort for the institution and the students. Once all program areas have been reviewed and assessed, the question of periodic review depends on the nature of the students and institutional requirements. Changes in student population and institutional mission need recognition. While it may be advisable to conduct annual reviews of evaluation data along with annual assessments, this is not always practical. However, some form of ongoing assessment activity is necessary and will be expected in the future from regional accrediting organizations.

The inability to demonstrate the relative value of an orientation program through periodic assessment will leave the program open to criticism and question. Is this program really necessary and can the institution afford it? These questions can only be answered through evaluation and assessment. A comprehensive evaluation and assessment program will allow you to answer questions before they arise and approach program development in a proactive manner.

Summary

To provide meaningful orientation experiences, staff must have at their disposal a comprehensive set of evaluation and assessment data that demonstrates the impact of the program on the participants and the institution. Orientation professionals must be able to determine which areas of evaluation in the CAS standards have priority at their own institution. Meeting the goals of the institution while contributing to the development of students will help increase the priority of the orientation program.

The establishment of comprehensive evaluation and assessment of orientation programs is one of the CAS standards. Yet developing such a tool is often overlooked or done on an "as needed" basis to support justifications for program modification. A comprehensive approach calls for an ongoing commitment to evaluation and assessment from many areas of the institution.

The comprehensive evaluation and assessment plan would make use of periodic reviews for specific areas and an overall review on an annual basis. Summative statements can be made at four- to six-year intervals. The comprehensive assessment plan can also be reviewed on an annual basis with recommendations forwarded as a part of the assessment of all programs at the institution. Without a comprehensive plan that is consistently implemented, orientation professionals have little basis for making program changes or justifying its continued existence.

References

Beal, P. E., & Noel, L. (1980). *What works in student retention?* Iowa City: American College Testing Program and National Center for Higher Education Management Systems.

Blimling, G. S., & Whitt, E. J. (1999). Using principles to improve practice. In G. S. Blimling, E. J. Whitt, & Associates (Eds.), *Good practice in student affairs: Principles to foster student learning* (pp. 179-204). San Francisco: Jossey-Bass.

Bryan, W. A., & Mullendore, R. H. (1991). Operationalizing CAS standards for program evaluation and planning. In W. A. Bryan, T. B. Winston, & T. K. Miller (Eds.), *Using professional standards in student affairs*. San Francisco: Jossey-Bass.

Busby, R. R., Jeffcoat, N. K., & Gammel, H. L. (2001, November). *Grades, graduation, and orientation: A longitudinal study of how new student programs relate to grade point averages and graduation.* Paper presented at the meeting of The National Orientation Directors Association Conference, Toronto, Canada.

Council for the Advancement of Standards (CAS) in Higher Education. (1997). *The role of student orientation programs and services.* Washington, DC: Author.

Council for the Advancement of Standards (CAS) in Higher Education. (1998). *CAS student orientation standards and guidelines: Self-assessment guide.* Washington, DC: Author.

Council for the Advancement of Standards (CAS) in Higher Education. (2002). *The role of student orientation programs and services.* Washington, DC: Author.

Fidler, D. S., & Henscheid, J. M. (2001). *Primer for research on the college student experience.* Columbia, SC: University of South Carolina, National Resource Center for The First-Year Experience and Students in Transition.

Forrest, A. (1982). *Increasing student competence and persistence: The best case for general education.* Iowa City: American College Testing Program and National Center for Advancement of Educational Practices.

Hansen, G. R. (1997). Using technology in assessment and evaluation. In C. M. Engstrom, & K. W. Krueger (Eds.), *Using technology to promote student learning: opportunities for today and tomorrow.* (pp. 31-44). San Francisco: Jossey-Bass.

Hossler, D., & Bean, J. P. (1990). *The strategic management of college enrollments.* San Francisco: Jossey-Bass.

Lewin, K. (1951). *Field theory in social science.* New York: Harper.

Mullendore, R. H. (1992). Standards-based programming in orientation. In D. P. Nadler (Ed.), *Orientation director's manual.* Statesboro, GA: National Orientation Directors Association.

Nadler, D. P. (Ed.). (1992). *Orientation director's manual.* Statesboro, GA: National Orientation Directors Association.

Nadler, D. P., & Miller, M. T. (1997). Student satisfaction with orientation: A program assessment and cultural satisfaction. *Journal of College Orientation and Transition, 5*(1), 7-14.

Pascarella, E. T., Terenzini, P. T., & Wolfle, L. M. (1986). Orientation to college and freshman year persistence/withdrawal decisions. *Journal of Higher Education, 57,* 155-174.

Robinson, D. D. G., Burns, C. F., & Gaw, K. F. (1996). The orientation program: A foundation for student learning and success. In S. C. Ender, F. B. Newton, & R. B. Caple (Eds.), *Contributing to learning: The role of student affairs* (pp. 55-68). San Francisco: Jossey-Bass.

Terenzini, P. T. (1989). Assessment with open eyes: Pitfalls in studying student outcomes. *Journal of Higher Education, 60*(6), 644-665.

Tinto, V. (1987). *Leaving college.* Chicago: University of Chicago Press.

Tinto, V. (1993). *Leaving college: Rethinking the causes and cures of student attrition* (2nd ed.). Chicago: University of Chicago Press.

Tremblay, C., & Nolan, T. V. (2001, November). *Venture beyond the boundaries: Using feedback to enhance leader performance.* Paper presented at the meeting of The National Orientation Directors Association Conference, Toronto, Canada.

Winston, R., & Moore, W. (1991). Standards and outcomes assessment: Strategies and tools. In W. A. Bryan, R. B. Winston, & T. K. Miller (Eds.), *Using professional standards in student affairs.* San Francisco: Jossey-Bass.

Suggested Readings

Astin, A. W. (1993). *What matters in college? Four critical years revisited.* San Francisco: Jossey-Bass.

Barr, M. J., & Keating, L. A. (1985). *Developing effective student services programs.* San Francisco: Jossey-Bass.

Light, R. J., & Pillemer, D. B. (1984). *Summing up the science of reviewing research.* Cambridge, MA: Harvard University Press.

Noel, L., & Saluri, D. (1983). Setting and assessing outcomes: A fresh approach. In J. E. Rouche (Ed.), *A new look at success programs.* San Francisco: Jossey-Bass.

Pace, C. R., & Friedlander, J. (1978). Approaches to evaluation: Models and perspectives. In G. R. Hanson (Ed.), *Evaluation program effectiveness.* San Francisco: Jossey-Bass.

Sims, R. R., & Sims, S. J. (1991). *Managing institutions of higher education into the 21st Century: Issues and implications.* Westport, CT: Greenwood.

Upcraft M. L., & Schuh, J. H. (1996). *Assessment in student affairs: A guide for practitioners.* San Francisco: Jossey Bass.

Wholey, J. S., Hatry, H. P., & Newcomer, K. (Eds.) (1994). *Handbook of practical program evaluation.* San Francisco: Jossey-Bass.

Reflections on the Future of Orientation

John N. Gardner and Dave A. Hansen

The profiles of student populations expected to enter higher education during the next 10 years will be influenced by the changing ethnic diversity of Americans and the disparities in intellectual and social preparation. International issues will play a significant role as changes in global leadership reposition where and how those pursuing college degrees realize their goals.

Global issues will also be intrinsically related to the degrees, programs, and services colleges and universities provide. Therefore, orientation programs need to accurately reflect the missions of institutions; accommodate the needs and interests of audiences in transition; and define a focus on student satisfaction, academic success, and persistence that mirrors these expected changes. The challenges presented by global changes and student diversity are also opportunities for colleges and universities. Ultimately, this monograph is written to help orientation professionals understand the theoretical and philosophical foundations of orientation, provide insights into expected programmatic changes, and appreciate the opportunities these changes present.

To close the monograph, we present the thoughts and reflections of two noted higher educational professionals on how orientation has influenced learning, success, and social adjustment for students in college prior to the new millennium and what students and colleges and universities will need in the future as national and global issues and priorities change. We thank them for taking the time to reflect on where orientation has been and what they predict the future will entail.—Jeanine Ward-Roof and Cathie Hatch, Editors

The Importance of Collegiate Orientation

The campuses of today are very different types of environments for students, faculty, and administrators than they once were. Designing effective transitions for students through orientation is one of the most important challenges facing American campuses. This monograph is dedicated to the proposition that effective orientation is indispensable to ensuring greater success of America's college students for the following reasons:

- The first few weeks of college are essential to student success. Research suggests that new students who participate in orientation are more likely to earn higher grades and graduate than those who do not participate.
- Orientation can serve as a critical step in making the most out of the student's investment of hopes, dreams, time, energy, and financial resources in the college experience.
- Progressive orientation programs are comprehensive, extended transitional programs that set a serious academic tone. Orientation not only helps new students make friends and learn their way around campus, but it also increases their comfort level and reduces their anxiety. Orientation provides needed information about campus resources and policies, testing, advising, class scheduling, initial registration, and often offers

187

student success sessions on such issues as wellness, safety, civility, diversity, student responsibilities, expectations, and the role of the family.

◆ Orientation can provide new students with important opportunities to develop relationships with college faculty, student affairs professionals, and administrators. Such relationships are an important ingredient in college success.

◆ An effective orientation provides an opportunity for the new student to initiate another critical relationship, that with the academic adviser, who in many cases will be a faculty member.

◆ Orientation provides new students with important academic information as well as a structural framework for connecting to admissions, advising, and registration functions through a concept of extended enrollment management. Advances in technology improve the ability of institutions to help students make these connections and the accessibility of needed resources to students studying on the campus and those at a distance.

◆ Another dimension of college success is the participation of family members in a partnership with the institution to support the new student. Orientation programs lay the groundwork for this partnership.

◆ Orientation is a mirror, a symbol, and a metaphor for what the campus represents, as well as what the institution has to offer. It is an opportunity for the institution to introduce students to the climate of the campus, unique aspects of the campus culture, and community norms.

◆ Orientation provides an opportunity to connect the admissions process to the actual campus environment, thus solidifying the concept of extended enrollment management and increasing the likelihood that new students will matriculate at the institution.

◆ Simultaneously, orientation shapes students' expectations of the particular institution and, hopefully, gives them a more realistic expectation of what lies ahead. This involves raising student expectations about the academic realities of the collegiate experience.

◆ Orientation programs have the opportunity to use current technology to connect prospective students to the campus regardless of their location, time, or circumstances as they prepare to attend college.

◆ Orientation provides a great opportunity to develop meaningful partnerships among faculty, student affairs professionals, academic administrators, and students.

Lessons Learned from the Evolution of College and University Orientation

The refinement of orientation programming has been significantly influenced by student development theory, longitudinal research, practice, changing student demographics, institutional needs, mandated legislation, academic/student affairs realignment trends, the accountability movement and resulting assessment data, and the ideas inherent in *The Student Learning Imperative* (American College Personnel Association, 1996). These influences, as listed below, also provide a glimpse of the directions in which orientation programs will evolve.

◆ College and university campuses will realize dramatic and continuing changes in the characteristics of students attending postsecondary institutions. For example, one in three students enrolled will be nonwhite. Students will be more diverse by race, ethnicity, ability, age, gender, sexual orientation, and national origin. They will be more likely to enroll part-time, take more than four years to graduate, and commute to campus. They will also likely have a much wider range of academic abilities, academic preparation, personal health and wellness, family support and stability, and learning styles.

♦ College and university administrators, faculty, and staff will shift from planning enrollments to *managing* enrollments. Increasingly limited resources, the increasing pool of potential applicants, earlier admissions deadlines, enrollment limits, and a stronger commitment to meeting the changing needs of new students will drive the move from planning to managing enrollment.

♦ Orientation programs will have to be more responsive to external mandates and include them in orientation programs, services, and publications. Such mandates include reporting campus crime statistics and meeting the requirements of various laws including the Drug Free Schools and Communities Act, the Americans with Disabilities Act, the Student Right-to-Know and Campus Security Act, and civil rights legislation.

♦ Orientation programs must reflect institutional mission and goals and be funded adequately through institutional resources and creative funding mechanisms such as participant fees, supplemental grants, and parent and family support.

♦ Orientation programs must demonstrate their impact on students. That is, assessment data must define needs, inform programs, and show an impact on such student outcomes as academic achievement, persistence to graduation, and personal and social development.

♦ More involvement of faculty in orientation programs and more partnerships between academic affairs and student affairs will continue to evolve as the whole institution communicates to new students what is expected of them and what is required to succeed. The administrative control of this partnership will move away from a separate "stand alone" program or office toward a focus on a more integrated, coherent, coordinated, and comprehensive approach to the first-college year. There is also significant probability that administrative authority and direction will be increasingly channeled through academic affairs.

♦ Access will continue to be an issue, and orientation will be extended not only beyond matriculation, but before matriculation as well. For example, "summer bridge" programs, institutes for "at-risk" students, and high school-college collaboration programs will continue to be vital links to increasing access to higher education.

♦ A renewed focus will be on students attending two-year colleges, not only to provide orientation programs that help students make a successful transition to college but also to help them transfer to four-year institutions. Transfer centers similar to the California model will continue to emerge, requiring changes in academic practices, inter-institutional faculty collaboration, curriculum development, and an ongoing commitment to support the adjustment and success of students who transfer.

Changes in Orientation Delivery—Meeting Students' Needs and Interests

Memories of orientation differ depending on the time, location, size, and type of educational institution and on the role that one played while at the college or university (as a student, family member, educator, or administrator). Yet orientation has become one of the most dynamic, rapidly changing components of students' college experience. To put this in perspective, we vividly recall the college orientation of the 1960s. Our experiences were typical of that of many senior administrators who now lead America's colleges and universities and who, unfortunately, have little contact with the highly professional and comprehensive orientation programs of today. In contrast, just four decades ago, we recall that college was primarily an experience for the White, male, Christian, middle-class student. Orientation often reflected the sexist and racist assumptions of these times. On many campuses, separate orientation sessions were held for men and women, and little if anything unique was offered for the few minority students on American campuses.

For example, John Gardner recalls attending a nominally private and non-sectarian college in which the first orientation session was held in the sanctuary of the local Baptist church. Imagine the disillusionment of the Jewish students when they were introduced to college in the sanctuary of a Christian church, after being admitted to a college described in its recruitment literature as private and non-sectarian. Even then, students rapidly learned whether or not institutions were going to deliver what they promised.

Further, orientation programs often reflected a kind of academic social Darwinism where only the fittest would and should survive. Hence, generations of college students were told by their college presidents to "look to the left and look to the right. The two students you just looked at won't be there four years from now when you graduate!" The message was clear: "It is our charge as administrators to identify those who may not have the potential to succeed."

Also, orientation programs were almost completely social, with little academic content and absolutely no contact with faculty. Contact with student affairs professionals was also limited and primarily for the purpose of making students aware of the prescriptive rules of conduct designed to promote proper morality and civility. These policies were based on the concept of *in loco parentis*, and students were warned that the rules would be rigorously enforced.

In the orientation programs of that era, there was certainly no concept of a continuing or extended orientation program beyond the beginning of classes. There were very few, if any, first-year seminars, and when they did exist, they were focused on "adjustment to college" themes with little or no academic content or rigor. The bottom line is that it may be very difficult for many of today's college administrators and faculty, because of their own experiences in the 1950s, 1960s, or 1970s, to understand what an effective, progressive orientation program should be or to have an awareness of the relationship of orientation to academic success.

Orientation: Four Decades of Change

Orientation programming must address a changing student population in response to the tremendous growth in numbers of women, ethnic minorities, adult students, and diverse student groups that colleges and universities are experiencing. As students change, so must the programs that orient them to the life of the campus. For example,

- ♦ Orientation is based on sound student development models and extensive empirical research, much of which is described in this monograph.
- ♦ Orientation is now a highly sophisticated component of the concept of enrollment management that links admissions, orientation, advising, registration, matriculation, and the process of actually starting and continuing through the collegiate academic experience.
- ♦ As a component of American higher education, orientation has been supported, since 1976, by the National Orientation Directors Association, a strong, viable professional association that provides information and support for institutional orientation services and programs as well as orientation staff.

♦ Since 1982, the concepts of extended orientation and the first-year seminar have been advocated by the University of South Carolina through its conferences on student transitions and its National Resource Center for The First-Year Experience and Students in Transition. On nearly three quarters of college campuses today, orientation is now extended beyond the first few days to the first six weeks or the entire first semester or year through first-year seminars. Substantial evidence suggests that new students who successfully complete these courses are more likely to earn higher grades, graduate, and feel more involved than those who do not enroll (Barefoot, 1993; Barefoot, Warnock, Dickinson, Richardson, & Roberts, 1998; Davis, 1992; Fidler, 1991; Fidler & Godwin, 1994; Fidler & Hunter, 1989; Fidler & Moore, 1996; Hunter & Linder, in press; Raymond & Napoli, 1998; Shanley & Witten, 1990; Simmons, 1995).

♦ The Council for the Advancement of Standards (CAS) in Higher Education provides nationally endorsed criteria to help institutions develop and assess effective orientation programs. These standards are provided in the Appendix.

♦ Orientation is now conducted by a combination of student affairs professionals, academic affairs administrators, faculty, and outstanding student orientation leaders. The student personnel professional component of that leadership team usually exercises primary responsibility for orientation.

♦ The demographic characteristics of those who participate in college orientation programs are profoundly more diverse by race, ethnicity, age, gender, and other factors that may influence college success. Each group presents a unique set of needs and challenges for the institution. Thus, orientation on many campuses is offered to a number of highly segmented, targeted, differentiated populations including family members and transfer students.

♦ As such, orientation is no longer designed to reflect sexist and racist assumptions. Rather, it now assumes that all students want to participate equally in the American dream of higher education and have equal access to first-year college opportunities. Special efforts are now made in many college orientation programs to provide focused supplementary orientation sessions and programs for under-represented students.

♦ No longer are college orientation programs the platforms for making negative predictions (with pride) about the potential failures of students. To the contrary, orientation is used as a vehicle for promoting and supporting positive outcomes for successful student learning.

♦ At many colleges, orientation is now a required experience that takes place before students arrive for the fall term. Often students who do not participate cannot be advised and registered through the normal channels.

Orientation of Today and Tomorrow: A Comprehensive Program

New student orientation programs have many variables reflective of individual campus characteristics and environments. The following reflect our thoughts on changes that are certain within orientation regardless of the type of institution.

♦ On some campuses, orientation is provided on a no-cost basis to entering students and members of their families. On many other campuses, orientation is provided on a fee basis. However, even in the instances when there is a fee, it is regarded as a "bargain." What consumer would not be willing to invest relatively few dollars, in effect, to purchase a warranty or owner's manual to learn how to make the most of this tremendously expensive investment called a college education? Ultimately, financial pressures at public and private institutions alike will influence institutions to pass more of the cost of orientation, like all other costs, on to program participants in order to become more self-supporting.

♦ More institutions will require orientation of all new students. We believe and hope this trend will ultimately permeate all sectors of American higher education—public and private, for-profit, and traditional versus virtual delivery modes.

♦ There will be even greater opportunities for student-to-student contact through the use of student orientation leaders, in part because they are cost effective *and* effective interpersonally. More important, they will be used more extensively because of the realization that they may have a more powerful influence on new student decision-making processes and role modeling than the professional educators also involved in orientation.

♦ More institutions will combine orientation with first-year seminars and with academic advising by integrating advising into the first-year seminar. In these situations, the seminar instructor could also serve as the academic adviser for students in the seminar.

♦ Technology will play a critical role in the years to come. While the computer will never replace the power of face-to-face interaction on campus, programs must be designed to provide students with maximum access to information, advising, and registration opportunities from sites throughout the world. Realizing that technology can connect people to the campus from anywhere on any given day, programs must be designed to capture the student in an optimal learning situation after he or she arrives at the institution. New student seminar courses provide this type of learning environment and should be strongly considered as the way to bring students together with key support personnel after they matriculate.

♦ Assessment of orientation programs must receive greater attention and emphasis. This will lead to further changes and refinements in orientation approaches. Effective programs will be evaluated based on the documented evidence of the needs of the student and the institution. The era of "thinking and feeling" what is right to do for the student is being replaced by local assessment data, student profile information, and research data based on personal, academic, and cultural findings.

♦ Orientation programs possibly may be incorporated into larger structures that span institutional boundaries such as undergraduate instruction and support programs, enrollment management divisions, advising centers, and university or general colleges. Such restructuring will have the consequence of moving many orientation programs further from traditional student affairs divisions in which they may have originated. It is imperative that orientation programs of the future be an integral part of the larger picture of setting a serious academic tone for students in terms of expectations, standards, and behaviors.

♦ Due to the long-term consequences of the financial challenges of contemporary higher education and the disproportionate reductions being experienced in student affairs staff, less mobility of orientation staff may be realized. As a result, the status of orientation professionals, ironically, may increase because more orientation professionals will remain in those positions longer and their seniority will increase. Simultaneously, orientation positions increasingly will be combined with other important university student support service functions such as advising, testing, and enrollment management, as well as academic affairs positions in undergraduate instruction and undergraduate university colleges.

Recommendations

This monograph has reviewed many ways in which orientation professionals are currently designing successful transition experiences for new students. As we consider the challenges facing higher education in future years, we offer the following recommendations to those leading orientation programs and to institutional policy makers whose decisions will determine the direction and effectiveness of future orientation programming.

♦ Orientation programs need to move away from the stereotypical "fun and games" approach that is based primarily on social integration. Rather, they need to develop a more serious academic tone and to stress that succeeding in college and making the most of an investment of consumer dollars is serious business indeed. The clear trend in orientation course work is to move away from addressing primarily social, personal adaptation issues to a much greater emphasis on academic orientation and introduction to the college experience. We commend and encourage this trend. Ultimately, orientation programs must raise student expectations for higher academic engagement and performance and should include some specific academic components involving, for example, readings, discussions, and faculty-student interaction.

♦ Although orientation programs need to continue acknowledging the differences of students, they need to focus especially and primarily on what students have in common. This is to say that while we commend the approach of many campuses to target unique sub-populations for special orientations, nevertheless, orientation should continue to be one of those few common core elements which students encounter to build a basis for community and bringing together all students in a common undertaking (i.e., the components of a common culture).

♦ Orientation needs to move from an optional to a required status in all higher education environments, regardless of institution type, but especially in community colleges.

♦ Ideally, extended orientation activities and concepts need to be incorporated into first-year seminars, learning communities, and summer bridge programs so as to increase the extent of student participation in extended orientation programs, in general.

♦ Colleges and universities need to communicate more directly with immediate and extended family members that they should encourage their new students to take an active part in orientation. Family members should be viewed and treated as an important support system for the student, especially during the first year at college.

♦ Faculty need strongly to encourage their student advisees to participate in the optional, extended orientation activities that are commonplace on campuses during the first few days, the first few weeks, or throughout the first year of the college experience.

♦ Institutions need to provide orientation for the transfer student as part of the larger effort to create a more "friendly" transfer student campus culture. Academic and student services units should work closely together to address transfer and support service articulation issues. For example, institutions that now offer first-year seminars should reconstitute those as "new student" seminars open to transfer students. In addition, transfer centers could provide support and programming on an extended basis.

♦ Periodically, an independent assessment should be made of the effectiveness of orientation programming by someone who is not connected with the administration of the orientation program under review. Such an assessment, based on outcome measures such as academic achievement, retention, personal development, and other variables, will provide a basis for improving orientation, as well as build greater credibility among the college community for orientation.

♦ This monograph has recognized that contemporary orientation work is based on sound theoretical assumptions. These theoretical principles, however, need to be shared more widely with the academic members of the community. Therefore, orientation professionals need to communicate to members of the academic community, especially the faculty, the philosophies and the literature base which influence their thinking. For example, if the campus offers a first-year seminar, one of the ideal contexts in which to communicate theories essential for successful instruction would be through professional development activities designed to prepare and support instructors.

♦ Obviously, not all the myriad needs of students can be addressed after they arrive on campus. Like many other aspects of improving the first-year experience, we need to initiate the orientation process during the secondary school experience. The college-school partnership movement as orchestrated by the Education Trust has made tremendous strides to increase the level of high school student motivation and preparedness for the ultimate college experience. We recommend that colleges and universities work more carefully with high schools to extend college orientation back into the high school years, or at the very least, during the senior year of high school. Perhaps the most effective way to do this would be to offer a concurrent college orientation course for high school seniors that would carry college-level credit. Admittedly, certain aspects of collegiate orientation cannot be accomplished until students actually arrive on a college campus. However, many issues can be dealt with prior to the first term, such as the acquisition of certain study skills.

♦ Technology has begun and will continue to play a significant role in the delivery of information and services. Distance education will be an important factor in the years to come. While colleges inevitably will use more and more technology in accomplishing orientation (e.g., video presentations, interactive media, computer assisted registration), it must never be forgotten that the most powerful components of orientation are the "high touch" elements that can only be provided by direct human contact.

♦ Orientation needs to be regarded by senior campus policy makers as a total campus re-sponsibility requiring a total campus commitment. It also needs to be viewed as perhaps the best partnership vehicle between academic administrators, faculty, student affairs administrators, and student leaders. Every campus should have a senior-level standing committee that serves as an advisory group to the orientation program.

♦ Given the tremendous importance of orientation in creating student satisfaction and enhancing student retention, institutions should *not* make the position of orientation director an entry level position. This merely perpetuates the historic American practice of conferring low status on those educators who deal primarily with new students. There have been enormous strides made in the orientation profession during the past two decades to increase the status and seniority of orientation professionals and we commend this trend.

♦ We encourage every post-secondary institution have at least one individual active in the National Orientation Directors Association in order to help further professionalize the campus' orientation programming.

♦ Senior institutional leaders (i.e., the chief executive officer, the chief academic officer, the chief student affairs officer, senior faculty) should be highly visible as participants in orientation. They should seize the opportunity to communicate the institutional message to new students of what is expected and required of them in terms of roles, responsibilities, and outcomes.

♦ Despite the tremendous temptation in this era of cost containment and reductions, we believe it is absolutely imperative not to reduce efforts to provide a comprehensive student orientation. The new students who are reaching campuses in increasing numbers are unique in nature, and they need and deserve a professional college orientation more than ever. We believe that there is a moral imperative to provide the most thorough and effective orientation possible to all students in order to strengthen the students' commitment to learning and increase the probability of their success.

♦ The identification, selection, and professional development support to facilitate participation of faculty members in orientation is very important. They play a key role in the introduction of the campus to the student, just as they do in the student satisfaction level with the institution. Faculty must be actively involved in the orientation program. They need to know the profile of the new student, as well as the academic regulations and requirements of the institution.

♦ Orientation programs will continue to use student-to-student contact as an effective delivery system. Students will be used in greater numbers as mentoring and peer advising initiatives become more commonplace. The composition of the student staff (paid or volunteer) must reflect the demographics of the student population in order for the students to "reach" diverse student populations and sub-groups effectively.

Accepting the Challenge

This monograph cites example after example of the exciting challenges and opportunities that face institutions of higher education in the new millennium. Campus faculty, administrators, and staff need to work with students to create a campus environment that promotes human and cultural civility, treats members of the college community equally while acknowledging differences, and creates a campus environment that encourages students to assume responsibility for their learning *and* personal development. A comprehensive, extended orientation program can and must set the tone for the campus and provide a medium to address these issues.

We believe that the goal of every educational institution should be to elicit 100% participation of students in their orientation programs to assist in new student transition. We endorse the premise that every American college student should have as a basic right the opportunity to a thorough, effective orientation. Based on the significant accumulation of evidence that a first-year seminar enhances the probability of student retention, graduation, use of student services, involvement in co-curricular activities, and other positive outcomes simultaneously, we believe that one very effective method of providing such an orientation can be

> *"We believe that the goal of every educational institution should be to elicit 100% participation of students in their orientation programs to assist in new student transition."*

through a degree-applicable, credit-bearing college course. We encourage the administration of every institution of higher education to accept this challenge as an institutional goal.

Looking to the future, as we reflect on the exciting changes that have taken place in orientation programming over the course of our lives as both undergraduate students and as educators in higher education, we conclude this reflection with optimism that the sophistication and professionalism of collegiate orientation can, must, and will continue. We expect the readership of this monograph to understand and embrace the important role that a meaningful, comprehensive orientation process plays in the academic success of new students in higher education in America. Clearly, we all have a stake in getting new students off to a good start. More important, we have an ethical and moral obligation to do so.

References

American College Personnel Association. (1996). *The student learning imperative.* Washington, DC: Author.

Barefoot, B. (Ed.). (1993). *Exploring the evidence: Reporting outcomes of freshman seminars.* (Monograph No. 11). Columbia, SC: University of South Carolina, National Resource Center for The Freshman Year Experience.

Barefoot, B., Warnock, C., Dickinson, M., Richardson, S., & Roberts, M. (1998). *Exploring the evidence: Reporting outcomes of first-year seminars, Volume II* (Monograph No. 25). Columbia, SC: University of South Carolina, National Resource Center for The First-Year Experience & Students in Transition.

Davis, B. (1992). Freshman seminar: A broad spectrum of effectiveness. *Journal of The Freshman Year Experience, 4*(1), 79-94.

Fidler, P. (1991). Relationship of freshman orientation seminars to sophomore return rates. *Journal of The Freshman Year Experience, 3*(1), 101-106.

Fidler, P., & Godwin, M. (1994). Retaining African-American students through the freshman seminar. *Journal of Developmental Education, 17*(3), 34-40.

Fidler, P., & Hunter, M. (1989). How seminars enhance student success. In M. L. Upcraft & J. N. Gardner (Eds.), *The freshman year experience: Helping students survive and succeed in college* (pp. 216-237). San Francisco: Jossey-Bass.

Fidler, P., & Moore, P. (1996). A comparison of effects of campus residence and freshman seminar attendance on freshman dropout rates. *Journal of The Freshman Year Experience & Students in Transition, 8*(2), 7-16.

Hunter, M. & Linder, C. (in press). First-year seminars. In M. L. Upcraft, J. N. Gardner, & B. O. Barefoot (Eds.), *Meeting challenges and building support: Creating a climate for first-year student success.* San Francisco: Jossey-Bass.

Raymond, L., & Napoli, A. (1998). An examination of the impact of a freshman seminar course on student academic outcomes. *Journal of Applied Research in the Community College, 6*(1), 27-34.

Shanley, M., & Witten, C. (1990). University 101 freshman seminar course: A longitudinal study of persistence, retention, and graduation rates. *NASPA Journal, 27*(4), 344-352.

Simmons, G. (1995). The effects of a freshman seminar on at-risk, under-, over-, and low achievers. *NACADA Journal, 15*(1), 8-14.

The Role of Student Orientation Programs and Services – CAS Standards Contextural Statement

Council for the Advancement of Standards in Higher Education

To understand current trends in student orientation it is helpful to view today's practice within an historical context. The history of orientation programs in the United States is virtually as old as the history of the country's higher education. Harvard College was the first to formalize a system by which experienced students assisted new students in their transition to the institution. In addition to a personalized support system, students also experienced certain rites of passage which, from today's perspective, would likely be considered hazing. Clearly the system was flawed, but it was the beginning of the formalization of orientation as a process that includes support of students as they make the transition to the higher education.

Later in the 19th century, Harvard institutionalized faculty-student contact by assigning faculty members educational and administrative responsibilities outside the classroom. One of these responsibilities was the orientation of new students. Soon other colleges were taking an interest in those problems specific to freshman students.

Increases in the number and diversity of college students in the mid-1900s posed issues that many institutions had not previously considered. Today's orientation programs have responded to these demographics, recognizing that women, people of color, and nontraditional students have clearly changed institutional agendas across the nation. These programs have evolved from simply providing individualized faculty attention to focusing on a multitude of important issues while responding to the needs of an increasingly diverse student population.

Today, most orientation programs seek to provide a clear and cogent introduction to an institution's academic community. Orientation is viewed by most as an important tool for improving student retention. Many institutions have included academic advising in their orientation programs as an impetus for active participation. Many institutions are implementing continuing orientation programs via a freshman orientation course. Because of such changes, colleges and universities are taking steps to encourage student and parent attendance by formalizing and marketing orientation programs from a clearly academic perspective.

The most important change that has occurred in orientation programs in the last decade is that orientation is now viewed as a comprehensive process rather than as a simplistic program. Schools across the country are developing ongoing orientation programs that truly address the transitional needs of students.

What trends will guide future approaches to student orientation? It is clear that retention will continue to be a major force in the development of orientation programs. Likewise, attempts to foster an environment responsive to the individual needs of students will also continue to have a profound effect on orientation programming. Very likely, funding for orientation programs will continue to be an issue of concern. Demographic changes in institutions of higher education

Appendix

and in the society at large will require institutional and programmatic accommodations. Simply maintaining current orientation programs by reacting to change will satisfy neither students, parents, or other constituents nor institutional leaders and the public in the years to come. New and creative programs must be assessed, planned, and ultimately implemented if the personal and educational needs of new and transfer students and their families are to be met.

The CAS Student Orientation Programs and Services Standards and Guidelines that follow have utility for institutions of all types and size and provide criteria to judge the quality and appropriateness of student orientation programs.

References, Readings, and Resources

National Orientation Directors Journal
National Orientation Directors Association
University of Michigan-Flint
375 University Center
Flint, MI 48502-1950

National Orientation Directors Data Bank
National Orientation Directors Association
University of Michigan-Flint
375 University Center
Flint, MI 48502-1950

Orientation Planning Manual
National Orientation Directors Association
University of Michigan-Flint
375 University Center
Flint, MI 48502-1950

STUDENT ORIENTATION *CAS* Standards and Guidelines

Part 1: MISSION

The student orientation program must develop, record, disseminate, implement, and regularly review its mission and goals. Mission statements must be consistent with the mission and goals of the institution and with the standards in this document.

The mission of the student orientation program must include . . .
♦ facilitating the transition of new students into the institution
♦ preparing new students for the institution's educational opportunities
♦ initiating the integration of new students into the intellectual, cultural, and social climate of the institution

Part 2. PROGRAM

Orientation is an ongoing process that begins when a student decides to attend a particular institution. The process should aid students in understanding the nature and purpose of the institution, their membership in the academic community, and their relationship to the intellectual, cultural, and social climate of the institution. The orientation process should include pre-enrollment, entry, and post-matriculation activities. Components may include credit and non-credit courses, comprehensive mailings, electronic communications, and campus visitations and may be administered through multiple institutional offices.

The formal education of students is purposeful, holistic, and consists of the curriculum and the co-curriculum. Student orientation programs must be (a) intentional, (b) coherent, (c) based on theories and knowledge of learning and human development, (d) reflective of developmental and demographic profiles of the student population, and (e) responsive to special needs of individuals.

Student orientation programs must promote learning and development in students by encouraging outcomes such as intellectual growth, ability to communicate effectively, realistic self-appraisal, enhanced self-esteem, clarification of values, appropriate career choices, leadership development, health and physical fitness, meaningful interpersonal relations, ability to work independently and collaboratively, social responsibility, satisfying and productive lifestyles, appreciation of aesthetic and cultural diversity, and achievement of personal goals.

The student orientation program must . . .

♦ Be based on stated goals and objectives

A comprehensive orientation program should be based on clearly defined and delineated goals and objectives that include service to both the student and the institution.

♦ Be coordinated with the relevant programs and activities of other institutional units

♦ Be available to all students new to the institution.

First-year, transfer, and entering graduate students should be served as distinct population groups with specific attention given to the special needs of sub-groups (e.g., students with disabilities, athletes, adult learners, traditionally under-represented students, honor students, and international students).

♦ Assist new students in understanding the purposes of higher education and the mission of the institution

New students should have a clear understanding of the overall purpose of higher education and how this general purpose translates to the institution they are attending. The roles, responsibilities, and expectations of faculty, staff, and students should be included.

♦ Assist new students in understanding their responsibilities within the educational setting

The student orientation program should set forth the institution's expectations of students (e.g., scholarship, integrity, conduct, financial obligations, ethical use of technology) and should provide information that clearly identifies relevant administrative policies and procedures.

♦ Provide new students with information about academic policies, procedures, requirements, and programs sufficient to make well-reasoned and well-informed choices

Class scheduling and registration processes should be explained and assistance should be provided by qualified faculty, staff, or peer academic advisors for developing educational plans.

♦ Inform new students about the availability of services and programs

The student orientation program should identify appropriate referral resources (e.g., counselors and advisors) and provide information about relevant services and programs.

♦ Assist new students in becoming familiar with the campus and local environment

The student orientation program should provide information about the physical layout of the campus, including the location and purposes of academic facilities, support services, co-curricular venues, and administrative offices. Information about personal health, safety and security should also be included.

♦ Provide intentional opportunities for new students to interact with faculty, staff, and continuing students

The student orientation program should design and facilitate opportunities for new students to discuss their expectations and perceptions of the campus and to clarify their educational goals.

♦ Provide new students with information and opportunities for self-assessment

Assist students in the selection of appropriate courses and course levels making use of placement examinations, career interest inventories, and study skills evaluations.

♦ Provide relevant orientation information and activities to the new students' primary support groups (e.g., parents, guardians, spouses, children)

Part 3. LEADERSHIP

Effective and ethical leadership is essential to the success of all organizations. The institution must appoint, position, and empower leaders within the administrative structure to accomplish stated missions. Leaders at various levels must be selected on the basis of formal education and training, relevant work experience, personal attributes, and other professional credentials. The institution must determine expectations of accountability for its leaders and fairly assess their performance.

Leaders of student orientation programs must exercise authority over resources for which they are responsible to achieve their respective missions. Leaders must articulate vision for their organization; set goals and objectives; prescribe and practice ethical behavior; recruit, select, supervise, and develop others in the organization; manage, plan, budget, and evaluate; communicate effectively; and marshal cooperative action from colleagues, employees, other institutional constituencies, and persons outside the organization. Leaders must address individual, organizational, or environmental conditions that inhibit goal achievement. Leaders must improve programs and services continuously in response to changing needs of students and institutional priorities

Part 4. ORGANIZATION and MANAGEMENT

The student orientation program must be structured purposefully and managed effectively to achieve stated goals. Evidence of appropriate structure must include current and accessible policies and procedures, written performance expectations for all employees, functional work flow graphics and organizational charts, and service delivery expectations. Evidence of effective management must include clear sources and channels of authority, effective communication practices, decision-making and conflict resolution procedures, responsiveness to changing conditions, accountability systems, and recognition and reward processes.

The student orientation program must provide channels for regular review of administrative policies and procedures.

There must be written policies and procedures regarding program delivery that are reviewed regularly.

All institutional offices involved in program delivery should be involved in the review. Coordination of the student orientation program should occur even though a number of offices may be involved in the delivery of structured activities. The size, nature, and complexity of the institution should guide the administrative scope and structure of the orientation program.

Part 5. HUMAN RESOURCES

The student orientation program must be staffed adequately by individuals qualified to accomplish its mission and goals. The student orientation program must establish procedures for staff selection, training, and evaluation; set expectations for supervision; and provide appropriate professional development opportunities.

Professional staff members must hold an earned graduate degree in a field relevant to the position description or must possess an appropriate combination of education and experience.

Degree or credential seeking interns or others in training must be qualified by enrollment in an appropriate field of study and relevant experience. These individuals must be trained and supervised adequately by professional staff members.

Student employees and volunteers must be carefully trained, supervised, and evaluated. When their knowledge and skills are not adequate for particular situations, they must refer students in need of assistance to qualified professional staff.

The student orientation program must have secretarial and technical staff adequate to accomplish its mission. Such staff must be technologically proficient, skilled in human relations and qualified to perform activities including reception duties, office equipment operation, records maintenance, and mail handling.

Salary levels and fringe benefits for staff members must be commensurate with those for comparable positions within the institution, in similar institutions, and in the relevant geographic area. Compensation for paraprofessional staff must be fair and voluntary services recognized adequately.

The student orientation program must intentionally employ a diverse staff to reflect the diversity of the institution's student population, to ensure the existence of readily identifiable role models for students and to enrich the campus community. Affirmative action must occur in hiring and promotion practices to ensure diverse staffing profiles as required by institutional policies and local, state/provincial, and federal law.

Faculty involvement in the development and delivery of the student orientation program is essential to its success. Faculty should be included as part of the overall staffing pattern.

Part 6. FINANCIAL RESOURCES

The student orientation program must have adequate funding to accomplish its mission and goals. Priorities, whether set periodically or as a result of extraordinary conditions, must be determined within the context of the stated mission, goals, and resources.

Money to underwrite expenses for the student orientation program should be allocated on a permanent basis. In additional to institutional funding through general funds, other funding sources may be considered, including state appropriations, student fees, user fees, donations, contributions, fines, concession and store sales, rentals, and dues.

Overnight programs may require students and their families to stay on campus. Although recovering room and board costs directly from participants is an acceptable practice, the student orientation program should be designed so as to impose as little financial burden on students and their families as possible.

Part 7. FACILITIES, TECHNOLOGY, and EQUIPMENT

The student orientation program must have adequate, suitably located facilities and equipment to support its mission and goals. Facilities, technology, and equipment must be in compliance with relevant federal, state, provincial, and local requirements to provide for access, health and safety.

Cooperation from within the campus community is necessary to provide appropriate facilities. Whenever possible, a single office location to house personnel and provide adequate work space should be conveniently located and suitable for its high interaction with the public.

Part 8. LEGAL RESPONSIBILITIES

Staff members must be knowledgeable about and responsive to law and regulations that relate to their respective program or service. Sources for legal obligations and limitations include constitutional, statutory, regulatory, and case law; mandatory laws and orders emanating from federal, state, provincial and local governments; and the institution through its policies.

Staff members must use reasonable and informed practices to limit the liability exposure of the institution, its officers, employees, and agents. Staff members must be informed about institutional policies regarding personal liability and related insurance coverage options.

The institution must provide access to legal advice for staff members as needed to carry out assigned responsibilities.

The institution must inform staff and students, in a timely and systematic fashion, about extraordinary or changing legal obligations and potential liabilities.

Part 9: EQUAL OPPORTUNITY, ACCESS, and AFFIRMATIVE ACTION

Staff members must ensure that the student orientation program is provided on a fair and equitable basis. The student orientation program must be accessible. Hours of operation must be responsive to the needs of all students.

The student orientation program must adhere to the spirit and intent of equal opportunity laws. The program must not be discriminatory on the basis of age, ancestry, color, disability, gender, national origin, race, religious creed, sexual orientation, and/or veteran status. Exceptions are appropriate only where provided by relevant law and institutional policy.

Consistent with its mission and goals, the student orientation program must take affirmative action to remedy significant imbalances in student participation and staffing patterns.

Part 10. CAMPUS and COMMUNITY RELATIONS

The student orientation program must establish, maintain, and promote effective relations with relevant campus offices and external agencies.

The student orientation program should be an institution-wide process that systematically involves student affairs, academic affairs, and other administrative units, such as campus police, physical plant, and the business office.

The student orientation program should disseminate information relating to other programs and services on campus. These services should, in turn, provide the media and human resources necessary to accomplish the transmission of information.

Part 11. DIVERSITY

Within the context of the institution's unique mission, multi-dimensional diversity enriches the community and enhances the collegiate experience for all; therefore, the student orientation program must nurture environments where similarities and differences among people are recognized and honored.

The student orientation program must promote cultural educational experiences that are characterized by open and continuous communication; that deepen understanding of one's culture and heritage; and that respect and educate about similarities, differences, and histories of cultures.

The student orientation program must address the characteristics and needs of a diverse population when establishing and implementing policies and procedures

Part 12. ETHICS

All persons involved in the delivery of the student orientation program must adhere to the highest principles of ethical behavior. The student orientation program must develop or adopt statements of ethical practice to address their unique issues. These statements must be published, implemented, and reviewed periodically.

Ethical standards of relevant professional associations should be considered.

Orientation staff members must ensure that confidentiality is maintained with respect to all communications and records considered confidential unless exempted by law.

Information disclosed in individual counseling sessions must remain confidential, unless written permission to divulge the information is given by the student. However, all staff members must disclose to appropriate authorities information judged to be of an emergency nature, especially when the safety of the individual or others is involved. Information contained in students' educational records must not be disclosed to noninstitutional third parties without appropriate consent unless classified as "Directory" information or when the information is subpoenaed by law. The student orientation program must apply a similar dedication to privacy and confidentiality to research data concerning individuals.

Staff members must be aware of and comply with the provisions contained in the institution's human subjects research policy and in other relevant institutional policies addressing ethical practices.

Orientation staff members must recognize and avoid personal conflict of interest or appearance thereof in their transactions with students and others. Staff members must strive to ensure the fair objectives and impartial treatment of all persons with whom they deal.

When handling institutional funds, staff members must ensure that such funds are managed in accordance with established and responsible accounting procedures.

Staff members must maintain the highest standards of ethical behavior in the use of technology.

Staff members must not participate in any form of harassment that demeans people or creates an intimidating, hostile, or offensive campus environment.

Orientation staff members must perform their duties within the limits of their training, expertise, and competence. When these limits are exceeded, individuals in need of further assistance must be referred to persons possessing appropriate qualifications.

Staff members must use suitable means to confront and otherwise hold accountable other staff members who exhibit unethical behavior.

Staff members must maintain the highest principles of ethical behavior in the use of technology.

Part 13. ASSESSMENT and EVALUATION

The student orientation program must regularly conduct systematic qualitative and quantitative evaluations of program quality to determine whether and to what degree the stated mission and goals are being met. Although methods of assessment vary, the student orientation program must employ a sufficient range of measures to ensure objectivity and comprehensiveness. Data collected must include responses from students and other significant constituencies. Results of these evaluations must be considered when revising and improving the student orientation program and in recognizing staff performance.

Evaluation of student and institutional needs, goals, objectives, and the effectiveness of the student orientation program should occur on a periodic basis. A representative cross-section of appropriate people from the campus community should be involved in reviews of the student orientation program.

About the Contributors

Jimmy W. Abraham

Abraham was the director of orientation for 20 years at Mississippi State University before being named vice president for student affairs in 2000. He has been very involved in NODA and has presented many programs at both regional and annual NODA conferences. Additionally, Abraham has served as the chair of two Southern Regional Orientation workshops and is well-known for his knowledge in the area of training student orientation leaders. He received a bachelor's degree (1975) and a master's of education (1977) from Mississippi State University and a doctorate (1985) from the University of Mississippi.

Diane M. Austin

Austin is the dean of student affairs at Lasell College in Newton, Massachusetts. She has also served as the associate dean of student affairs/director of new student programs at Bentley College. She has made more than 45 presentations at NODA's national and regional conferences as well as at National Resource Center for The First-Year Experience and Student in Transition's conferences. Her other NODA activities include serving as historian (1988-1996), annual conference program chair (1990), vice-president (1984-1986), national membership chair (1981-1984), member of the board of directors (1980-1983), and member of the annual conference planning committees (1996, 1990, 1982). Austin received bachelor's (1973) and master's degrees (1976) from SUNY-Plattsburgh.

Gary Biller

Gary Biller currently serves as vice president for student services at Arkansas Tech University. For more than two decades, he has worked in a variety of student affairs administrative positions, maintaining a focus on orientation and retention services. He received his bachelor's (1975) and master's (1976) degrees at Oklahoma State University and his doctorate (1986) from the University of Kansas. He has served as director of orientation at Wichita State University, and his NODA activities include serving as a member of the Board of Directors (1987-90) and as editor of the *Orientation Review* (1990-92).

Brian S. Bowen

As a graduate assistant at the University of North Texas, Bowen was responsible for the enhancement of numerous aspects of the parent orientation program and for helping student orientation participants understand their rights and responsibilities. A former teacher, he has recently returned from a work assignment in London and has also studied abroad in Madrid. Bowen is a member of the American College Personnel Association and a recipient of a Texas Association of College and University Student Personnel Administrators scholarship. Bowen earned bachelor's degrees in secondary education, mathematics, and Spanish (1998) from Kansas State University and master's (2001) in higher education from the University of North Texas. He will enter law school at the University of Texas this fall.

Richard Brackin

Brackin is retired from his job as assistant to the dean of University College at The Ohio University in Athens, Ohio. During his tenure, he was director of orientation for 17 years and director of the bachelor of specialized studies degree program for 25 years. He worked with the orientation program for 27 years and was active in NODA for most of those years as a member of the board of directors, director of regions, and editor of the *First Timer's Handbook,* now titled *New Member Handbook.* He has attended and presented at more than 20 NODA conferences and at several National Resource Center for The First-Year Experience and Students in Transition conferences. In 1999 he was called out of retirement to become the director of the Ohio University Degree Programme in Hong Kong for three years. In June 2002, Brackin retired for the second time. He earned a bachelor's degree from Capital University and a master's degree and doctorate from The Ohio University.

Ralph Busby

Busby is the director of counseling and career services at Stephen F. Austin State University in Nacogdoches, Texas. He has been on the planning committees for the NODA annual conferences in Fort Worth, Kansas City (pre-conference program chair), and Austin (program chair). He has attended and presented at many of the annual and regional NODA conferences, served on faculty at the Regional Orientation Professionals Institute, and has written articles and conducted research on orientation. Busby received a bachelor's degree (1970) from Dallas Baptist University and a master's degree (1971) in education from Stephen F. Austin State University. Thirty-one years in higher education has increased his resolve to provide the best possible beginning for those entering this process.

Tony W. Cawthon

Cawthon is the unit coordinator and associate professor of counselor education and student affairs at Clemson University. Prior to becoming a faculty member, he worked for more than 13 years in university housing. He has been active in the American College Personnel Association, the Association of College and University Housing Officers-International, and the Southern Association of College Student Affairs and has published numerous articles on the first-year experience and orientation. Cawthon received a bachelor's degree (1977) and a master's degree (1981) from the University of Tennessee-Knoxville and a doctorate (1995) from Mississippi State University.

Les Cook

Cook currently serves as the special assistant to the vice president at the University of Utah. His prior positions include associate vice president for student life at the University of the Pacific in Stockton, California and several positions at the University of Utah, including director of orientation and leadership development, director of orientation and student involvement, and associate director of recruitment and high school services. Cook has also worked at Salt Lake Community College and the University of Nebraska. He has an education doctorate in educational leadership from Brigham Young University and a master's degree in social science and a bachelor's in political science from Utah State University. Cook has been significantly involved in a number of professional associations, including the National Association of Student Personnel Administrators, the National Orientation Directors Association, and LeaderShape Institute. His commitment to the profession was recently acknowledged when he received a national award at the 2003 NASPA Conference.

Betty R. Cully

Cully is the director of the Success Center at Enterprise State Junior College in Enterprise, Alabama, and has been a NODA member for 14 years. She has served as NODA's Two-Year College Network chair and presented at many NODA Region 6 (Southern Regional Orientation Workshop) conferences. In 1991, Cully was selected as an Outstanding Freshman Advocate, a national award sponsored by the National Resource Center for The First-Year Experience and Students in Transition at the University of South Carolina and Houghton Mifflin. In 1994, she co-wrote a chapter, "Academic Advising Programs," in *Technology in Student Affairs: Issues, Applications, and Trends*, published by the American College Personnel Association. Cully has presented numerous student-oriented workshops within the Alabama Postsecondary College System. She has a bachelor's degree (1969) from West Virginia University, a master's degree (1979) from Troy State University, and an education doctorate (1995) from the University of Alabama.

Michael Dannells

Dannells is a professor and the director of the higher education doctoral program at Bowling Green State University. In a former life he was, among other things, director of new student programs at Northern Arizona University. He received a bachelor's degree (1971) from Bradley University and a doctorate (1978) from the University of Iowa.

John N. Gardner

Gardner is founder and senior fellow of the National Resource Center for The First-Year Experience and Students in Transition and distinguished professor emeritus of library and information science at the University of South Carolina. From 1974 to 1999, Gardner served as executive director of the National Resource Center and of the nationally acclaimed University 101 program at USC. He currently serves as the executive director of the Policy Center on the First Year of College, located in Brevard, North Carolina and funded by grants from The Atlantic Philanthropies, The Pew Charitable Trusts, and The Lumina Foundation (2003-2004).

David A. Hansen

Hansen is assistant vice president for student success services at the University of Nevada, Reno, and a long-standing member of NODA. From 1984-1986, he served the association's president. For almost 30 years, Hansen has dedicated his entire professional career to higher education in student affairs. He has been involved in several professional associations at the state, regional, and national levels, has made numerous presentations, and has published several articles associated with retention and recruitment. Hansen earned a doctorate (1985) from the University of Nevada, Reno, in the area of educational administration, higher education.

Cathie Hatch

Hatch has worked in the field of orientation for more than 20 years. In 2002, she received the NODA Award for Outstanding Contributions to the Orientation Profession. Hatch has published a book on the first-year experience and has written more than 30 articles on nontraditional students, parent orientation, academic advising, and student success issues. She co-authored *Helping Your First-Year College Student Succeed: A Guide for Parents*. Hatch has been an associate editor for NODA's *Journal on Orientation and Transition* for seven years and has served as the chairperson for the Adult Learner Network for 14 years. She has presented on first-year transition issues and orientation programs at more than 50 national and regional conferences. Hatch received a bachelor's degree from the University of Michigan, Ann Arbor and a master's degree from Bemidji State University.

Valerie M. Hodge

Hodge is vice president for student affairs at East Stroudsburg University of Pennsylvania. Previously, she served as assistant vice president of student affairs, assistant dean of students, and director of orientation. During this time she helped develop the ESU Residence Life Program. Hodge is a member of Phi Delta Kappa, the National Educational Society, the National Orientation Directors Association, and the American Association of University Women. Hodge has been presented with the Martin Luther King, Jr. University Award in recognition of her leadership and commitment to students. She has also received the ESU Women of Distinction Award, The State System of Higher Education of PA-Council of Chief Student Affairs Officers Distinguished Service Award, and The National Orientation Directors Association's President's Award. Hodge graduated with honors from Adelphi University with a bachelor's degree in history and from SUNY at Albany with a master's degree in counseling and student personnel services in higher education.

Deneece Huftalin

Huftalin is the dean of students at Salt Lake Community College and has worked in the student affairs field for 17 years. In addition to working with orientation programs, she has been very involved in student leadership development, learning communities on campus, and service-learning initiatives. Huftalin earned a bachelor's degree at the University of Utah and a master's degree at University of California, Los Angeles.

Mary Stuart Hunter

As director of the National Resource Center for The First-Year Experience and Students in Transition at the University of South Carolina, Hunter's work centers on providing educators with resources to develop personal and professional skills while creating and refining innovative programs designed to increase student success. In addition to her administrative and teaching responsibilities, she conducts workshops on the first-year experience, first-year seminars, and teaching. Hunter has published on the first-year experience, first-year seminars, and academic advising, and she edited a monograph on instructor training. Beyond the university, she serves on the national advisory boards of the Policy Center on the First Year of College, the National Society of Collegiate Scholars, the Columbia Pastoral Counseling Center, and sits on the Council of Advisers for the Network of Colleges and Universities Committed to the Elimination of Drug and Alcohol Abuse. She was honored in 2001 as the Outstanding Alumnae of the Year by USC's Student Personnel/Higher Education department.

Bonita C. Jacobs

Jacobs is the vice president for student development and associate professor of higher education at the University of North Texas. She served as the editor of the *Journal of College Orientation and Transition* from 1997-2000 and received the 1999 NODA President's Award and the 2000 NODA Award for Outstanding Scholarly Contributions to the Orientation Profession. In addition, she was very active as a member of the NODA board of directors and was the program chair for NODA's annual conference in 1993, the pre-conference program chair for the 1987 annual conference, and the program chair for NODA Region 6 (SROW) in 1991 and 1995. She is a former chairperson of ACPA Commission II (Admissions and Orientation) and has published extensively on orientation. Jacobs holds a bachelor's degree and a master's of education from Stephen F. Austin State University and a doctorate from Texas A&M University.

Patricia A. Kashner

Kashner is assistant to the vice president for student affairs at East Stroudsburg University of Pennsylvania. During her tenure in higher education, she has served as assistant director of admissions at Lock Haven University of Pennsylvania, director of the program of return to advanced learning at Cedar Crest College, and county services director of LeHigh-Carbon Community College. She has been active on the board of NODA, Leadership Pocono, and the LeHigh Valley Association for Academic Women. She is a member of Pi Sigma Alpha National Honor Society and has received a Certificate of Merit for Outstanding Advising of Students from the National Academic Advising Association. Kashner received a bachelor's degree (1977) from Lock Haven University of Pennsylvania and a master's of public affairs (1992) from Kutztown University of Pennsylvania.

Gary L. Kramer

Kramer is associate dean of admissions and records and a professor in the counseling psychology department at Brigham Young University. In addition to his current position, Kramer has also served as the dean of students at Trident Technical College in Charleston, South Carolina. He has published 70 refereed journal articles, book chapters, book reviews, monographs, grant proposals, ERIC documents, and institutional reports; and 45 scholarly papers in nine different refereed journals. He is the editor of four monographs, has written six monograph chapters and chapters in books published by Jossey-Bass and SCUP, and delivered more than 100 professional papers including keynote addresses for nine different professional organizations. In process are two books, one for Anker Publishing (2002) and another for Jossey-Bass (2003). Kramer received a doctorate from Oregon State University

Carrie W. Linder

As coordinator of research and project development at the National Resource Center for The First-Year Experience and Students in Transition at the University of South Carolina, Linder organizes Center research projects and initiatives, assists educators and visiting scholars with their research efforts and requests, and maintains the Center's database on first-year seminar programs across the United States. She also teaches, each fall, a section of the University 101 first-year seminar or University 101 peer leader seminar. Linder holds a bachelor's degree in communication studies from the University of Florida and a master's degree in student personnel services from the University of South Carolina.

Michael T. Miller

Miller is the associate dean of the college of education at San Jose State University, and he currently serves as the editor of the NODA journal, *Journal of College Orientation and Transition*. He was previously chair of the higher education administration program at the University of Alabama and has served on the faculty of the University of Nebraska. Miller has also worked in the areas of alumni relations and fundraising.

Richard H. Mullendore

Mullendore is vice president for student affairs, associate provost, and professor of college student affairs administration at the University of Georgia. He is also a fellow of the National Resource Center for The First-Year Experience and Students in Transition at the University of South Carolina. Mullendore is a past president of the National Orientation Directors Association and former editor of the *Orientation Planning Manual*. He is co-editor of the first edition of *Designing Successful Transitions: A Guide for Orienting Students to College* and co-author of *Helping Your First-Year College Student Succeed: A Guide for Parents*. He has written numerous articles and book chapters on such topics as orientation, retention, professional standards, students rights and freedoms, planning and assessment, and job satisfaction.

Bryan G. Nesbit

Nesbit is the associate director of enrollment services at Mississippi State University, where he also serves as director of orientation as well as the NODA Region VI state coordinator for Mississippi. His first experience with orientation was in 1994, where he served as an orientation leader for Mississippi State University. After serving four years as an enrollment counselor and coordinator of transfer student recruiting, Nesbit was named director of orientation in July, 2001. Nesbit received a bachelor's (1996) from Mississippi State University and is currently working toward a master's degree in public policy administration, also from MSU.

Greg Sharer

Sharer is the dean of student services at Butler University. He began working at Butler in 1994 after having the privilege of working in orientation at the University of Maryland with Gerry Strumpf and prior to that at the University at Albany with Mary Schimley. He was involved in NODA as co-editor of the *NODA Data Bank* and co-chair of a regional conference in 1995. Sharer received his bachelor's and master's degrees from the University at Albany. He recently earned his juris doctorate from Indiana University.

Tracy L. Skipper

Skipper is editorial projects coordinator for the National Resource Center for The First-Year Experience and Students in Transition at the University of South Carolina. Prior to her work at the Center, she served as director of residence life and judicial affairs at Shorter College (Rome, Georgia) where her duties included teaching in the college's first-year seminar program and serving as an academic advisor for first-year students. Skipper has taught first-year English and University 101 at USC. She holds a bachelor's degree in psychology from USC, a master's degree in higher education from Florida State University, and a master's degree in American literature from USC. She is currently pursuing a doctorate in composition and rhetoric and has a research interest in the teaching of writing in first-year seminar courses.

Rebecca F. Smith

Smith is associate dean of students at Otterbein College in Westerville, Ohio. She serves in the capacity of the director of orientation and campus center and is responsible for community service, commuters, student activities, commencement, and the common book program. Smith served on the NODA board of directors from 1986-1996 and served as NODA president from 1992-1994. Smith received a bachelor's degree (1981) from Otterbein College and a master's degree (1984) from Bowling Green State University.

Gerry Strumpf

Strumpf is director of orientation at the University of Maryland, College Park. She served as the representative to the Council for the Advancement of Standards (CAS) in Higher Education for NODA and has written numerous articles on orientation and freshman transition issues. She also served as the editor of the *NODA Data Bank* from 1982-2000.

M. Lee Upcraft

Upcraft is an assistant vice president emeritus for student affairs, affiliate professor emeritus of higher education, and a senior research scientist in the Center for the Study of Higher Education at the Pennsylvania State University. During his nearly 40 years in higher education, Upcraft has served in various student affairs administrative and faculty positions. He is the author/editor of nine books and 75 book chapters and has refereed journal articles on topics such as residence halls, the first-year experience, academic advising, student affairs administration, and assessment. He has received recognition for his professional accomplishments from several national and regional professional organizations and is a Senior Scholar Diplomate of the American College Personnel Association. He received a bachelor's degree (1960) in history and a master's degree (1961) in guidance and counseling from SUNY-Albany, and a doctorate (1967) in student personnel administration from Michigan State University.

Jeanine A. Ward-Roof

Ward-Roof is the director of student development services and an adjunct instructor in the school of education at Clemson University. She has worked with orientation programs since 1985 and currently directs the program at Clemson. She has been active in NODA, having served as the orientation review editor, board of directors member, director of regions, regional and annual conference chair, regional Orientation Professionals Institute coordinator and faculty member, inter-association liaison, and president. Ward-Roof has also received the NODA New Professionals Award and President's Award. In addition, she has published several articles and presented many programs and keynotes about orientation and leadership. She received a bachelor's degree from Ohio University (1988), a master's degree from Bowling Green State University (1990), and is currently pursuing a doctorate at Clemson University.

Matthew R. Wawrzynski

Wawrzynski worked at the University of Maryland as the assistant director of new student programs and research. During that time, he was a consultant for the 2000 *NODA Data Bank*. He has presented at numerous National Resource Center for The First-Year Experience and Students in Transition, American College Personnel Association, and National Association of Student Personnel Administrator conferences. Wawrzynski received a bachelor's degree (1985) from Canisius College, a master's of education (1991) from Indiana University, and a doctorate (1991) from the University of Maryland. He is currently an AERA post-doctoral fellow and adjunct faculty member at Indiana University.

Maureen E. Wilson

Wilson is assistant professor of college student personnel and higher education administration at Bowling Green State University in Ohio. Wilson received a bachelor's degree (1985) from Aquinas College (Michigan), a master's degree (1987) from Michigan State University, and a doctorate (1998) from Ohio State University.

Jim Zakely

Zakely is a health professions adviser at Colorado State University and has directed orientation at Northern Colorado and the University of Utah. He has served in many NODA capacities including president (1988-1990), board of directors (1981-82, 1984-1987), annual conference host (1981), and annual conference planning committee (1997). Jim received an associate's degree (1970) from Mesa Community College, a bachelor's degree (1975) from Colorado State University, a master's degree (1977) from Western Illinois University, and is working on a doctorate from Colorado State University.

Monograph 36. *Involvement in Campus Activities and the Retention of First-Year College Students. Tracy L. Skipper and Roxanne Argo,* Editors. Produced in association with the National Association for Campus Activities. Campus activities programs have long been considered an important vehicle for connecting students to the institution and for delivering educational content not found in the traditional curriculum. But as our student populations and campus cultures change, our activities programming must change as well. Chapter authors argue for a broadened definition of campus activities that will lead to heightened social and intellectual engagement for college students. Specific topics include community building on commuter campuses, engaging distance learners, changing campus culture, developing curricular and co-curricular leadership programs, and assessing the effect of activities programs. 2003. ISBN 1-889271-40-3 $30.00

Monograph 35. *2000 National Survey of First-Year Seminar Programs: Continuing Innovations in the Collegiate Curriculum.* This volume reviews national data on first-year seminars in nearly 750 regionally accredited colleges and universities in the United States. Information is offered on both the structure and content of these courses, with a discussion of how the seminar has changed over the last decade. Brief descriptions of courses representing the five most common seminar types are also provided. Data and course descriptions can be used to design, refine, or build support for the first-year seminar on a variety of campuses. 128 pages. ISBN 1-889271-39-X. $30.00. 2002.

Monograph 32. *Peer Leadership: A Primer on Program Essentials. Suzanne L. Hamid,* Editor. This volume focuses on the use of peer leaders in the first-year seminar classroom and also includes examples of undergraduates fulfilling a variety of academic and social support roles on campus. Topics include a historical overview of research on peer leadership and information on emerging leadership trends; a discussion of recruitment, selection, and training for successful programs; recommendations for effective program management; practical examples from a variety of campuses; and comprehensive appendices, including sample applications, contracts, job descriptions, training agendas and syllabi, team building activities, and evaluations. 155 pages. ISBN 1-889271-36-X. $30.00. 2001.

Strengthening First-Year Student Learning at Doctoral/Research-Extensive Universities: Examples of Current Practice. Marc Cutright. This monograph is a selection of 25 narratives submitted by Carnegie Doctoral/Research-Extensive Universities to a web-based database created by the Policy Center on the First Year of College. The monograph highlights a variety of efforts gaining strength at research universities, including learning communities, disciplined-based first-year seminars, and Supplemental Instruction. 100 pages. ISBN 0-9726527-1-X $25.00. 2002.

Helping Your First-Year College Student Succeed: A Guide for Parents. Richard H. Mullendore and Cathie Hatch. Parents may be the most powerful untapped resource for helping new students make the transition to college. This guide, published in conjunction with the National Orientation Directors Association, offers practical advice on how parents can help children make a successful transition to college. This is an ideal resource to incorporate into summer and fall orientation programs, admissions open houses, and parents programs. 28 pages. ISBN 1-889271-31-4. $3.00 each or $2.00 each per 100-unit lot. 2000.

A Family Guide to Academic Advising. Donald C. Smith and Virginia N. Gordon. This guide is an easy-to-read overview of one of the most important educational programs colleges and universities provide their students— academic advising. Written by a college faculty member and a veteran academic advisor, the *Guide* is a great resource for highlighting the role of academic advising in college success, promoting advising and other student support services on campus, and enlisting family members as partners and referral agents in their students' college careers. 32 pages. ISBN 1-889271-42-X. $3.00 each or $2.00 each per 100-unit lot. 2003.

Use the order form on the next page to order any of these titles from the National Resource Center.

Use this form to order additional copies of this monograph or to order other titles from the National Resource Center for The First-Year Experience & Students in Transition.

Prices advertised in this publication are subject to change.

Item	Quantity	Price	Total
Monograph 13. *Designing Successful Transitions*, 2nd Edition		$35.00	
Monograph 36. *Involvement in Campus Activities and the Retention of First-Year College Students*		$30.00	
Monograph 35. *2000 National Survey of First-Year Seminar Programs*		$30.00	
Monograph 32. *Peer Leadership*		$30.00	
Strengthening First-Year Student Learning at Doctorial/Research-Extensive Universities: Example of Current Practice.		$25.00	
Helping Your First-Year College Student Succeed		$3.00 each or $2.00 each per* 100-unit lot	
A Family Guide to Academic Advising		$3.00 each or $2.00 each per* 100-unit lot	
		Shipping and Handling	
		Total	

Call for shipping charges on this item.

Shipping Charges:	Order Amount	Shipping Cost
U.S.	$0 - $50	$ 6.50 US
	$50 - $150	$10.00 US
	over $150	$15.00 US

Customers outside the U.S. will be billed exact shipping charges plus a $5.00 processing fee. Fax or e-mail us to obtain a shipping estimate. Be sure to include a list of items you plan to purchase and to specify your preference for Air Mail or UPS delivery.

Name _____ Department_____

Institution_____ Telephone_____

Mailing Address_____

City_____ State/Province_____ Postal Code _____

E-mail Address_____

Select your option payable to the University of South Carolina:

☐ Check Enclosed   ☐ Institutional Purchase Order   Purchase Order No._____

Credit Card: ☐ VISA   ☐ MasterCard   ☐ DISCOVER   Expiration Date: _____

Card No._____

Name of Cardholder_____

Signature_____

Mail this form to: National Resource Center for The First-Year Experience & Students in Transition, University of South Carolina, 1728 College Street, Columbia, SC 29208. Phone (803) 777-6229. FAX (803) 777-4699. E-mail burtonp@gwm.sc.edu Federal ID 57-6001153.